Supreme Court DRAMA

Cases That Changed America

Supreme Court DRAMA

Cases That Changed America

Daniel E. Brannen, &
Dr. Richard Clay Hanes

Elizabeth Shaw, Editor

VOLUME 2
CAPITAL PUNISHMENT
CRIMINAL LAW AND PROCEDURE
FAMILY LAW
JURIES
JUVENILE LAW AND JUSTICE
SEARCH AND SEIZURE

AN IMPRINT OF THE GALE GROUP
DETROIT · NEW YORK · SAN FRANCISCO
LONDON · BOSTON · WOODBRIDGE, CT

Supreme Court Drama:
Cases That Changed America

DANIEL E. BRANNEN
RICHARD CLAY HANES

Staff

Elizabeth M. Shaw, U·X·L Editor
Carol DeKane Nagel, U·X·L Managing Editor
Thomas L. Romig, U·X·L Publisher

Shalice Shah-Caldwell, Permissions Associate (Pictures)
Maria Franklin, Permissions Manager
Robyn Young, Imaging and Multimedia Content Editor

Rita Wimberley, Senior Buyer
Evi Seoud, Assistant Manager, Composition Purchasing and Electronic Prepress
Dorothy Maki, Manufacturing Manager
Mary Beth Trimper, Production Director
Michelle DiMercurio, Senior Art Director

Pamela A. Reed, Imaging Coordinator
Randy Basset, Image Database Supervisor
Barbara Yarrow, Imaging and Multimedia Content Manager

Linda Mahoney, LM Design, Typesetting

Cover photographs: Reproduced by permission of the Library of Congress and the Supreme Court of the United States.

Library of Congress Cataloging-in-Publication Data

Brannen, Daniel E., 1968-
    Supreme Court drama: cases that changed the nation / Daniel E. Brannen, Jr. and Richard Clay Hanes ; Elizabeth M. Shaw, editor.
        p. cm.
    Includes bibliographical references and index.
    ISBN 0-7876-4877-9 (set) – ISBN 0-7876-4878-7 (v.1) – ISBN 0-7876-4879-5 (v.2) –ISBN 0-7876-4880-9 (v.3) – ISBN 0-7876-4881-7 (v.4)
        1.Constitutional law–United States–Cases–Juvenile literature. 2. United States. Supreme Court–Juvenile Literature. [1. Constitutional law–United States–Cases. 2. United States. Supreme Court.] I. Hanes, Richard Clay, 1946- II. Shaw, Elizabeth M., 1973- III. Title.

    KF4550.Z9 B73 2001
    347.73'26'0264–dc21

                                                            00-056380

Contents

VOLUME 1: INDIVIDUAL LIBERTIES

FREEDOM OF ASSEMBLY

Contents

Contents

VOLUME 2: CRIMINAL JUSTICE AND FAMILY LAW

Contents

CAPITAL PUNISHMENT

CRIMINAL LAW AND PROCEDURE

Contents

JUVENILE COURTS AND LAW

SEARCH AND SEIZURE

VOLUME 3: EQUAL PROTECTION AND CIVIL RIGHTS

AFFIRMATIVE ACTION

ASSISTED SUICIDE/ RIGHT TO DIE

CIVIL RIGHTS AND EQUAL PROTECTION

RIGHTS OF IMMIGRANTS, GAYS, LESBIANS AND THE DISABLED

SEGREGATION AND DESEGREGATION

FEDERAL POWERS AND SEPARATION OF POWERS

times to justify presidential initiatives in foreign affairs and contributed greatly to the growth of the power of the presidency in modern times.

public enterprise, which the state may regulate, and private enterprise, which it may not.

LABOR AND LABOR PRACTICES

Contents

Trials Alphabetically

F

G

H

I

**Trials
Alphabetically**

N

O

P

R

S

T

Trials
Alphabetically

U

V

W

**Trials
Alphabetically**

Y

Trials Chronologically

1979

1980

1981

1982

1984

1985

1986

1987

1988

1989

1990

1991

1992

1993

1994

1995

1996

1997

**Trials
Chronologically**

Reader's Guide

U.S. citizens take comfort and pride in living under the rule of law. Our elected representatives write and enforce the laws that cover everything from family relationships to the dealings of multi-billion-dollar corporations, from the quality of the air to the content of the programs broadcast through it. But it is the judicial system that interprets the meaning of the law and makes it real for the average citizen through the drama of trials and the force of court orders and judicial opinions.

The four volumes of *Supreme Court Drama: Cases that Changed America* profile approximately 150 cases that influenced the development of key aspects of law in the United States. The case profiles are grouped according to the legal principle on which they are based, with each volume covering one or two broad areas of the law as follows:

- **Volume : Individual Liberties** includes cases that have influenced such First Amendment issues as freedom of the press, religion, speech, and assembly. It also covers the right to privacy.

- **Volume 2: Criminal Justice and Family Law** covers many different areas of criminal law, such as capital punishment, crimnal procedure, family law, and juvenile law.

- **Volume 3: Equal Protection and Civil Rights** includes cases in the areas of affirmative action, reproductive rights segregation, and voting rights, as well as areas of special concern such as immigrants, the disabled, and gay and lesbian citizens. Sexual harassment and the right to die are also represented in this volume.

- **Volume 4: Business and Government Law** also encompasses two major spheres of the law. Monopolies, antitrust, and labor-related cases supplement the business fundamentals of corporate law. The government cases document the legal evolution of the branches of the federal government as well as the federal government's relation to state power. Separate topics address military issues, taxation, and legal history behind some Native American issues.

- **Appendixes** to all volumes also present the full text of the U.S. Constitution and its amendments and a chronological table of Supreme Court justices.

Coverage

Issue overviews, averaging 2,000 words in length provide the context for the case profiles that follow. Case discussions range from 750 to 2,000 words according, to their complexity and importance. Each provides the background of the case and issues involved, the main arguments presented by each side, and an explanation of the Supreme Court's decision, as well as the legal, political, and social impact of the decision. Excerpts from the Court's opinions are often included. Within each issue section, the cases are arranged from earliest to most recent.

When a single case could be covered under several different areas—the landmark reproductive rights decision in *Roe v. Wade,* for example, is also based upon an assertion of privacy rights—the case is placed with the issue with which it is most often associated. Users should consult the cumulative index that appears in each volume to find cases throughout the set that apply to a particular topic.

Additional Features

- The issues and proceedings featured in *Supreme Court Drama* are presented in language accessible to middle school users. Legal terms must sometimes be used for precision, however, so a Words to Know section of more than 300 words and phrases appears in each volume.

- A general essay providing a broad overview of the Supreme Court of the United States and the structure of the American legal system.

- **Bolded** cross-references within overview and case entries that point to cases that appear elsewhere in the set.

- Tables of contents to locate a particular case by name or in chronological order.

- A cumulative index at the end of each volume that includes the cases, people, events and subjects that appear throughout *Supreme Court Drama.*

Suggestions Are Welcome

We welcome your comments on *Supreme Court Drama: Cases That Changed America.* Please write, Editors, *Supreme Court Drama,* U•X•L, 27500 Drake Road, Farmington Hills, MI 48331-3535; call toll-free: 1-800-877-4253; fax to 248-414-5043; or send e-mail via http://www.galegroup.com.

Advisors

The editor is grateful for all the assistance and insight offered by the advisors to this product.

- Mary Alice Anderson, Media Specialist, Winona Middle School, Winona, Minnesota
- Sara Brooke, Librarian, Ellis School, Pittsburgh, Pennsylvania
- Marolynn Griffin, Librarian, Desert Ridge Middle School, Albuquerque, New Mexico
- Dr. E. Shane McKee, Instructor, The Putney School at Elm Lea Farm, Putney, Vermont

The editor and writers would also like to acknowledge the tireless review and copy editing work done by:

- Aaron Ford, The Ohio State University, Columbus, Ohio
- Kathleen Knisely, Franklin County Courts, Columbus, Ohio
- Courtney Mroch, Freelance Writer, Jacksonville, Florida
- Melynda Neal, Franklin County Courts, Columbus, Ohio
- Berna Rhodes-Ford, Franklin County Courts, Columbus, Ohio
- Gertrude Ring, Freelance Writer, Los Angeles, California
- Lauren Zupnic, Franklin County Courts, Columbus, Ohio

Guide to the Supreme Court
of the United States

The United States Supreme Court is the highest court in the judicial branch of the federal government. That means the Supreme Court is equal in importance to the president, who heads the executive branch, and Congress, which heads the legislative branch. Congress makes laws, the president enforces them, and the Supreme Court interprets them to make sure they are properly enforced.

The Supreme Court's main job is to review federal (national) and state cases that involve rights or duties under the U.S. Constitution, the document outlining the laws and guidelines for lawmaking and enforcement in the United States. The Court does this to make sure that all federal and state governments are obeying the Constitution.

For example, if Congress passes a law that violates the First Amendment freedom of speech, the Supreme Court can strike the law down as unconstitutional. If the president violates the Fourth Amendment by having the Federal Bureau of Investigation search a person's home without a warrant, the Supreme Court can fix the violation. If a state court violates the Constitution by convicting someone of a crime in an unfair trial, the Supreme Court can reverse the conviction.

As the highest court in the United States government, the Supreme Court also has the job of interpreting federal law. Congress creates law to regulate crimes, drugs, taxes, and other important issues across the nation. When someone is accused of violating a federal law, a federal court must interpret the law to decide whether the accused has broken the law. In this role, the Supreme Court makes the final decision about what a federal law means.

The Federal Court System

The Supreme Court was born in 1789, when the United States adopted the Constitution. Article III of the Constitution says, "The judicial Power of the United States, shall be vested in one supreme Court, and in such inferior Courts as the Congress may from time to time ordain and establish." With this sentence, the Constitution made the Supreme Court the highest Court in the judicial branch of the federal government. It also gave Congress the power to create lower courts.

Congress used that power to create a large judicial (court) system. The system has three levels. Trial courts, called federal district courts, are at the lowest level. There are ninety-four federal district courts covering different areas of the country. Each federal district court handles trials for cases in its area.

Federal district courts hold trials in both criminal and civil cases. Criminal trials involve cases by the government against a person who is accused of a crime, like murder. Civil trials involve cases between private parties, such as when one person accuses another of breaking a contract or agreement.

When a party loses a case in federal district court, she usually may appeal the decision to a U.S. court of appeals. Federal courts of appeals are the second level in the federal judicial system. There are twelve courts of appeals covering twelve areas, or circuits, of the country. For example, the district courts in Connecticut, New York, and Vermont are part of the Second Circuit. Appeals from district courts in those states go to the U.S. Court of Appeals for the Second Circuit.

During an appeal, the losing party asks the court of appeals to reverse or modify the trial court's decision. In essence, she argues that the trial court made an error when it ruled against her.

The party who loses before the court of appeals must decide whether to take her case to the U.S. Supreme Court. The Supreme Court is the third and highest level of the federal judicial system. The process of taking a case to the U.S. Supreme Court is described below.

State Court Systems

Most states have a judicial system that resembles the federal system. Trial courts hold trials in both criminal and civil cases. Most states also have special courts that hear only certain kinds of cases. Family, juvenile, and traffic courts are typical examples. There also are state courts, such as justices of the peace and small claims courts, that handle minor matters.

Appeals from all lower courts usually go to a court of appeals. The losing party there may take her case to the state's highest court, often called the state supreme court. When a case involves the U.S. Constitution or federal law, the losing party sometimes may take the case from the state supreme court to the U.S. Supreme Court.

Bringing a Case to the U.S. Supreme Court

There are three main ways that cases get to the U.S. Supreme Court. The most widely used method is to ask the Supreme Court to hear the case. This is called filing a petition for a writ of *certiorari*. The person who files the petition, usually the person who lost the case in the court of appeals, is called the petitioner. The person on the other side of the case is called the respondent. The Court only grants a small percentage of the writ petitions it receives each year. It usually tries to accept the cases that involve the most important legal issues.

The second main way to bring a case to the Supreme Court is by appeal. An appeal is possible only when the law that the case involves says the parties may appeal to the Supreme Court. The losing party who files the appeal is called the appellant, while the person on the other side of the case is a called the appellee.

The third main way to bring a case to the Supreme Court is by filing a petition for a writ of habeas corpus. This petition is mainly for people who have been imprisoned in violation of the U.S. Constitution. For example, if an accused criminal is convicted and jailed after the police beat him to get a confession (a police act that is illegal), the prisoner may ask the Supreme Court to release him by filing a petition for a writ of habeas corpus. The person who files the petition is called the petitioner, while the person holding the petitioner in jail is called the respondent.

The process of arguing and deciding a case in the Supreme Court is similar no matter how the case gets there. The parties file briefs that explain why they think the lower court's decision in their case is either right or wrong. The Supreme Court reviews the briefs along with a record of the evidence presented during trial in the federal district court or state trial court. The Supreme Court also may allow the parties to engage in oral argument, which is a chance for the lawyers to explain their clients' cases. During oral argument, the Supreme Court justices can ask questions to help them make the right decision.

After the justices read the briefs, review the record, and hear oral argument, they meet privately in chambers to discuss the case. Eventually, the nine justices vote for the party they think should win the case. A party must receive votes from five of the nine justices to win the case. The justices who cast the votes for the winning party are called the majority, while the justices who vote for the losing party are called the minority.

After the justices vote, one justice in the majority writes an opinion to explain the Court's decision. Other justices in the majority may write concurring opinions that explain why they agree with the Court's decision. Justices in the minority may write dissenting opinions to explain why they think the Court's decision is wrong.

The Supreme Court's decision is the final word in a case. Parties who are unhappy with the result have no place to go to get a different ruling. The only way to change the effect of a Supreme Court decision is to have Congress change the law, have the entire nation change, or amend, the Constitution, or have the president appoint a different justice to the Court when one retires or dies. This is part of the federal government's system of checks and balances, which prevents one branch from becoming too strong.

Supreme Court Justices

Supreme Court justices are among the greatest legal minds in the country. Appointment to the job is usually the high point of a career that involved some combination of trial work as a lawyer, teaching as a professor, or service as a judge on a lower court.

Under the Constitution, the president appoints Supreme Court justices with the advice and consent of the Senate when one of the nine justices retires, dies, or is removed from office. Supreme Court justices cannot be removed from office except by impeachment and conviction by Congress for serious crimes. That means the process of appointing a new justice usually begins when one of the justices retires or dies.

The president begins the process by nominating someone to fill the empty seat on the Court. The president usually names someone who he thinks will interpret the Constitution favorably to his political party's wishes. In other words, democratic presidents typically nominate liberal justices, while republican presidents nominate conservative justices.

The next step in the process is for the Senate Judiciary Committee to review the president's recommendation. If the Senate is controlled by the president's political party, the review process usually results in Senate approval of the president's selection.

If the president's political opposition controls the Senate, the review process can be fierce and lengthy. The Judiciary Committee calls the nominee before it to answer questions. The Committee's goal is to determine whether the nominee is qualified to be a Supreme Court justice. The Committee also uses the investigation to try to figure out how the nominee will decide controversial cases, such as cases involving abortion. After its investigation, the Committee recommends whether the Senate should confirm or reject the president's nomination. Two-thirds of the senators must vote for the nominee to confirm him as a new Supreme Court justice.

The Supreme Court has changed greatly over the years. One of the Court's greatest liberal periods was when Chief Justice Earl Warren headed the Court from 1953 to 1969. In 1954, the Warren Court decided one of its most famous cases, *Brown v. Board of Education,* in which it forced public schools to end the practice of separating black and white students in different schools.

The Warren Court was followed by one of the Court's greatest conservative periods, under Chief Justice Warren E. Burger from 1969 to 1986, followed by Chief Justice William H. Rehnquist from 1986 onward. In one of the Rehnquist Court's most important decisions, *Clinton v. Jones* (1997), the Court said the president may be sued while in office for conduct unrelated to his official duties. The decision allowed Paula Jones to sue President William J. Clinton for sexual harassment.

Unfortunately, the justices on the highest court in a nation of diversity have not been very diverse themselves. Until 1916, all Supreme Court justices were white, Christian men. That year, Louis D. Brandeis became the first Jewish member of the Supreme Court. In 1967, Thurgood Marshall became the first African American justice. Clarence Thomas became just the second in 1991. In 1981, President Ronald Reagan nominated Sandra Day O'Connor to be the first woman on the Supreme Court. Ruth Bader Ginsburg joined her there in 1993.

Research and Activity Ideas

Activity 1: New School Rule

Assignment: Imagine that your school principal has just announced a new school rule for detention. Students who get detention are not allowed to explain themselves, even if they did nothing wrong. Instead, they must sit in the principal's office during lunch. They are not allowed to eat lunch, not allowed to talk at all, and must listen to Frank Sinatra music during the entire period. Your teacher has asked you to prepare a written report on whether this new rule violates the U.S. Constitution.

Preparation: Begin your research by reading the Bill of Rights, which contains the first ten amendments to the U.S. Constitution, along with the Fourteenth Amendment. These amendments contain many rights that might apply to the principal's new rule. Do you see any that might help? Continue your research by looking in *Supreme Court Drama: Cases That Changed America* for essays and cases on the freedom of speech, cruel and unusual punishment, and students' rights in school. Consult the library and Internet web sites for additional research material. Does it seem to matter whether you are in a public or private school?

Presentation: After you have gathered your information, prepare a report that explains what you found. Does the principal's new rule violate the Constitution? Why or why not? Explain your conclusions by refer-ring to specific amendments from the Constitution and specific cases from *Supreme Court Drama*.

**Research
and Activity
Ideas**

Activity 2: Taking a Case to Court

Assignment: Pretend you were in a bookstore that was being robbed. When the police arrived to arrest the criminal, they accidentally arrested you. During the arrest they treated you roughly and broke your arm. Your lawyer has informed you that you may sue the police to recover damages in either state or federal court. Before deciding which court system to use, you must do some research about both systems.

Preparation: Begin by reading the Introduction to *Supreme Court Drama: Cases That Changed America* so you can learn about the federal and state court systems in general. Continue with library and Internet research for more information about these systems. Then figure out which courts you need to use for your case. For the state system, use the library and Internet to find your local trial court for civil cases. Then find your state court of appeals and supreme courts in case you lose in the trial court. For the federal system, find the federal district court and U.S. court of appeals for your area. Write to the state supreme court and the U.S. court of appeals to find out what percentage of cases make it from those courts to the U.S. Supreme Court each year.

Presentation: Write a letter to your attorney explaining what you found. Tell her where you need to file your case if you choose the state system, and where you need to take appeals in that system. Do the same for the federal system. Tell her what your chances are of getting to the U.S. Supreme Court with your case.

Activity 3: Oral Argument

Activity: Imagine that a new religious group called Planterism has moved into your community. Planters are a group of men who worship trees, flowers, and other plant life. Once every week they hold an all-night ceremony during which they burn a tree as a sacrifice for all living plants. The ceremony disturbs neighbors who are trying to sleep and threatens to eliminate rare trees in your town.

Your mayor or other local leader decides he does not like Planters, so he enacts the following law:

> **Everyone in this town must follow Christianity, Judaism, or some other popular religion. Anyone who follows a false religion, including Planterism, is guilty of a felony. Anyone who burns a tree as a**

sacrifice during a religious ceremony is guilty of a felony. Anyone who disturbs the peace with a religious ceremony at night is guilty of a felony.

Violation of this law by men is punishable by life in prison without a trial. If the local police suspect a man is violating this law, they shall enter his house immediately without a warrant, arrest him, and take him to jail for imprisonment. Violation of this law by women is punishable by thirty days in jail only after a jury finds the woman guilty in a fair trial.

Your teacher has instructed the class to convene a Supreme Court to determine whether this law violates the U.S. Constitution.

Preparation: Select nine members of your class to be justices on the Court. The rest of your class should divide into three teams. One team will represent the mayor, who will argue in favor of the law. The second team will represent a group of Planters who want to challenge the law. The third team will represent a group of Christians, who want to burn palms on Palm Sunday, a religious holiday that happens once a year.

The justices and all three teams should begin by reading the Bill of Rights and the Fourteenth Amendment of the U.S. Constitution. Continue by reading *Supreme Court Drama: Cases That Changed America* for essays and cases on the freedom of religion, the establishment clause, search and seizure, cruel and unusual punishment, governmental power, due process of law, and gender discrimination. Supplement this with research from library materials and Internet web sites. You may want to assign small groups from each team to handle specific issues.

Presentation: When everyone has completed the research, all three teams should prepare to argue before the Supreme Court. The team representing the mayor should explain why the law should be upheld. The teams representing the Planters and the Christians should explain why the law should be struck down as unconstitutional. During the argument, the justices are allowed to ask questions of each team. After every team has made its argument, the justices should meet to discuss the case and to make a ruling. Is the law unconstitutional? Which parts are valid and which are not?

Words to Know

A

Accessory Aiding or contributing in a secondary way to a crime or assisting in or contributing to a crime.

Accomplice One who knowingly and voluntarily helps commit a crime.

Acquittal When a person who has been charged with committing a crime is found not guilty by the courts.

Admissible A term used to describe information that is allowed to be used as evidence or information in a court case.

Adultery Voluntary sexual relations between an individual who is married and someone who is not the individual's spouse.

Affidavit A written statement of facts voluntarily made by someone in front of an official or witness.

Affirmative action Employment programs required by the federal government designed to eliminate existing and continuing discrimination, to remedy lingering effects of past discrimination, and to create systems and procedures to prevent future discrimination; commonly based on population percentages of minority groups in a particular area. Factors considered are race, color, sex, creed (religious beliefs), and age.

Age of consent The age at which a person may marry without parental approval.

Age of majority The age at which a person, formerly a minor or an infant, is recognized by law to be an adult, capable of managing his or her own affairs and responsible for any legal obligations created by his or her actions.

Aggravated assault A person is guilty of aggravated assault if he or she tries to cause serious bodily injury to another or causes such injury purposely, knowingly, or recklessly without any concern for that person or without remorse.

Alien Foreign-born person who has not been naturalized to become a U.S. citizen under federal law and the Constitution.

Alimony Payment a family court may order one person in a couple to make to the other when the couple separates or divorces.

Amendment An addition, deletion, or change to an original item, such as the additions to the Constitution.

Amicus curiae Latin for "friend of the court"; a person with strong interest in, views on, or knowledge of the subject matter of a case, but is not a party to the case. A friend of the court may petition the court for permission to file a statement about the situation.

Amnesty The action of a government by which all persons or certain groups of persons who have committed a criminal offense—usually of a political nature that threatens the government (such as treason)—are granted immunity from prosecution.

Appeal Timely plea by an unsuccessful party in a lawsuit to an appropriate superior court that has the power to review a final decision on the grounds that the decision was made in error.

Appellate court A court having jurisdiction to review decisions of a lower court.

Apportionment The process by which legislative seats are distributed among those who are entitled to representation; determination of the number of representatives that each state, county, or other subdivision may send to a legislative body.

Arbitration Taking a dispute to an unbiased third person and agreeing in advance to comply with the decision made by that third person, after both parties have had a chance to argue their side of the issue.

Arraignment The formal proceeding where the defendant is brought before the trial court to hear the charges against him or her and to enter a plea of guilty, not guilty, or no contest.

Arrest The taking into custody of an individual for the purpose of answering the charges against him or her.

Arrest warrant A written order issued by an authority of the state and commanding that the person named be taken into custody.

Arson The malicious burning or exploding of a house, building, or property.

Assault Intentionally harming another person.

Attempt Unsuccessfully preparing and trying to carry out a deed.

B

Bail An amount of money the defendant needs to pay the court to be released while waiting for a trial.

Bankruptcy A federally authorized procedure by which an individual, corporation, or municipality is relieved of total liability for its debts by making arrangements for the partial repayment of those debts.

Battery An intentional, unpermitted act causing harmful or offensive contact with another person.

Beneficiary One who inherits something through the last will and testament (will) of another; also, a person who is entitled to profits, benefits, or advantage from a contract.

Bigamy The offense of willfully and knowingly entering into a second marriage while married to another person.

Bill A written declaration that one hopes to have made into a law.

Bill of rights The first ten amendments to the U.S. Constitution, ratified (adopted by the states) in 1791, which set forth and guaranteed certain fundamental rights and privileges of individuals, including freedom of religion, speech, press, and assembly; guarantee of a speedy jury trial in criminal cases; and protection against excessive bail and cruel and unusual punishment.

Black codes Laws, statutes, or rules that governed slavery and segregation of public places in the South prior to 1865.

Bona fide occupational qualification An essential requirement for performing a given job. The requirement may even be a physical condition beyond an individual's control, such as perfect vision, if it is absolutely necessary for performing a job.

Brief A summary of the important points of a longer document.

Burden of proof The duty of a party to convince a judge or jury of their position, and to prove wrong any evidence that damages the position of the party. In criminal cases the party must prove their case beyond a reasonable doubt.

Burglary The criminal offense of breaking and entering a building illegally for the purpose of committing a crime.

Bylaws The rules and regulations of an association or a corporation to provide a framework for its operation and management.

C

Capacity The ability, capability, or fitness to do something; a legal right, power, or competency to perform some act. An ability to comprehend both the nature and consequences of one's acts.

Capital punishment The lawful infliction of death as a punishment; the death penalty.

Cause A reason for an action or condition. A ground of a legal action.

Censorship The suppression of speech or writing that is deemed obscene, indecent, or controversial.

Certiorari Latin for "to be informed of"; an order commanding officers of inferior courts to allow a case pending before them to move up to a higher court to determine whether any irregularities or errors occurred that justify review of the case. A device by which the Supreme Court of the United States exercises its discretion in selecting the cases it will review.

Change of venue The removal of a lawsuit from one county or district to another for trial, often permitted in criminal cases in which the court finds that the defendant would not receive a fair trial in the first location because of negative publicity.

Charter A grant from the government of ownership rights of land to a person, a group of people, or an organization, such as a corporation.

Circumstantial evidence Information and testimony presented by a party in a civil or criminal case that allows conclusions to be drawn about certain facts without the party presenting concrete evidence to support their facts.

Citation A paper commonly used in various courts that is served upon an individual to notify him or her that he or she is required to appear at a specific time and place.

Citizens Those who, under the Constitution and laws of the United States, owe allegiance to the United States and are entitled to the enjoyment of all civil rights awarded to those living in the United States.

Civil law A body of rules that spell out the private rights of citizens and the remedies for governing disputes between individuals in such areas as contracts, property, and family law.

Civil liberties Freedom of speech, freedom of press, freedom from discrimination, and other rights guaranteed and protected by the Constitution, which were intended to place limits on government.

Civil rights Personal liberties that belong to an individual.

Class action A lawsuit that allows a large number of people with a common interest in a matter to sue or be sued as a group.

Clause A section, phrase, paragraph, or segment of a legal document, such as a contract, deed, will, or constitution, that relates to a particular point.

Closing argument The final factual and legal argument made by each attorney on all sides of a case in a trial prior to the verdict or judgment.

Code A collection of laws, rules, or regulations that are consolidated and classified according to subject matter.

Collective bargaining agreement The contractual agreement between an employer and a labor union that controls pay, hours, and working conditions for employees which can be enforced against both the employer and the union for failure to comply with its terms.

Commerce Clause The provision of the U.S. Constitution that gives Congress exclusive power over trade activities between the states and with foreign countries and Native American tribes.

Commercial speech The words used in advertisments by commercial companies and service providers. Commercial speech is protected under the First Amendment as long as it is not false or misleading.

Common law The principles and rules of action, embodied in case law rather than legislative enactments, applicable to the government and protection of persons and property, Common laws derive their authority from the community customs and traditions that evolved over the centuries as interpreted by judicial tribunals (types of courts).

Common-law marriage A union of two people not formalized in the customary manner but created by an agreement by the two people to consider themselves married followed by their living together.

Community property The materials and resources owned in common by a husband and wife.

Complaint The possible evidence that initiates a civil action; in criminal law, the document that sets in motion a person's being charged with an offense.

Concurring opinion An opinion by one or more judges that provides separate reasoning for reaching the same decision as the majority of the court.

Conditional Subject to change; dependent upon the occurrence of a future, uncertain event.

Confession A statement made by an individual that acknowledges his or her guilt of a crime.

Conflict of interest A term used to describe the situation in which a public official exploits his or her position for personal benefit.

Consent Voluntary agreement to the proposal of another; the act or result of reaching an agreement.

Conspiracy An agreement between two or more persons to engage in an unlawful or criminal act, or an act that is innocent in itself but becomes unlawful when done by those participating.

Constituent A person who gives another person permission to act on his or her behalf, such as an agent, an attorney in a court of law, or an elected official in government.

Constitution of the United States A document written by the founding fathers of the United States that has been added to by Congress over the centuries that is held as the absolute rule of action and decision for all branches and offices of the government, and which all subsequent laws and ordinances must be in accordance. It is enforced by representatives of the people of the United States, and can be changed only by a constitutional amendment by the authority that created it.

Contempt An act of deliberate disobedience or disregard for the laws or regulations of a public authority, such as a court or legislative body.

Continuance The postponement of an action pending (waiting to be tried) in a court to a later date, granted by a court in response to a request made by one of the parties to a lawsuit.

Corporations Business entities that are treated much like human individuals under the law, having legally enforceable rights, the ability to acquire debt and pay out profits, the ability to hold and transfer property, the ability to enter into contracts, the requirement to pay taxes, and the ability to sue and be sued.

Counsel An attorney or lawyer.

Court of appeal An intermediate court of review that is found in thirteen judicial districts, called circuits, in the United States. A state court of appeal reviews a decision handed down by a lower court to determine whether that court made errors that warrant the reversal of its final decision.

Covenant An agreement, contract, or written promise between two individuals that frequently includes a pledge to do or refrain from doing something.

Criminal law A body of rules and statutes that defines behavior prohibited by the government because it threatens and/or harms public safety, and establishes the punishments to be given to those who commit such acts.

Cross-examination The questioning of a witness or party during a trial, hearing, or deposition by the opposing lawyer.

Cruel and unusual punishment Such punishment as would amount to torture or barbarity, any cruel and degrading punishment, or any fine, penalty, confinement, or treatment so disproportionate to the offense as to shock the moral sense of the community.

Custodial parent The parent to whom the court grants guardianship of the children after a divorce.

D

Death penalty See Capital punishment.

De facto Latin for "in fact"; in deed; actually.

Defamation Any intentional false communication, either written or spoken, that harms a person's reputation; decreases the respect, regard, or confidence in which a person is held; or causes hostile or disagreeable opinions or feelings against a person.

Defendant The person defending or denying; the party against whom recovery is sought in an action or suit, or the accused in a criminal case.

Defense The forcible reaction against an unlawful and violent attack, such as the defense of one's person, property, or country in time of war.

De jure Latin for "in law"; legitimate; lawful, as a matter of law. Having complied with all the requirements imposed by law.

Deliberate Willful; purposeful; determined after thoughtful evaluation of all relevant factors. To act with a particular intent, which is derived from a careful consideration of factors that influence the choice to be made.

Delinquent An individual who fails to fulfill an obligation or otherwise is guilty of a crime or offense.

Domestic partnership laws Legislation and regulations related to the legal recognition of nonmarital relationships between persons who are romantically involved with each other, have set up a joint residence, and have registered with cities recognizing said relationships.

Denaturalization To take away an individual's rights as a citizen.

Deportation Banishment to a foreign country, attended with confiscation of property and deprivation of civil rights.

Deposition The testimony of a party or witness in a civil or criminal proceeding taken before trial, usually in an attorney's office.

Desegregation Judicial mandate making illegal the practice of segregation.

Disclaimer The denial, refusal, or rejection of a right, power, or responsibility.

Discrimination The grant of particular privileges to a group randomly chosen from a large number of people in which no reasonable difference exists between the favored and disfavored groups. Federal laws prohibit discrimination in such areas as employment, housing, voting rights, education, access to public facilities, and on the bases of race, age, sex, nationality, disability, or religion.

Dismissal A discharge of an individual or corporation from employment.

Dissent A disagreement by one or more judges with the decision of the majority on a case before them.

Divorce A court decree that terminates a marriage; also known as marital dissolution.

Double jeopardy A second prosecution for the same offense after acquittal or conviction or multiple punishments for the same offense. The evil sought to be avoided by prohibiting double jeopardy is double trial and double conviction, not necessarily double punishment.

Draft A mandatory call of persons to serve in the military.

Due process of law A fundamental, constitutional guarantee that all legal proceedings will be fair and that one will be given notice of the proceedings and an opportunity to be heard before the government acts to take away one's life, liberty, or property. Also, a constitutional guarantee that a law shall not be unreasonable, random, or without consideration for general well-being.

Duress Unlawful pressure exerted upon a person to force that person to perform an act that he or she ordinarily would not perform.

Words to Know

E

Emancipation The act or process by which a person is liberated from the authority and control of another person.

Entrapment The act of government agents or officials that causes a person to commit a crime he or she would not have committed otherwise.

Equal Pay Act Federal law that commands the same pay for all persons who do the same work without regard to sex, age, race, or ability.

Equal protection The constitutional guarantee that no person or class of persons shall be denied the same protection of the laws that is enjoyed by other persons or other classes in like circumstances in their lives, liberty, property, and pursuit of happiness.

Establishment Clause The provision in the First Amendment that provides that there will be no laws created respecting the establishment of a religion, inhibiting the practice of a religion, or giving preference to any or all religions. It has been interpreted to also denounce the discouragement of any or all religions.

Euthanasia The merciful act or practice of terminating the life of an individual or individuals inflicted with incurable and distressing diseases in a relatively painless manner.

Exclusionary rule The principle based on federal constitutional law that evidence illegally seized by law enforcement officers in violation of a suspect's right to be free from unreasonable searches and seizures cannot be used against the suspect in a criminal prosecution.

Executive agreement An agreement made between the head of a foreign country and the president of the United States. This agreement does not have to be submitted to the Senate for consent, and it supersedes any contradicting state law.

Executive orders When the president uses some part of a law or the Constitution to enforce some action.

Executor The individual legally named by a deceased person to administer the provisions of his or her will.

Ex parte Latin for "on one side only"; done by, for, or on the application of one party alone.

Expert witness A witness, such as a psychological statistician or ballisticsexpert, who possesses special or superior knowledge concerning the subject of his or her testimony.

Ex post facto laws Latin for "after-the-fact laws"; laws that provide for the infliction of punishment upon a person for some prior act that, at the time it was committed, was not illegal.

Extradition The transfer of a person accused of a crime from one state or country to another state or country that seeks to place the accused on trial.

F

Family court A court that presides over cases involving: (1) child abuse and neglect; (2) support; (3) paternity; (4) termination of custody due to constant neglect; (5) juvenile delinquency; and (6) family offenses.

Federal Relating to a national government, as opposed to state or local governments.

Federal circuit courts The twelve circuit courts making up the U.S. Federal Circuit Court System. Decisions made by the federal district courts can be reviewed by the court of appeals in each circuit.

Federal district courts The first of three levels of the federal court system, which includes the U.S. Court of Appeals and the U.S. Supreme Court. If a participating party disagrees with the ruling of a federal district court in its case, it may petition for the case to be moved to the next level in the federal court system.

Felon An individual who commits a felony, a crime of a serious nature, such as burglary or murder.

Felony A serious crime, characterized under federal law and many state statutes as any offense punishable by death or imprisonment in excess of one year.

First degree murder Murder committed with deliberately premeditated thought and malice, or with extreme atrocity or cruelty. The difference between first and second degree murder is the presence of the specific intention to kill.

Fraud A false representation of a matter of fact—whether by words or by conduct, by false or misleading allegations, or by concealment of what should have been disclosed—that deceives and is intended to deceive another so that the individual will act upon it to her or his legal injury.

Freedom of assembly See Freedom of association.

Freedom of association The right to associate with others for the purpose of engaging in constitutionally protected activities, such as to peacefully assemble.

Freedom of religion The First Amendment right to individually believe and to practice or exercise one's religious belief.

Freedom of speech The right, guaranteed by the First Amendment to the U.S. Constitution, to express beliefs and ideas without unwarranted government restriction.

Freedom of the press The right, guaranteed by the First Amendment to the U.S. Constitution, to gather, publish, and distribute information and ideas without government restriction; this right encompasses freedom from prior restraints on publication and freedom from censorship.

Fundamental rights Rights that derive, or are implied, from the terms of the U.S. Constitution, such as the Bill of Rights, the first ten amendments to the Constitution.

G

Gag rule A rule, regulation, or law that prohibits debate or discussion of a particular issue.

Grandfather clause A portion of a statute that provides that the law is not applicable in certain circumstances due to preexisting facts.

Grand jury A panel of citizens that is convened by a court to decide whether it is appropriate for the government to indict (proceed with a prosecution against) someone suspected of a crime.

Grand larceny A category of larceny—the offense of illegally taking the property of another—in which the value of the property taken is greater than that set for petit larceny.

Grounds The basis or foundation; reasons sufficient in law to justify relief.

Guardian A person lawfully invested with the power, and charged with the obligation, of taking care of and managing the property and rights of a person who, because of age, understanding, or lack of self-control, is considered incapable of administering his or her own affairs.

Guardian ad litem A guardian appointed by the court to represent the interests of infants, the unborn, or incompetent persons in legal actions.

H

Habeas corpus Latin for "you have the body"; a writ (court order) that commands an individual or a government official who has restrained another to produce the prisoner at a designated time and place so that the court can determine the legality of custody and decide whether to order the prisoner's release.

Hate crime A crime motivated by race, religion, gender, sexual orientation, or other prejudice.

Hearing A legal proceeding in which issues of law or fact are tried and evidence is presented to help determine the issue.

Hearsay A statement made out of court that is offered in court as evidence to prove the truth of the matter asserted.

Heir An individual who receives an interest in, or ownership of, land or tenements from an ancestor who died through the laws of descent and distribution. At common law, an heir was the individual appointed by law to succeed to the estate of an ancestor who died without a will. It is commonly used today in reference to any individual who succeeds to property, either by will or law.

Homicide The killing of one human being by another human being.

Hung jury A trial jury selected to make a decision in a criminal case regarding a defendant's guilt or innocence that is unable to reach a verdict due to a complete division in opinion.

I

Immunity Exemption from performing duties that the law generally requires other citizens to perform, or from a penalty or burden that the law generally places on other citizens.

Impeachment A process used to charge, try, and remove public officials for misconduct while in office.

Inalienable Not subject to sale or transfer; inseparable.

Incapacity The absence of legal ability, competence, or qualifications.

Income tax A charge imposed by government on the annual gains of a person, corporation, or other taxable unit derived through work, business pursuits, investments, property dealings, and other sources determined in accordance with the Internal Revenue Code or state law.

Indictment A written accusation charging that an individual named therein has committed an act or admitted to doing something that is punishable by law.

Indirect tax A tax upon some right, privilege, or corporation.

Individual rights Rights and privileges constitutionally guaranteed to the people as set forth by the Bill of Rights; the ability of a person to pursue life, liberty, and property.

Infant Persons who are under the age of the legal majority—at common law, twenty-one years, now generally eighteen years. According to the sense in which this term is used, it may denote the age of the person, the contractual disabilities that nonage entails, or his or her status with regard to other powers or relations.

Inherent rights Rights held within a person because he or she exists.

Inheritance Property received from a person who has died, either by will or through state laws if the deceased has failed to execute a valid will.

Injunction A court order by which an individual is required to perform or is restrained from performing a particular act. A writ framed according to the circumstances of the individual case.

In loco parentis Latin for "in the placeof a parent"; the legal doctrine under which an individual assumes parental rights, duties, and obligations without going through the formalities of legal adoption.

Insanity defense A defense asserted by an accused in a criminal prosecution to avoid responsibility for a crime because, at the time of the crime, the person did not comprehend the nature or wrongfulness of the act.

Insider Relating to the federal regulation of the purchase and sale of stocks and bonds, anyone who has knowledge of facts not available to the general public.

Insider trading The trading of stocks and bonds based on information gained from special private, privileged information affecting the value of the stocks and bonds.

Intent A determination to perform a particular act or to act in a particular manner for a specific reason; an aim or design; a resolution to use a certain means to reach an end.

Intermediate courts Courts with general ability or authority to hear a case (trial, appellate, or both) but are not the court of last resort within the jurisdiction.

Intestate The description of a person who dies without making a valid will.

Involuntary manslaughter The act of unlawfully killing another human being unintentionally.

Irrevocable Unable to cancel or recall; that which is unalterable or irreversible.

J

Judicial Relating to courts and the legal system.

Judicial discretion Sound judgment exercised by a judge in determining what is right and fair under the law.

Judicial review A court's authority to examine an executive or legislative act and to invalidate (cancel) that act if it opposes constitutional principles.

Jurisdiction The geographic area over which authority (such as a cout) extends; legal authority.

Jury In trials, a group of people selected and sworn to inquire into matters of fact and to reach a verdict on the basis of evidence presented to it.

Jury nullification The ability of a jury to acquit the defendant despite the amount of evidence against him or her in a criminal case.

Just cause A reasonable and lawful ground for action.

Justifiable homicide The killing of another in self-defense or in the lawful defense of one's property; killing of another when the law demands it, such as in execution for a capital crime.

Juvenile A young individual who has not reached the age whereby he or she would be treated as an adult in the area of criminal law. The age at which the young person attains the status of being a legal majority varies from state to state—as low as fourteen years old, as high as eighteen years old; however, the Juvenile Delinquency Act determines that a youthful person under the age of eighteen is a juvenile in cases involving federal jurisdiction.

Juvenile court The court presiding over cases in which young persons under a certain age, depending on the area of jurisdiction, are accused of criminal acts.

Juvenile delinquency The participation of a youthful individual, one who falls under the age at which he or she could be tried as an adult, in illegal behavior.

L

Larceny The unauthorized taking and removal of the personal property of another by a person who intends to permanently deprive the owner of it; a crime against the right of possession.

Legal defense A complete and acceptable response as to why the claims of the plaintiff should not be granted in a point of law.

Legal tender All U.S. coins and currencies—regardless of when coined or issued—including (in terms of the Federal Reserve System) Federal Reserve notes and circulating notes of Federal Reserve banks and national banking associations that are used for all public and private debts, public charges, taxes, duties, and dues.

Legislation Lawmaking; the preparation and enactment of laws by a legislative body.

Liability A comprehensive legal term that describes the condition of being actually or potentially subject to (responsible for) a legal obligation.

Libel and slander The communication of false information about a person, a group, or an entity, such as a corporation. Libel is any defamation that can be seen, such as in print or on a film or in a representation such as a statued. Slander is any defamation that is spoken and heard.

Litigation An action brought in court to enforce a particular right; the act or process of bringing a lawsuit in and of itself; a judicial contest; any dispute.

Living will A written document that allows a patient to give explicit instructions about medical treatment to be administered when the patient is terminally ill or permanently unconscious; also called an advance directive.

Lobbying The process of influencing public and government policy at all levels: federal, state, and local.

M

Magistrate Any individual who has the power of a public civil officer or inferior judicial officer, such as a justice of the peace.

Majority Full age; legal age; age at which a person is no longer a minor. The age at which, by law, a person is capable of being legally responsible for all of his or her acts (i.e., contractual obligations) and is entitled to manage his or her own affairs and to the enjoy civic rights (i.e., right to vote). Also the status of a person who is a major in age.

Malice The intentional commission of a wrongful act, without justification, with the intent to cause harm to others; conscious violation of the law that injures another individual; a mental state indicating a disregard of social responsibility.

Malpractice When a professional, such as a doctor or lawyer, fails to carry out their job correctly and there are bad results.

Mandate A judicial command or order from a court.

Manslaughter The unjustifiable, inexcusable, and intentional killing of a human being without deliberation, premeditation, or malice.

Material Important; significant; substantial. A description of the quality of evidence that possesses such value as to establish the truth or falsity of a point in issue in a lawsuit.

Mediation Settling a dispute or controversy by setting up an independent person between the two parties to help them settle their disagreement.

Minor An infant or person who is under the age of legal competence. In most states, a person is no longer a minor after reaching the age of eighteen (though state laws might still prohibit certain acts until reaching a greater age; i.e., purchase of liquor).

Misdemeanor Offenses lower than felonies and generally those punishable by fine, penalty, or imprisonment other than in a penitentiary.

Mistrial A courtroom trial that has been ended prior to its normal conclusion. A mistrial has no legal effect and is considered an invalid trial. It differs from a new trial, which recognizes that a trial was completed but was set aside so that the issues could be tried again.

Mitigating circumstances Circumstances that may be considered by a court in determining responsibility of a defendant or the extent of damages to be awarded to a plaintiff. Mitigating circumstances do not justify or excuse an offense but may reduce the charge.

Monopoly An economic advantage held by one or more persons or companies because they hold the exclusive power to carry out a particular business or trade or to manufacture and sell a particular task or produce a particular product.

Moratorium A suspension (ending) of activity or an authorized period of delay or waiting. A moratorium is sometimes agreed upon by the interested parties, or it may be authorized or imposed by operation of law.

Motion A written or oral application made to a court or judge to obtain a ruling or order directing that some act be done in favor of the applicant.

Motive An idea, belief, or emotion that causes a person to act in a certain way, either good or bad.

Murder The unlawful killing of another human being without justification or excuse.

N

National origin The country in which a person was born or from which his or her ancestors came. One's national origin is typically calculated by employers to provide equal employment opportunity statistics in accordance with the provisions of the Civil Rights Act.

Naturalization A process by which a person gains nationality and becomes entitled to the privileges of citizenship. While groups of individuals have been naturalized in history by treaties or laws of Congress, such as in the case of Hawaii, typically naturalization occurs on the individual level upon the completion of a list of requirements.

Necessary and Proper Clause The statement contained in Article I, Section 8, Clause 18 of the U.S. Constitution that gives Congress the power to pass any laws that are necessary and proper to carrying out its specifically granted powers.

Negligence Conduct that falls below the standards of behavior established by law for the protection of others against unreasonable risk of harm.

Nonprofit A corporation or an association that conducts business for the benefit of the general public rather than to gain profits for itself.

Notary public A public official whose main powers include administering oaths and witnessing signatures, both important and effective ways to minimize fraud in legal documents.

O

Obscenity An act, spoken word, or item tending to offend public morals by its indecency or lewdness.

Ordinance A law, statute, or regulation enacted by a municipality.

P

Palimony The settlement awarded at the end of a non-marital relationship, where the couple lived together for a long period of time and where there was an agreement that one partner would support the other in return for the second making a home and performing domestic duties.

Pardon When a person in power, such as a president or governor, offers a formal statement of forgivenss for a crime and takes away the given punishment.

Parental liability A statute (law), enacted in some states, that makes parents responsible for damages caused by their children if it is found that the damages resulted from the parents' lack of control over the acts of the child.

Parole The release of a person convicted of a crime prior to the end of that person's term of imprisonment on the condition that they will follow certain strict rules for their conduct, and if they break any of those rules they will return to prison.

Patents Rights granted to inventors by the federal government that permit them to keep others from making, using, or selling their invention for a definite, or restricted, period of time.

Peremptory challenge The right to challenge the use of a juror in a trial without being required to give a reason for the challenge.

Perjury A crime that occurs when an individual willfully makes a false statement during a judicial proceeding, after he or she has taken an oath to speak the truth.

Petition A formal application made to a court in writing that requests action on a certain matter.

Petit larceny A form of larceny—the stealing of another's personal property—in which the value of the property that is taken is generally less than $50.

Words to Know

Plaintiff The party who sues in a civil action.

Plain view doctrine In the context of searches and seizures, the principle that provides that objects that an officer can easily see can be seized without a search warrant and are fair to use as evidence.

Plea The phase in a court case where the defendant has to declare whether they are guilty or not guilty.

Police power The authority that states to employ a police force and give them the power to enforce the laws and protect the community.

Poll tax A specified sum of money to be paid by each person who votes.

Polygamy The offense of having more than one wife or husband at the same time.

Precedent A court decision that is cited as an example to resolve similar questions of law in later cases.

Preponderance of evidence A rule that states that it is up to the plaintiff to convince the judge or the jury of their side of the case in or to win the case.

Prima facie [*Latin,* On the first appearance.]A fact presumed to be true unless it is disproved.

Prior restraint Government violating freedom of speech by not allowing something to be published.

Privacy In constitutional law, the right of people to make personal decisions regarding intimate matters; under the common law, the right of people to lead their lives in a manner that is reasonably secluded from public scrutiny, whether such scrutiny comes from a neighbor's prying eyes, an investigator's eavesdropping ears, or a news photographer's intrusive camera; and in statutory law, the right of people to be free from unwarranted drug testing and electronic surveillance.

Privilege An advantage or benefit possessed by an individual, company, or class beyond those held by others.

Privileges and immunities Concepts contained in the U.S. Constitution that place the citizens of each state on an equal basis with citizens of other states with respect to advantages resulting from citizenship in those states and citizenship in the United States.

Probable cause Apparent facts discovered through logical inquiry that would lead a reasonably intelligent person to believe that an accused person has committed a crime.

Probate court Called Surrogate or Orphan's Court in some states, the probate court presides over wills, the administration of estates, and, in some states, the appointment of guardians or approval of the adoption of minors.

Probation A sentence whereby a convict is released from confinement but is still under court supervision; a testing or a trial period. It can be given in lieu of a prison term or can suspend a prison sentence if the convict has consistently demonstrated good behavior.

Procedural due process The constitutional guarantee that one's liberty and property rights may not be affected unless reasonable notice and an opportunity to be heard in order to present a claim or defense are provided.

Property A thing or things owned either by government—public property—or owned by private individuals, groups, or companies—private property.

Prosecute To follow through; to commence and continue an action or judicial proceeding to its conclusion. To proceed against a defendant by charging that person with a crime and bringing him or her to trial.

Prosecution The proceedings carried out before a court to determine the guilt or innocence of a defendant. The term also refers to the government attorney charging and trying a criminal case.

Punitive damages Money awarded to an injured party that goes beyond that which is necessary to pay for the individual for losses and that is intended to punish the wrongdoer.

Q

Quorum A majority of an entire body; i.e., a quorum of a legislative assembly.

Quota The number of persons or things that must be used, or admitted, or hired in order to be following a rule or law.

R

Rape A criminal offense defined in most states as forcible sexual relations with a person against that person's will.

Ratification The confirmation or adoption of an act that has already been performed.

Reapportionment The realignment of voting districts done to fulfill the constitutional requirement of one person, one vote.

Referendum The right reserved to the people to approve or reject an act of the legislature, or the right of the people to approve or reject legislation that has been referred to them by the legislature.

Refugees Individuals who leave their native country for social, political, or religious reasons, or who are forced to leave as a result of any type of disaster, including war, political upheaval, and famine.

Rehabilitation Work to restore former rights, authority, or abilities.

Remand To send back.

Replevin A legal action to recover the possession of items of personal property.

Reprieve The temporary hold put on a death penalty for further review of the case.

Rescind To declare a contract void—of no legal force or binding effect—from its beginning and thereby restore the parties to the positions they would have been in had no contract ever been made.

Reservation A tract of land under the control of the Bureau of Indian Affairs to which a Native American tribe retains its original title of ownership, or that has been set aside from the public domain for use by a tribe.

Reserve Funds set aside to cover future expenses, losses, or claims. To retain; to keep in store for future or special use; to postpone to a future time.

Resolution The official expression of the opinion or will of a legislative body.

Retainer A contract between attorney and client specifying the nature of the services and the cost of the services.

Retribution Punishment or reward for an act. In criminal law, punishment is based upon the theory that every crime demands payment.

Reverse discrimination Discrimination against a group of people that is generally considered to be the majority, usually stemming from the enforcement of some affirmative action guidlelines.

Revocation The recall of some power or authority that has been granted.

Robbery The taking of money or goods in the possession of another, from his or her person or immediate presence, by force or intimidation.

S

Sabotage The willful destruction or impairment of war material or national defense material, or harm to war premises or war utilities. During a labor dispute, the willful and malicious destruction of an employer's property or interference with his or her normal operations.

Search warrant A court order authorizing the examination of a place for the purpose of discovering evidence of guilt to be used in the prosecution of a criminal action.

Second degree murder The unlawful taking of human life with malice, but without premeditated thought.

Sedition A revolt or an incitement to revolt against established authority, usually in the form of treason or defamation against government.

Seditious libel A written communication intended to incite the overthrow of the government by force or violence.

Segregation The act or process of separating a race, class, or ethnic group from a society's general population.

Self-defense The protection of one's person or property against some injury attempted by another.

Self-incrimination Giving testimony in a trial or other legal proceeding that could subject one to criminal prosecution.

Sentencing The post-conviction stage of a criminal justice process, in which the defendant is brought before the court for penalty.

Separate but equal The doctrine first accepted by the U.S. Supreme Court in *Plessy v. Ferguson* establishing that different facilities for blacks and whites was valid under the Equal Protection Clause of the Fourteenth Amendment as long as they were equal.

Separation of church and state The separation of religious and government interest to ensure that religion does not become corrupt by government and that government does not become corrupt by religious conflict. The principle prevents the government from supporting the practices of one religion over another. It also enables the government to do what is necessary to prevent one religious group from violating the rights of others.

Separation of powers The division of state and federal government into three independent branches.

Settlement The act of adjusting or determining the dealings or disputes between persons without pursuing the matter through a trial.

Sexual harassment Unwelcome sexual advances, requests for sexual favors, and other verbal or physical conduct of a sexual nature that tends to create a hostile or offensive work environment.

Share A portion or part of something that may be divided into components, such as a sum of money. A unit of stock that represents ownership in a corporation.

Shield laws Statutes that allow journalists not to disclose in legal proceedings confidential information or sources of information obtained in their professional capacities.

Statutes that restrict or prohibit the use of certain evidence in sexual offense cases, such as evidence regarding the lack of chastity of the victim.

Shoplifting Theft of merchandise from a store or business establishment.

Small claims court A special court that provides fast, informal, and inexpensive solutions for small claims.

Solicitation The criminal offense of urging someone to commit an unlawful act.

Statute An act of a legislature that declares, or commands something; a specific law, expressed in writing.

Statute of limitations A type of federal or state law that restricts the time within which legal proceedings may be brought.

Statutory law A law which is created by an act of the legislature.

Statutory rape Sexual intercourse by an adult with a person below a designated age.

Subpoena Latin for "under penalty"; a formal document that orders a named individual to appear before an officer of the court at a fixed time to give testimony.

Suffrage The right to vote at public elections.

Summons The paper that tells a defendant that he or she is being sued and asserts the power of the court to hear and determine the case. A form of legal process that commands the defendant to appear before the court on a specific day and to answer the complaint made by the plaintiff.

Supreme court The highest court in the U.S. judicial system.

Surrogate mother A woman who agrees under contract to bear a child for an infertile couple. The woman is paid to have a donated fertilized egg or the fertilized egg of the female partner in the couple (usually fertilized by the male partner of the couple) artificially placed into her uterus.

Suspended sentence A sentence that states that a criminal, in waiting for their trial, has already served enough time in prison.

Symbolic speech Nonverbal gestures and actions that are meant to communicate a message.

T

Testify To provide evidence as a witness in order to establish a particular fact or set of facts.

Testimony Oral evidence offered by a competent witness under oath, which is used to establish some fact or set of facts.

Trade secret Any valuable commercial information that provides a business with an advantage over competitors who do not have that information.

Trade union An organization of workers in the same skilled occupation or related skilled occupations who act together to secure for all members favorable wages, hours, and other working conditions.

Treason The betrayal of one's own country by waging war against it or by consciously or purposely acting to aid its enemies.

Treaty A compact made between two or more independent nations with a view to the public welfare.

Trespass An unlawful intrusion that interferes with one's person or property.

Trial A judicial examination and determination of facts and legal issues arising between parties to a civil or criminal action.

Trial court The court where civil actions or criminal proceedings are first heard.

Truancy The willful and unjustified failure to attend school by one required to do so.

Words to Know

U

Unenumerated rights Rights that are not expressly mentioned in the written text of a constitution but instead are inferred from the language, history, and structure of the constitution, or cases interpreting it.

Unconstitutional That which is not in agreement with the ideas and regulations of the Constitution.

Uniform commercial code A general and inclusive group of laws adopted, at least partially, by all of the states to further fair dealing in business.

V

Valid Binding; possessing legal force or strength; legally sufficient.

Vandalism The intentional and malicious destruction of or damage to the property of another.

Venue A place, such as a city or county, from which residents are selected to serve as jurors.

Verdict The formal decision or finding made by a jury concerning the questions submitted to it during a trial. The jury reports the verdict to the court, which generally accepts it.

Veto The refusal of an executive officer to approve a bill that has been created and approved by the legislature, thereby keeping the bill from becoming a law.

Voir dire Old French for "to speak the truth"; the preliminary examination of possible jurors to determine their qualifications and suitability to serve on a jury, in order to ensure the selection of a fair and impartial jury.

Voluntary manslaughter The unlawful killing of a person where there is no malice, premeditation or deliberate intent but too near to these standards to be classified as justifiable homicide.

W

Waive To intentionally or voluntarily give up a known right or engage in conduct that caused your rights to be taken away.

Ward A person, especially an infant or someone judged to be incompetent, placed by the court in the care of a guardian.

Warrant A written order issued by a judicial officer commanding a law enforcement officer to perform a duty. This usually includes searches, seizures and arrests.

White collar crime Term for nonviolent crimes that were committed in the course of the offender's occupation.

Will A document in which a person explains the management and distribution of his or her estate after his or her death.

Workers' compensation A system whereby an employer must pay, or provide insurance to pay, the lost wages and medical expenses of an employee who is injured on the job.

Writ An order issued by a court requiring that something be done.

Z

Zoning Assigning different areas within a city or county different uses, whereby one area cannot be used for any other purpose other than what it is designated. For example, if an area is assigned as residential, an office building could not be built there.

Words to Know

CAPITAL PUNISHMENT

Capital punishment, also called the death penalty, means killing a person as punishment for a crime. By the end of 1999, thirty-eight states and the federal government allowed the death penalty for criminal homicide, or murder. The District of Columbia and the following states did not allow the death penalty: Alaska, Hawaii, Iowa, Maine, Massachusetts, Michigan, Minnesota, North Dakota, Rhode Island, Vermont, West Virginia, and Wisconsin.

In 1999 ninety-eight executions occurred in the United States, up from sixty-eight in 1998. Ninety-four were by lethal injection, which kills the criminal with a deadly chemical solution. Three were by electrocution in an electric chair. Just one was with lethal gas, by which the state locks the criminal in a room with deadly gas. The only other methods allowed in the United States, hanging and firing squad, were not used in 1999.

History

Colonists brought the death penalty to America from England. The first recorded execution in America happened in the Jamestown Colony of

Virginia in 1608. Death penalty laws varied widely in the colonies. In 1636, the Massachusetts Bay Colony allowed capital punishment for a long list of crimes that included witchcraft and blasphemy. Pennsylvania, by contrast, initially allowed the death penalty only for treason and murder.

In the wake of the American Revolution in 1776, eleven colonies became states with new constitutions. Nine of the states prohibited cruel and unusual punishment, but all allowed the death penalty. In 1790, the first U.S. Congress passed a law allowing the death penalty for crimes of robbery, rape, murder, and forgery of public securities (notes and bonds for the payment of money). Under most of these laws, the death penalty was an automatic punishment for murder and other serious crimes.

Ever since the United States was established, many Americans have opposed the death penalty. In 1845, the American Society for the Abolition of Capital Punishment was formed. In 1847, Michigan became the first state to abolish capital punishment for all crimes except treason. By 1850, nine states had societies working to abolish capital punishment. Reflecting this trend, many states and other countries began to reduce the crimes punishable by death to murder and treason. Nevertheless, nearly 1400 recorded executions took place in the United States in the 1800s.

The movement to abolish capital punishment had both high and low points in the 1900s. On the up side, by the beginning of the century most states had changed their laws. Instead of making the death penalty automatic, new laws allowed juries to choose between death or imprisonment.

A low point, however, was in the 1930s and 1940s when between one hundred and two hundred prisoners were executed each year. Executions then declined in the 1950s and 1960s, partly because more prisoners began fighting their sentences in court. This trend led to a series of U.S. Supreme Court cases in the 1970s about whether the death penalty violates the U.S. Constitution.

Cruel and unusual punishment

The Eighth Amendment of the U.S. Constitution says that the government may not use "cruel and unusual punishments." Death penalty opponents say that this makes capital punishment unlawful. However, supporters argue that the Eighth Amendment only prevents torture and other barbaric punishments. They point out that the Fifth and Fourteenth Amendments say that the government may not take a person's life without "due process of law." Due process of law means using fair procedures to give a defendant a fair trial. For death penalty supporters, this means capital punishment is lawful if the government follows fair procedures.

Beginning in 1967, the nation stopped executions so the courts could examine whether the death penalty violated the U.S. Constitution. At that time, no guidelines were in effect to help juries decide between life or death. Studies showed that juries randomly chose the death penalty. For example, in cases that were similar some defendants got the death penalty, while others just went to prison.

Other studies suggested that the death penalty treated whites better than blacks. Blacks were sentenced to death more often than whites. Criminals who killed white people received the death penalty more often than those who killed black people.

In *Furman v. Georgia* (1972), the defendant argued to the Supreme Court that these random and racial results made the death penalty unconstitutional. With a 5–4 decision, the Supreme Court agreed. Justice William O. Douglas said that death penalty laws are cruel and unusual when they are unfair to African Americans and to poor, uneducated, and mentally ill people. Justice Douglas said America's laws were unfair because they did not give juries any guidance for choosing between life or death.

States reacted to *Furman* in two different ways. Some states passed new laws that made the death penalty automatic. In other words, if a defendant was found guilty of murder, he automatically got the death penalty. This was a return to the system that existed in 1776.

Most states passed new laws that created a two–phase approach to the death penalty. In the first phase, the jury decided whether the defendant was guilty, just like in a regular trial. In the second phase, the jury heard new evidence to determine if the defendant deserved the death penalty. This new evidence would tell the jury about the defendant's character, childhood, criminal record, and other background information, plus information about the severity of the murder. The jury then had to follow certain guidelines to decide whether to choose the death penalty.

In 1976, the Supreme Court heard a series of cases involving the new laws. In *Woodson v. California* (1976), the Court said that automatic death penalty laws are unconstitutional because they do not respect human dignity, as they do not consider each defendant's case on its own merits. In *Gregg v. Georgia* (1976), however, the Court said the new two–phase system in most states was constitutional. The two–phase system was a good way to make sure defendants facing the death penalty got a fair trial. Justice Potter Stewart specifically said that the death penalty is not a "cruel and unusual" punishment. Rather, it is a severe punishment fit for a severe crime.

One year later, in *Coker v. Georgia* (1977), the Supreme Court said that the death penalty is an unfair punishment for rape. (Rape is when a person forces someone else to have sexual intercourse.) After *Coker,* the death penalty in the United States is mostly limited to murder cases.

Death penalty debate

Between 1976 and the end of 1999, there were 598 exccutions in the United States. As of September 1, 1999, there were 3,625 inmates on death row waiting to be executed.

Studies suggest that seventy-five percent of Americans support the death penalty. Whether America should keep the death penalty, however, is a hotly debated question. Supporters say the death penalty makes the punishment fit the crime. Opponents say that killing murderers does not teach people that killing is wrong. Here are some of the issues that divide Americans in this debate.

Accuracy

Death penalty opponents argue that the system is not entirely accurate. They fear that innocent people are put to death when judges and juries make mistakes, and when the government frames the wrong person. Sometimes after a defendant is convicted, for instance, another person admits to being the real murderer. For instance, in 1999 alone, eight people were released from death row after new evidence suggested they were not guilty. In one of these cases in Illinois, Anthony Porter came within hours of being executed before he was released. Death penalty opponents wonder how many innocent people are not saved in time.

Death penalty supporters say the chance for an innocent person to be executed is small. On the other hand, they say murderers who are allowed to live are likely to kill again. For them, the death penalty is a choice between victims and criminals.

Fairness

As noted above, studies in the mid-1900s suggested that the death penalty treated whites better than blacks. Some say that the situation has not improved under the new laws after *Furman*. While African Americans make up less than fifteen percent of the general population, they made up 42 percent of the death row population in 1997. Although blacks and whites are murder victims in roughly equal numbers, for the ninety-eight people executed in 1999, one hundred and four of their victims were white, while only fifteen were black. Death penalty opponents say that these statistics show that the system treats whites better than blacks, and punishes people who murder whites more severely.

Data also suggests a gender bias in the death penalty system. Although women commit thirteen percent of all murders, they account for only two percent of all death sentences and less than one percent of actual executions. Death penalty opponents also say that poor people are executed more often than wealthy people, and uneducated people more than educated people. As Supreme Court Justice William O. Douglas said in *Furman* when referring to wealthy people, "The Leopolds and Loebs are given prison terms, not sentenced to death."

Death penalty supporters reject this data. They say studies show that people who get the death penalty are the ones who commit the worst murders, such as murder during rape, murder of children, and murder of more than one person.

In *McCleskey v. Kemp* (1987), the U.S. Supreme Court rejected a racial bias challenge to the death penalty. The Court said that as long as the system is designed to be fair, and as long as a jury does not convict a defendant just because of his race, the death penalty is constitutional. Numerical studies that suggest the system is unfair do not mean that it is.

Juveniles

In the United States, most young people are minors, or juveniles, until they reach the age of eighteen. The Supreme Court, however, has said that people who are sixteen when they commit murder may receive the death penalty. In the 1990s, the United States was one of only six countries to allow juvenile offenders to be executed. The other countries were Iran, Nigeria, Pakistan, Saudi Arabia, and Yemen.

Death penalty opponents say that it is barbaric to execute juvenile offenders. They say juveniles are too young to understand what they are doing when they kill another person. Some juvenile murderers are themselves victims of crime, including physical and sexual child abuse. Death penalty opponents say these juveniles need love, caring, and reform to nurture them into responsible adults.

Death penalty supporters argue that a person who is old enough to kill is old enough to die for it. They also say gangs use juveniles for crimes if juveniles cannot get the death penalty. In 1999, just one juvenile offender was executed in the United States.

Cost

Death penalty cases spend many years in the court system because defendants appeal their convictions and sentences many times. The average inmate spends eleven years on death row during this process. Because the state often pays expenses for both the prosecution and defense, one estimate says that death penalty cases cost states between two and four million dollars per inmate. By comparison, it costs about one million dollars to keep a criminal in prison for life. Opponents say that death penalty cases are wasting taxpayer dollars.

Death penalty supporters disagree with these numbers. They say inmates on death row are costly and take up valuable space in already overcrowded jails.

In 1996, Congress passed the Anti -Terrorism and Effective Death Penalty Act. The law is designed to speed up death penalty cases so they do not take as long or cost as much. Some fear, however, that quicker executions will cause more mistakes.

Prevention

Death penalty supporters say that capital punishment prevents murderers from killing again and discourages other people from ever killing. They point to the example of Kenneth McDuff, who was sentenced to death for two murders in 1966. When the Supreme Court temporarily got rid of the death penalty in *Furman* in 1972, McDuff's sentence was reduced to life in prison. After being released on parole in 1989, McDuff raped, tortured, and murdered at least nine women before being caught again in 1992.

Death penalty opponents argue that capital punishment does not stop criminals from committing murder. They point to studies that show that the murder rate in states without the death penalty is half the murder rate of states with capital punishment. For death penalty opponents, this is evidence that capital punishment increases violence in society by setting a bad example.

Suggestions for further reading

Almonte, Paul. *Capital Punishment.* New York: Crestwood House, 1991.

"Death Penalty." *Issues and Controversies on File.* May 1, 1998.

Gottfried, Ted. *Capital Punishment: The Death Penalty Debate.* Enslow Publishers, Inc., 1997.

Nardo, Don. *Death Penalty.* Lucent Books, 1992.

O'Sullivan, Carol. *The Death Penalty: Identifying Propaganda Techniques.* San Diego: Greenhaven Press, 1989.

Steins, Richard. *The Death Penalty: Is It Justice?* Twenty First Century Books, 1995.

Wawrose, Susan C. *The Death Penalty: Seeking Justice in a Civilized Society.* Millbrook Press, 2000.

Winters, Paul A., ed. *The Death Penalty: Opposing Viewpoints.* San Diego: Greenhaven Press, 1997.

Wolf, Robert V. *Capital Punishment.* Philadelphia: Chelsea House Publishers, 1997.

Furman v. Georgia
1972

Appellant: William Henry Furman

Appellee: State of Georgia

Appellant's Claim: That the Georgia death penalty was cruel and unusual punishment under the Eight and Fourteenth Amendments.

Chief Lawyer for Appellant: Anthony G. Amsterdam

Chief Lawyer for Appellee: Dorothy T. Beasley, Assistant Attorney General of Georgia

Justices for the Court: William J. Brennan, Jr., William O. Douglas, Thurgood Marshall, Potter Stewart, Byron R. White

Justices Dissenting: Harry A. Blackmun, Warren E. Burger, Lewis F. Powell, Jr., William H. Rehnquist

Date of Decision: June 29, 1972

Decision: Georgia's death penalty statute was unconstitutional.

Significance: *Furman* said death penalty laws that allow random, racial results are unconstitutional.

O n the night of August 11, 1967, 29-year-old William Joseph Micke, Jr., came home from work to his wife and five children in Savannah, Georgia. He went to bed around midnight. Two hours later, the Mickes were awakened by strange noises in the kitchen. Thinking that one of his children was sleepwalking, William Micke went to the kitchen to investigate.

Micke found 26-year-old William Henry Furman in the kitchen. Furman was a poor, uneducated, mentally ill African American who had broken into the house and was carrying a gun. When he saw Micke, Furman fled the house, shooting Micke as he left. The bullet hit Micke in the chest, killing him instantly.

Micke's family immediately called the police. Within minutes, the police searched the neighborhood and found Furman still carrying his gun. Furman was charged with murder. Before Furman's trial, the court committed Furman to the Georgia Central State Hospital for psychological examination. After studying Furman, the hospital decided he was mentally ill and psychotic.

Furman v. Georgia

On Trial

Furman's trial was on September 20, 1968. Because he was poor, Furman got a poor man's trial. His court-appointed lawyer, B. Clarence Mayfield, received the regular court-approved fee of just $150. Furman testified in his own defense. He said that when Micke caught him in the kitchen, he started to leave the house backwards and tripped over a wire. When Furman tripped, the gun fired. Furman said he did not mean to kill anyone.

Although murder cases can be complicated, Furman's trial lasted just one day. The court rejected Furman's insanity plea and the jury found Furman guilty of murder. Although the evidence suggested Furman killed Micke accidentally, the jury sentenced Furman to death.

Furman Appeals

Furman appealed his conviction and sentence. The Georgia Supreme Court affirmed both on April 24, 1969. On May 3, however, the court stayed (delayed) Furman's execution so Furman could appeal to the U.S. Supreme Court. Because Furman's case attracted a lot of publicity, several lawyers, including Anthony G. Amsterdam, joined Mayfield to help with the appeal.

Before the Supreme Court on January 17, 1972, Amsterdam argued that the death penalty in Georgia violated the Eighth Amendment of the U.S. Constitution. The Eighth Amendment says the federal government may not use "cruel and unusual punishments." States, including Georgia, must obey the Eighth Amendment under the Due Process Clause of the Fourteenth Amendment.

CAPITAL PUNISHMENT

Amsterdam said the death penalty was "cruel and unusual" for several reasons. At the time, juries received no guidance about choosing the death penalty. They simply listened to the evidence on guilt or innocence and decided whether the defendant deserved to die. Studies showed that juries acted randomly when choosing the death penalty. In cases that were similar, some defendants got the death penalty while others just went to prison.

Other studies showed that defendants who were black, uneducated, poor, or mentally ill received the death penalty more often than those who were white, educated, wealthy, and mentally healthy. Amsterdam said these random, racial, unfair results made the death penalty cruel and unusual.

Supreme Court Rules

With a 5–4 decision, the Supreme Court reversed Furman's conviction. Five of the justices agreed that Furman's death sentence was cruel and unusual punishment. The justices, however, could not agree on a reason for their decision. All five justices in the majority, then, wrote separate opinions explaining the result.

Justice William O. Douglas wrote an opinion that best explained the Court's decision. Justice Douglas reviewed the history of the death penalty in England and America. He noted that under English law, the death penalty was unfair if it was applied unevenly to minorities, outcasts, and unpopular groups. Douglas decided the death penalty in the United States is "unusual" under the Eighth Amendment if it discriminates against a defendant because of his "race, religion, wealth, social position, or class."

Douglas then reviewed many studies about how the death penalty was applied in America. He decided that African Americans and the poor, sick, and uneducated members of society received the death penalty most often. Douglas believed this happened because juries had no guidance when applying the death penalty. This allowed juries to act on their prejudices by targeting unpopular groups with the death penalty. Douglas suggested death penalty laws would have to be rewritten to prevent such results.

Justices William J. Brennan, Jr., and Thurgood Marshall also wrote opinions. They believed the death penalty was cruel and unusual punishment in all cases and should be outlawed forever. Four justices wrote dissenting opinions, meaning they disagreed with the Court's decision. Chief Justice Warren E. Burger said if the public did not like the death

FLORIDA'S ELECTRIC CHAIR

Debate over the death penalty heated up again in Florida in 1999. The issue was whether the electric chair is cruel and unusual punishment. In July 1999, blood poured from Allen Lee Davis's nose as he was executed in Florida's electric chair. The incident followed two others in Florida in 1990 and 1997, when inmates caught fire as they were killed in the chair.

Death penalty opponents said the electric chair is cruel and unusual punishment. They called for Florida to stop all such executions. Meanwhile, the U.S. Supreme Court agreed to review a case to determine whether Florida may continue to use the electric chair.

Death penalty supporters said the electric chair is a fair way to execute convicted murderers. Davis had been convicted of murdering a pregnant woman and her two young daughters. Florida Governor Jeb Bush said Davis's nosebleed was nothing compared to the savage murders he committed.

In January 2000, the Florida state legislature considered a law to switch the death penalty from the electric chair to lethal injection. Florida State Senator Locke Burt (R) once said he did not want to make the switch because "a painless death is not punishment." On January 7, 2000, however, the legislature passed the law, and Governor Bush was expected to sign it

penalty or thought it was being used unfairly, they could rewrite the law or get rid of it altogether.

Impact

Furman did not outlaw the death penalty. It just required states to prevent random, racial, unfair results by giving juries guidance to apply the death penalty fairly. After *Furman,* most states rewrote their death penalty laws to do this. The new laws created a two-phase system for death penalty

**CAPITAL
PUNISHMENT**

cases. In the first phase, the jury decides if the defendant is guilty of murder. In the second phase, the jury hears new evidence to decide if the defendant deserves the death penalty. The new laws gave juries guidance for making this decision. In *Gregg v. Georgia* (1976), the Supreme Court said the new laws were valid under the Eighth Amendment. America was allowed to keep the death penalty.

Some people believe the death penalty is still unfair under the new laws. For the ninety-eight people executed in the United States in 1999, 104 of their victims were white while only fifteen of their victims were black. Death penalty opponents say this means the system treats whites better by punishing their attackers more severely. Death penalty supporters disagree. They say studies prove that criminals who get the death penalty are the ones who commit the worst murders, such as murder during rape, murdering children, and murdering more than one person.

Suggestions for further reading

Almonte, Paul. *Capital Punishment.* New York: Crestwood House, 1991.

Bragg, Rick. "Florida's Messy Executions Put the Electric Chair on Trial." *New York Times,* November 18, 1999.

"Death Penalty." *Issues and Controversies on File.* May 1, 1998.

Gottfried, Ted. *Capital Punishment: The Death Penalty Debate.* Enslow Publishers, Inc., 1997.

Henson, Burt M., and Ross R. Olney. *Furman v. Georgia: The Death Penalty and the Constitution.* New York: Franklin Watts, Ind., 1996.

Herda, D.J. *Furman v. Georgia: The Death Penalty Case.* Enslow Publishers, Inc., 1994.

Nardo, Don. *Death Penalty.* Lucent Books, 1992.

O'Sullivan, Carol. *The Death Penalty: Identifying Propaganda Techniques.* San Diego: Greenhaven Press, 1989.

Steins, Richard. *The Death Penalty: Is It Justice?* Twenty First Century Books, 1995.

Wawrose, Susan C. *The Death Penalty: Seeking Justice in a Civilized Society.* Millbrook Press, 2000.

Winters, Paul A., ed. *The Death Penalty: Opposing Viewpoints.* San Diego: Greenhaven Press, 1997.

Wolf, Robert V. *Capital Punishment.* Philadelphia: Chelsea House Publishers, 1997.

Woodson v. North Carolina
1976

Petitioners: James Tyrone Woodson and Luby Waxton

Respondent: State of North Carolina

Petitioners' Claim: That North Carolina's automatic death penalty for first degree murder violated the Eighth Amendment.

Chief Lawyer for Petitioners: Anthony G. Amsterdam

Chief Lawyer for Respondent: Sidney S. Eagles, Jr., Special Deputy Attorney General of North Carolina

Justices for the Court: William J. Brennan, Jr., Thurgood Marshall, Lewis F. Powell, Jr., John Paul Stevens, Potter Stewart

Justices Dissenting: Harry A. Blackmun, Warren E. Burger, William H. Rehnquist, Byron R. White

Date of Decision: July 2, 1976

Decision: North Carolina's automatic death penalty was cruel and unusual punishment under the Eighth Amendment.

Significance: *Woodson* said death penalty laws must let juries choose between death and imprisonment. To make that decision, juries must consider the defendant's character, his prior criminal record, and the circumstances of the murder he committed.

Using the death penalty, governments kill people as punishment for crime. In the United States, most states allow the death penalty for first degree murder. Before 1972, most states allowed juries to decide death penalty cases with no guidance. Juries had total control to choose life or death for defendants who committed murder.

The Eighth Amendment prevents the government from using cruel and unusual punishments. In *Furman v. Georgia* (1972), the U.S. Supreme Court said death penalty laws that give juries total control are cruel and unusual under the Eighth Amendment. Many states, including North Carolina, changed their laws to take control away from juries. Under the new laws, defendants who were convicted of first degree murder automatically got the death penalty. In *Woodson v. North Carolina,* the question was whether these new laws were cruel and unusual.

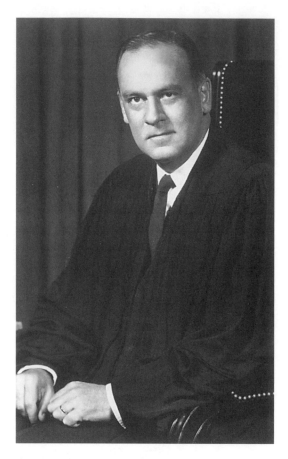

Associate Justice Potter Stewart.
Courtesy of the Supreme Court of the United States.

Killing for Cash

James Tyrone Woodson and three other men in North Carolina had discussed robbing a convenience food store. On June 3, 1974, Woodson had been drinking alcohol in his trailer. At 9:30 p.m., Luby Waxton and Leonard Tucker arrived at Woodson's trailer. Waxton hit Woodson in the face and threatened to kill him if he did not join the robbery.

Woodson got into the car and the three men drove to Waxton's trailer, where they met Johnnie Lee Carroll. Waxton got a handgun, Tucker gave Woodson a rifle, and the four men drove to a convenience food store in one car. Tucker and Waxton entered the store while Carroll and Woodson stayed in the car as lookouts.

Inside the store, Tucker bought a pack of cigarettes. Waxton also asked the clerk for cigarettes. When she handed them over, Waxton shot her at point blank range. Waxton then removed money from the cash register and gave it to Tucker, who rushed back to the parking lot. From outside, Tucker heard another shot and then saw Waxton appear holding a wad of money. The four men drove away together.

As it turned out, the clerk died and a customer was seriously wounded. This made it a case of first degree murder. Tucker and Carroll pled guilty to crimes lesser than murder in exchange for testifying for the prosecution at Woodson and Waxton's trial. At trial, Waxton claimed that Tucker, not he, had shot the clerk and customer. Woodson, who was forced to go along that night and sat in the car during the robbery, refused to admit to any wrongdoing.

The jury found both Woodson and Waxton guilty of first degree murder. Under North Carolina's new law, they automatically got the death penalty. The judge and jury had no choice. Woodson and Waxton appealed their death sentences. They argued that the death penalty is cruel and unusual punishment under the Eighth Amendment. The U.S. Supreme Court agreed to review their case.

Automatic Death Penalty Unconstitutional

With a 5–4 decision, the Supreme Court reversed Woodson and Waxton's death sentences. Writing for the Court, Justice Potter Stewart first decided that the death penalty is not cruel and unusual punishment in all cases. When a criminal commits first degree murder, the death penalty makes the punishment fit the crime.

The Court decided, however, that automatic death penalties are cruel and unusual punishment. Stewart said punishment is cruel and unusual when it offends America's standards of decency. To determine these standards, Justice Stewart analyzed the history of the death penalty.

Woodson v. North Carolina

CAPITAL PUNISHMENT

CRUEL AND UNUSUAL PUNISHMENT

The Eighth Amendment of the U.S. Constitution prevents the government from using cruel and unusual punishment. Most people agree that torture and other barbaric punishments are cruel and unusual. Does this mean the death penalty is cruel and unusual?

To answer this question, the Supreme Court uses the test from a non-death penalty case. In *Trop v. Dulles* (1958), Albert L. Trop lost his U.S. citizenship after deserting the U.S. army during World War II. The U.S. Supreme Court decided that taking away Trop's citizenship was cruel and unusual punishment under the Eighth Amendment. To decide what is cruel and unusual, the Court said it must consider American standards of decency as the country grows and matures.

In *Woodson,* the question was whether the death penalty is indecent in American society. The Court decided that when a criminal commits murder, the death penalty is not indecent. The death penalty cannot, however, be automatic. The law must allow juries to decide whether each criminal should live or die.

When the United States was born in 1776, many states had automatic death penalties for crimes such as murder, rape, and robbery. Juries, however, thought automatic death was too serious for certain crimes. This led most states to change their death penalty laws to give juries the choice between death and imprisonment. Stewart said this meant automatic death penalties offended American society.

In *Furman v. Georgia,* the U.S. Supreme Court struck down laws giving juries too much control over the death penalty. But Stewart said automatic death penalties did not solve the problem. Instead, juries needed to decide the death penalty in each case based on the defendant's character and criminal record and the circumstances of his crime. Only such individual consideration would respect the humanity of each defendant. Justice Stewart said the Eighth Amendment required such respect in a civilized society.

Impact

After *Furman* outlawed the death penalty in 1972, *Woodson* and other cases decided on July 2, 1976 made it legal again. From 1976 through 1999, 598 people were executed in the United States. Protesters still say the death penalty is cruel and unusual punishment in any case. Supporters say people who commit murder deserve to die. Under *Woodson,* juries deciding death penalty cases must be guided by the defendant's character and background and the circumstances of his murder.

Woodson v. North Carolina

Suggestions for further reading

Almonte, Paul. *Capital Punishment.* New York: Crestwood House, 1991.

Gottfried, Ted. *Capital Punishment: The Death Penalty Debate. Enslow Publishers, Inc., 1997.*

Henson, Burt M., and Ross R. Olney. *Furman v. Georgia: The Death Penalty and the Constitution.* New York: Franklin Watts, Inc., 1996.

Herda, D.J. *Furman v. Georgia: The Death Penalty Case.* Enslow Publishers, Inc., 1994.

Mikula, Mark, and L. Mpho Mabunda, eds. *Great American Court Cases.* Vol. II. Detroit: The Gale Group, 1999.

Nardo, Don. *Death Penalty.* Lucent Books, 1992.

O'Sullivan, Carol. *The Death Penalty: Identifying Propaganda Techniques.* San Diego: Greenhaven Press, 1989.

Steins, Richard. *The Death Penalty: Is It Justice?* Twenty First Century Books, 1995.

Tushnet, Mark. *The Death Penalty.* New York: Facts on File, 1994.

Wawrose, Susan C. *The Death Penalty: Seeking Justice in a Civilized Society.* Millbrook Press, 2000.

Winters, Paul A., ed. *The Death Penalty: Opposing Viewpoints.* San Diego: Greenhaven Press, 1997.

Wolf, Robert V. *Capital Punishment.* Philadelphia: Chelsea House Publishers, 1997.

Booth v. Maryland
1987

Petitioner: John Booth

Respondent: State of Maryland

Petitioner's Claim: That Maryland violated the Eighth Amendment by letting the jury hear evidence about how his crime affected his victim's family.

Chief Lawyer for Petitioner: George E. Burns, Jr.

Chief Lawyer for Respondent: Charles O. Monk II, Deputy Attorney General of Maryland

Justices for the Court: Harry A. Blackmun, William J. Brennan, Jr., Thurgood Marshall, Lewis F. Powell, Jr., John Paul Stevens

Justices Dissenting: Sandra Day O'Connor, William H. Rehnquist, Antonin Scalia, Byron R. White

Date of Decision: June 15, 1987

Decision: The Supreme Court reversed Booth's death sentence.

Significance: With *Booth,* the Supreme Court said it is cruel and unusual to let juries hear evidence about how a murder affected the victim's family.

Using the death penalty, governments kill people as punishment for crime. In the United States, most states allow the death penalty for first degree murder. Before 1972, most states allowed juries to decide death penalty cases with no guidance. Juries had total control to choose life or death for defendants who committed murder.

The Eighth Amendment prevents the government from using cruel and unusual punishments. In **Furman v. Georgia** (1972), the U.S. Supreme Court said death penalty laws that give juries total control are cruel and unusual. The Court said juries must be guided to decide between life or death based on the defendant's character, his background, and the circumstances of the murder he committed.

As violent crime increased in the 1980s, a victims rights movement began in the United States. The movement's goal was to make sure the criminal justice system takes care of victims instead of just protecting the rights of defendants and criminals. During this movement, many states passed laws allowing juries to hear victim impact evidence during the sentencing phase of death penalty cases. Victim impact evidence is information that tells the jury how a murder has affected the victim's family and community. In *Booth v. Maryland,* the U.S. Supreme Court had to decide whether victim impact evidence violates the Eighth Amendment.

**B o o t h   v.
M a r y l a n d**

Killing for Drugs

Irvin Bronstein, 78, and his wife Rose, 75, lived a happy life of retirement in West Baltimore, Maryland. John Booth lived three houses away in the same neighborhood. In 1983, Booth and Willie Reid entered the Bronsteins' home to steal money to buy heroin. During the crime, Booth and Reid bound and gagged the Bronsteins and then stabbed them to death with a kitchen knife. The Bronsteins' son found his dead parents two days later.

Booth and Reid faced separate trials in Maryland. The jury convicted Booth of two counts of first-degree murder, two counts of robbery, and conspiracy to commit robbery. Maryland's prosecutor requested the death penalty, and Booth chose to have the jury make the decision. A Maryland law required the prosecutor to prepare a victim impact statement (VIS) before the death penalty hearing. The purpose of the VIS was to describe the effect the crime had on the Bronsteins' family.

The prosecutor prepared a VIS based on interviews with the Bronsteins' son, daughter, daughter-in-law, and granddaughter. The Bronsteins' son, who discovered his murdered parents, said they were "butchered like animals." He said he suffered from lack of sleep and depression ever since finding them. The Bronsteins' daughter also suffered from lack of sleep and constant crying. She felt like a part of her died with her parents and that the joy in life was gone. The Bronsteins' granddaughter told how a family wedding four days after the murders was ruined. The Bronsteins expressed their desire that Booth be put to death.

The prosecutor read the VIS at Booth's death penalty hearing. Booth objected, arguing that it would prevent the jury from fairly deciding whether he deserved to die. The trial court rejected this objection and the jury sentenced Booth to death. Booth appealed to the Maryland Court of Appeals, again arguing that the VIS was cruel and unusual under the Eighth Amendment. The court disagreed and said the VIS helped the jury determine the punishment Booth deserved based on the harm he had done. Booth took his case to the U.S. Supreme Court.

Focus on the Criminal

With a 5–4 decision, the Supreme Court reversed Booth's death sentence. Writing for the Court, Justice Lewis F. Powell, Jr., said the jury's job in a death penalty case is to decide whether the criminal deserves to die based on his character and background and the circumstances of the murder. The jury is supposed to focus on the criminal's personal responsibility and moral guilt. Victim impact statements make the jury focus on the victim instead of the criminal.

Powell said murderers usually have no idea how their crimes will affect their victims' families. That means those effects have nothing to do with a criminal's blameworthiness. Victim impact evidence makes juries evaluate how much a victim is worth. That implies that people deserve to die more when they kill a valuable person who has a big family than when they kill a bad person who is alone. That did not feel right to the Supreme Court.

The Supreme Court said the death penalty is cruel and unusual when given by a jury that has been inflamed by victim impact evidence. Because the jury received such evidence in Booth's case, his death sentence violated the Eighth Amendment and had to be reversed.

Make the Punishment Fit the Crime

Four justices dissented, which means they disagreed with the Court's decision. Justice Byron R. White said that "just as the murderer should be considered as an individual, so too the victim is an individual whose death represents a unique loss to society and in particular to his family." Justice Antonin Scalia agreed. He said the jury's job is to determine

DRUGS AND CRIME

The murderers in *Booth v. Maryland* were stealing money to buy heroin, an illegal narcotic drug. Studies show a link between crime and frequent drug use. In a 1988 study, eighty-two percent of daily narcotic drug users said they committed some form of property crime, such as theft, shoplifting, and burglary. Violent crime, such as assault, robbery, rape, and murder, was less frequent among narcotic drug users.

Crime among non-narcotic drug users is a little different. Studies say cocaine users frequently commit both property and violent crime. In a 1991 study of 1,725 teenagers, cocaine users accounted for sixty percent of minor thefts, fifty-seven percent of felony thefts, forty-one percent of robberies, and twenty-eight percent of felony assaults. By contrast, people who use marijuana do not appear to commit more crime than non-users. In fact, there is evidence that marijuana use reduces violent crime.

whether a murderer deserves to die. How can the jury do that without knowing the harm the murderer did to his victim's family.

Impact

Booth was a setback for the victims rights movement in the United States. Four years later, however, the Supreme Court decided ***Payne v. Tennessee*** (1991). In *Payne,* the jury was allowed to hear evidence about how a mother's murder affected her son, who was with her and injured himself while his mother was killed. The Supreme Court said that because the boy was one of the victims, it did not violate the Eighth Amendment to tell the jury how the crime affected his life.

Suggestions for further reading

Almonte, Paul. *Capital Punishment.* New York: Crestwood House, 1991.

Gottfried, Ted. *Capital Punishment: The Death Penalty Debate.* Enslow Publishers, Inc., 1997.

**CAPITAL
PUNISHMENT**

Henson, Burt M., and Ross R. Olney. *Furman v. Georgia: The Death Penalty and the Constitution.* New York: Franklin Watts, Inc., 1996.

Herda, D.J. *Furman v. Georgia: The Death Penalty Case.* Enslow Publishers, Inc., 1994.

Jaffe, Jerome H., ed. *Encyclopedia of Drugs and Alcohol.* New York: Macmillan Library Reference USA, 1995.

Nardo, Don. *Death Penalty.* Lucent Books, 1992.

O'Sullivan, Carol. *The Death Penalty: Identifying Propaganda Techniques.* San Diego: Greenhaven Press, 1989.

Steins, Richard. *The Death Penalty: Is It Justice?* Twenty First Century Books, 1995.

Tushnet, Mark. *The Death Penalty.* New York: Facts on File, 1994.

Wawrose, Susan C. *The Death Penalty: Seeking Justice in a Civilized Society.* Millbrook Press, 2000.

Winters, Paul A., ed. *The Death Penalty: Opposing Viewpoints.* San Diego: Greenhaven Press, 1997.

Wolf, Robert V. *Capital Punishment.* Philadelphia: Chelsea House Publishers, 1997.

Thompson v. Oklahoma
1988

Appellant: William Wayne Thompson

Appellee: State of Oklahoma

Appellant's Claim: That executing him for committing murder when he was fifteen years old would be cruel and unusual punishment.

Chief Lawyer for Appellant: Harry F. Tepker, Jr.

Chief Lawyer for Appellee: David W. Lee

Justices for the Court: Harry A. Blackmun, William J. Brennan, Jr., Thurgood Marshall, Sandra Day O'Connor, John Paul Stevens

Justices Dissenting: William H. Rehnquist, Antonin Scalia, Byron R. White (Anthony M. Kennedy did not participate)

Date of Decision: June 29, 1988

Decision: The Supreme Court reversed Thompson's death sentence.

Significance: *Thompson* said the Eighth Amendment forbids executing people for crimes they commit when they are less than sixteen years old.

In 1983, when he was fifteen years old, William Wayne Thompson had a brother-in-law named Charles Keene. Keene was married to Thompson's sister, Vicki, whom Keene beat and abused. Thompson decided to end his sister's suffering.

On the night of January 22, 1983, Thompson left his mother's house with his half-brother and two friends to kill Charles Keene. In the early morning hours of January 23, a neighbor named Malcom "Possum" Brown was awakened by the sound of a gunshot on his porch. Someone pounded on Brown's door shouting, "Possum, open the door, let me in. They're going to kill me." Brown called the police and then opened the door to see Keene being beaten by four men. Before the police arrived, the four men took Keene away in a car.

Thompson and his friends shot Keene twice, cut his throat, chest, and stomach, broke one of his legs, chained him to a concrete block, and threw him into the Washita River. One of Thompson's friends said Thompson cut Keene "so the fish could eat his body." Authorities did not find Keene's body until almost four weeks after the murder.

Lawyer David W. Lee argued the state's case against William Thompson. Reproduced by permission of AP/Wide World Photos.

Child or Adult Murderer?

As most states do, Oklahoma had a juvenile justice system. The system's goal was to reform childhood criminals in juvenile justice centers rather than punish them in prisons. Oklahoma, however, allowed childhood murderers to be tried and punished as adults if they understood what they were doing and had no hope for reform.

Prior to the murder, Thompson had been arrested four times for assault and battery and once for attempted burglary. Mary Robinson, who worked for the juvenile justice system, said the counseling Thompson received in the juvenile justice system did not improve his behavior. The court decided Thompson understood the severity of murder and could not be reformed by the juvenile justice system. Thompson was tried as an adult, convicted of murder, and sentenced to death.

Thompson appealed his conviction and sentence. The Eighth Amendment of the U.S. Constitution prevents the federal government from using "cruel and unusual punishment." States, including Oklahoma, must obey the Eighth Amendment under the Due Process Clause of the Fourteenth Amendment. During his appeals, Thompson argued that executing him for a crime he committed when he was fifteen years old would be cruel and unusual.

The court of criminal appeals ruled in favor of Oklahoma. It said if Thompson was old enough to commit murder and old enough to be tried as an adult, he was old enough to be punished as an adult. Thompson appealed to the U.S. Supreme Court. The Child Welfare League of America and others filed briefs (official documents giving evidence on Thompson's behalf) urging the Court to outlaw the death penalty for juvenile offenders.

Court Spares Thompson's Life

With a 5–3 decision, the Supreme Court reversed Thompson's death sentence. Writing for the Court, Justice John Paul Stevens said executing people for childhood crimes is cruel and unusual punishment. In short, the Eighth Amendment forbids executing people for crimes they commit when under sixteen years old.

Justice Stevens said the Constitution does not explain what it means by "cruel and unusual punishment." Instead, the Supreme Court must decide based on what American society thinks is cruel and unusual. To do this, the Court reviewed laws affecting juveniles.

CAPITAL PUNISHMENT

In the United States at the time, eighteen states set sixteen as the minimum age for the death penalty. In most of the fifty states, people under sixteen could not vote, sit on a jury, marry, buy alcohol or cigarettes, drive, or gamble. Stevens said those laws meant people under sixteen lack the intelligence, experience, and education to make adult decisions. If children cannot make adult decisions, it is cruel and unusual to punish them as adults, especially when the punishment is death.

Cruel and Unusual Children

Three justices dissented, which means they disagreed with the Court's decision. Justice Antonin Scalia wrote a dissenting opinion. Scalia said the Eighth Amendment does not require a strict rule that nobody can be executed for crimes committed under sixteen. Scalia pointed out that when the United States adopted the Eighth Amendment, children could be executed for crimes committed at age fourteen.

Scalia said courts should be able to decide each case separately. The question is whether a childhood murderer has the ability to understand and control his conduct like an adult. If so, he should be punished like an adult. Scalia said the Court's decision would allow hardened criminals who are just one day short of sixteen to escape severe punishment for the most severe crimes. In a society that says people should pay for murder with their lives, that result may be cruel and unusual.

Suggestions for further reading

Almonte, Paul. *Capital Punishment.* New York: Crestwood House, 1991.

Gottfried, Ted. *Capital Punishment: The Death Penalty Debate.* Enslow Publishers, Inc., 1997.

Henson, Burt M., and Ross R. Olney. *Furman v. Georgia: The Death Penalty and the Constitution.* New York: Franklin Watts, Inc., 1996.

Herda, D.J. *Furman v. Georgia: The Death Penalty Case.* Enslow Publishers, Inc., 1994.

Nardo, Don. *Death Penalty.* Lucent Books, 1992.

O'Sullivan, Carol. *The Death Penalty: Identifying Propaganda Techniques.* San Diego: Greenhaven Press, 1989.

SEAN SELLERS

At age sixteen in 1985, Sean Sellers murdered his mother, step-father, and a convenience store clerk in Oklahoma. Around that time, Sellers worshiped Satan and played the game "Dungeons and Dragons." He told a friend that he killed the clerk just to know what it felt like to kill. There was evidence that Sellers killed his parents to escape their supervision.

Sellers, however, said his mother abused him verbally and physically. In 1992, a psychiatric test said Sellers suffered from multiple personality disorder. Some say this prevented Sellers from controlling his behavior when he committed murder.

In prison for his crimes, Sellers rejected Satan and became a Christian. He wrote poems and a Christian comic book. A Christian ministry helped Sellers make a video urging young people not to follow his bad deeds. His stepfather's family and prison guards, however, said Sellers' Christianity was an act to help him escape the death penalty.

If it was an act, it did not work. On February 4 1999, when Sellers was twenty-nine years old, Oklahoma executed him by lethal injection. It was the first time since 1959 that a state exe-cuted someone for committing murder at age sixteen. The execu-tion revived the debate over whether the death penalty is appro-priate for juvenile offenders.

Romano, Lois. "Reaching Out as Time is Running Out; Teenage Killer of 3 Becomes Christian Book Writer and Contributor to Web Site." *Washington Post,* January 22, 1999.

Steins, Richard. *The Death Penalty: Is It Justice?* Twenty First Century Books, 1995.

Tushnet, Mark. *The Death Penalty.* New York: Facts on File, 1994.

Wawrose, Susan C. *The Death Penalty: Seeking Justice in a Civilized Society.* Millbrook Press, 2000.

CAPITAL PUNISHMENT

Winters, Paul A., ed. *The Death Penalty: Opposing Viewpoints.* San Diego: Greenhaven Press, 1997.

Wolf, Robert V. *Capital Punishment.* Philadelphia: Chelsea House Publishers, 1997.

Penry v. Lynaugh
1989

Petitioner: Johnny Paul Penry

Respondent: James A. Lynaugh, Director, Texas Department of Corrections

Petitioner's Claim: That executing mentally retarded criminals is cruel and unusual punishment under the Eighth Amendment.

Chief Lawyer for Petitioner: Curtis C. Mason.

Chief Lawyer for Respondent: Charles A. Palmer, Assistant Attorney General of Texas

Justices for the Court: Harry A. Blackmun, William J. Brennan, Jr., Thurgood Marshall, Sandra Day O'Connor, John Paul Stevens

Justices Dissenting: Anthony M. Kennedy, William H. Rehnquist, Antonin Scalia, Byron R. White

Date of Decision: June 26, 1989

Decision: The Supreme Court reversed Penry's conviction and death sentence.

Significance: In *Penry,* the Supreme Court said it is not cruel and unusual to give the death penalty to mentally retarded criminals. Juries, however, must be allowed to decide whether defendants should get a prison sentence instead of the death penalty because of their mental retardation

Johnny Paul Penry was mildly mentally retarded. At age twenty-two, he had the mental age of a six year old child. Brain damage during his birth probably caused Penry's mental retardation. Penry's mother, however, beat and abused Penry when he was a child. The abuse also may have caused Penry's retardation.

On the morning of October 25, 1979, Pamela Carpenter was raped, beaten, and stabbed with a pair of scissors in her home in Livingston, Texas. She died a few hours later during emergency treatment. Before her death, Carpenter described her attacker to two sheriff's deputies. The deputies suspected Penry, who was on parole after raping another woman. Under questioning, Penry admitted to killing Carpenter.

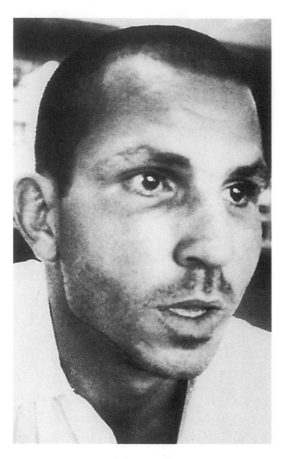

The Court decided that it would be cruel and unusual to sentence Johnny Paul Penry to death. Reproduced by permission of AP/Wide World Photos

Texas charged Penry with capital murder. At his trial, Penry's lawyer argued that Penry was innocent because he was insane and unable to control his behavior. As an expert witness, Dr. Jose Garcia testified that Penry had a limited mental capacity. Garcia said Penry did not know right from wrong and could not control his behavior to obey the law. The state of Texas presented its own testimony from two psychiatrists. The psychiatrists said that while Penry was mentally retarded, he was not insane and could control his behavior.

The jury rejected Penry's insanity defense and found him guilty of murder. The jury's next step was to decide whether Penry should get life in prison or the death penalty. Penry's lawyer argued that because of

Penry's mental retardation and childhood abuse, Penry did not deserve the death penalty. Under Texas law, however, the jury had to give the death penalty if it decided that Penry killed Carpenter on purpose, was not provoked, and probably would commit more crimes.

The jury answered all these questions in Texas's favor and sentenced Penry to death. Relying on the Eighth Amendment, which forbids cruel and unusual punishment, Penry's lawyer appealed the sentence. His lawyer said the jury should have been allowed to give Penry life in prison instead of the death penalty because of his mental retardation and childhood abuse. He also argued that executing mentally retarded people should be banned as cruel and unusual punishment. The Texas Court of Criminal Appeals and two federal courts rejected these arguments, so he took his case to the U.S. Supreme Court.

Executing mentally retarded murderers constitutional

With a 5–4 decision, the Supreme Court reversed Penry's death sentence. Writing for the Court, Justice Sandra Day O'Connor said the jury should have been allowed to consider mitigating evidence when it determined Penry's sentence. Mitigating evidence is information about a defendant's character and background that suggests he should not get the death penalty.

In Penry's case, the jury might have decided that because of his mental retardation and childhood abuse, Penry deserved less punishment than someone with a happy background and full mental ability. Under Texas's death penalty law, the jury was not allowed to make that decision. That made Penry's death sentence cruel and unusual punishment that had to be reversed.

The Supreme Court, however, decided that executing mentally retarded criminals is not always cruel and unusual under the Eighth Amendment. O'Connor said whether a punishment is cruel and unusual depends on the standards of decency in American society. To determine what those standards are, the Supreme Court looks at American laws. At the time, only two states made it illegal to execute mentally retarded criminals. That meant most Americans did not think such executions were cruel and unusual.

O'Connor said some mentally retarded people who cannot control their behavior should not get the death penalty. Courts can make those

FORD V. WAINWRIGHT

In 1974, a jury in Florida found Alvin Bernard Ford guilty of murder and sentenced him to death. Ford was not insane at the time. In early 1982, however, Ford's behavior changed while he awaited execution. Ford claimed he was the target of a conspiracy. He thought prison guards were killing people and sealing the bodies into concrete prison beds. Ford began calling himself Pope John Paul III.

Two doctors examined Ford and decided he had become insane. Ford's lawyer asked Florida to declare Ford legally insane and cancel Ford's execution. Florida's governor refused and, in April 1984, signed Ford's death warrant. Meanwhile, Ford's lawyer took the case to the Supreme Court. There he argued that executing insane people is cruel and unusual punishment under the Eighth Amendment.

The Supreme Court reversed Ford's death sentence. The Court said insane people are unable to defend themselves because they cannot tell their side of the story. Executing insane people will not prevent others from committing crimes. It also offends religion, because an insane person cannot make peace with God before being executed. For all these reasons, the Supreme Court ruled that executing insane people is cruel and unusual punishment that is outlawed by the Eighth Amendment.

decisions in individual cases. When a jury decides that a mentally retarded criminal was able to control his behavior, however, the jury is allowed to give the death sentence. Until more Americans decide it is cruel and unusual, executing mentally retarded criminals does not violate the Eighth Amendment.

Impact

When the Supreme Court decided *Penry* in 1989, only two states with the death penalty made it illegal to execute mentally retarded criminals. After *Penry,* organizations such as the American Association on Mental

Retardation (AAMR), the Association for Retarded Citizens (ARC), and the American Psychological Association (APA) formally spoke out against death sentences for the mentally retarded. Ten years later, twelve of the thirty-eight death penalty states outlawed death sentences for the mentally retarded.

If this trend continues, the Supreme Court might someday decide that such executions violate the Eighth Amendment. Meanwhile, thirty-four mentally retarded persons have been executed in the United States since the Supreme Court found the death penalty constitutional in 1976.

Penry v. Lynaugh

Suggestions for further reading

Almonte, Paul. *Capital Punishment.* New York: Crestwood House, 1991.

Gottfried, Ted. *Capital Punishment: The Death Penalty Debate.* Enslow Publishers, Inc., 1997.

Henson, Burt M., and Ross R. Olney. *Furman v. Georgia: The Death Penalty and the Constitution.* New York: Franklin Watts, Inc., 1996.

Herda, D.J. *Furman v. Georgia: The Death Penalty Case.* Enslow Publishers, Inc., 1994.

Mikula, Mark, and L. Mpho Mabunda, eds. *Great American Court Cases.* Vol. II. Detroit: Gale Group, 1999.

Nardo, Don. *Death Penalty.* Lucent Books, 1992.

O'Sullivan, Carol. *The Death Penalty: Identifying Propaganda Techniques.* San Diego: Greenhaven Press, 1989.

Steins, Richard. *The Death Penalty: Is It Justice?* Twenty First Century Books, 1995.

Tushnet, Mark. *The Death Penalty.* New York: Facts on File, 1994.

Wawrose, Susan C. *The Death Penalty: Seeking Justice in a Civilized Society.* Millbrook Press, 2000.

Winters, Paul A., ed. *The Death Penalty: Opposing Viewpoints.* San Diego: Greenhaven Press, 1997.

Wolf, Robert V. *Capital Punishment.* Philadelphia: Chelsea House Publishers, 1997.

Stanford v. Kentucky
1989

Petitioner: Kevin N. Stanford

Respondent: State of Kentucky

Petitioner's Claim: That executing him for committing murder when he was seventeen years old would be cruel and unusual punishment.

Chief Lawyer for Petitioner: Frank W. Heft, Jr.

Chief Lawyer for Respondent: Frederic J. Cowan, Attorney General of Kentucky

Justices for the Court: Anthony M. Kennedy, Sandra Day O'Connor, William H. Rehnquist, Antonin Scalia, Byron R. White

Justices Dissenting: Harry A. Blackmun, William J. Brennan, Jr., Thurgood Marshall, John Paul Stevens

Date of Decision: June 26, 1989

Decision: The Supreme Court affirmed Stanford's death sentence.

Significance: Under *Stanford,* the government may execute people who are sixteen years old or older when they commit murder.

On January 7, 1981, Kevin Stanford was seventeen years and four months old. That night, he and an accomplice robbed a gas station in Jefferson County, Kentucky, where Barbel Poore worked as an attendant. During the robbery Stanford and his accomplice repeatedly raped Poore. After taking 300 cartons of cigarettes, two gallons of fuel, and a small

Associate Justice Antonin Scalia.
Courtesy of the Supreme Court of the United States.

amount of cash, they drove Poore to a hidden area near the gas station. There Stanford killed Poore by shooting her once in the face and once in the back of the head.

After he was arrested, Stanford admitted to the murder to a corrections officer. Stanford said he killed Poore because she lived next door and would recognize him. The corrections officer said Stanford laughed when he told the story.

Kentucky state law allowed juveniles to be tried as adults for committing murder. A juvenile court conducted a hearing to determine if Stanford should be tried as an adult. The court learned that Stanford had a history of juvenile offenses and did not respond well to reform efforts. Because Stanford was charged with a disgusting murder, had many prior crimes, and did not seem capable of being reformed, the court ordered Stanford to be tried as an adult.

Stanford was convicted of murder and sentenced to death. The Eighth Amendment of the U.S. Constitution, however, prevents the government from using cruel and unusual punishment. Stanford used the Eighth Amendment to appeal his death sentence. He said it would be cruel and unusual to execute him for a crime he committed as a juvenile.

The Kentucky Supreme Court rejected Stanford's appeal. Relying on Stanford's criminal history and his failure to respond to reform, the court affirmed his death sentence. Stanford took his case to the U.S. Supreme Court.

Death penalty for juveniles approved

Just one year before the Supreme Court ruled in Stanford's case, it decided that executing people for crimes they commit under sixteen years old violates the Eighth Amendment. With a 5–4 decision, however, the Supreme Court affirmed Stanford's death sentence. Writing for the Court, Justice Antonin Scalia said executing people for crimes they commit when sixteen or older is not cruel and unusual punishment.

Scalia said whether a punishment is cruel and unusual depends on the standards of decency in American society. To determine what those standards were, Scalia studied American laws and cases.

In 1988, thirty-seven states had laws that allowed the death penalty. Twenty-two of those states allowed the death penalty to be given to people who committed crimes when they were sixteen or seventeen years old. In other words, most of the states with the death penalty allowed it to be given to juvenile offenders. Moreover, between 1982 and 1988, forty-five juvenile offenders received death sentences in the United States.

For Scalia, this data meant American society approved of executing juvenile offenders. If such executions do not offend the standards of decency in the United States, they do not violate the Eighth Amendment.

Children too young to know better

Four justices dissented, meaning they disagreed with the Court's decision. Justice William J. Brennan, Jr., wrote a dissenting opinion. Brennan believed it was cruel and unusual to take someone's life for committing a crime as a child. When he counted the states that outlawed the death penalty completely, Brennan found that a total of twenty-seven states said nobody under eighteen could get the death penalty. He also learned that between 1982 and 1988, less than three percent of death sentences in the United States were for juvenile crimes.

Brennan did not stop with analyzing the data. He pointed out that many important organizations opposed the death penalty for juvenile offenders. Most countries in the world had outlawed the death penalty completely or at least for juvenile offenders. The United States even had signed international treaties that prohibited juvenile death penalties.

Finally, Brennan said the reason for the death penalty is to punish offenders and discourage other criminals. Executing juvenile offenders

INTERNATIONAL LAW ON
JUVENILE OFFENDERS

Treaties and conventions are agreements between different countries. These agreements form an international law. If a country
ratifies a convention, it must obey the agreement or be in violation of international law.

Many international conventions prevent countries from using
the death penalty for juvenile offenders—people who commit
crimes and are under eighteen years old. The countries that ratify
these agreements believe children under eighteen are too young
to understand the meaning of their crimes. They also believe that
children can change and grow into lawful adults if the government helps rather than executes them.

Although the United States has signed and ratified some of
these agreements, it has reserved the right to execute juvenile
offenders. Since the U.S. Supreme Court approved the death
penalty in 1976, the United States has executed sixteen juvenile
murderers, including three in January 2000. At the start of 2000,
the only other countries that allowed the death penalty for juvenile offenders were Iran, Nigeria, Pakistan, and Saudi Arabia.

does not serve these purposes. Because juveniles are not old enough to
understand their crimes and control their conduct, reform is more appropriate than punishment. Because juveniles often believe they will never
die, the death penalty does not discourage them from committing murder.
In Brennan's opinion, the best thing to do with juvenile murderers is to
try to reform them into lawful adults.

Suggestions for further reading

Almonte, Paul. *Capital Punishment.* New York: Crestwood House, 1991.

Gottfried, Ted. *Capital Punishment: The Death Penalty Debate.* Enslow
    Publishers, Inc., 1997.

**CAPITAL
PUNISHMENT**

Henson, Burt M., and Ross R. Olney. *Furman v. Georgia: The Death Penalty and the Constitution.* New York: Franklin Watts, Inc., 1996.

Herda, D.J. *Furman v. Georgia: The Death Penalty Case.* Enslow Publishers, Inc., 1994.

Nardo, Don. *Death Penalty.* Lucent Books, 1992.

O'Sullivan, Carol. *The Death Penalty: Identifying Propaganda Techniques.* San Diego: Greenhaven Press, 1989.

Steins, Richard. *The Death Penalty: Is It Justice?* Twenty First Century Books, 1995.

Tushnet, Mark. *The Death Penalty.* New York: Facts on File, 1994.

Wawrose, Susan C. *The Death Penalty: Seeking Justice in a Civilized Society.* Millbrook Press, 2000.

Winters, Paul A., ed. *The Death Penalty: Opposing Viewpoints.* San Diego: Greenhaven Press, 1997.

Wolf, Robert V. *Capital Punishment.* Philadelphia: Chelsea House Publishers, 1997.

Payne v. Tennessee
1991

Petitioner: Pervis Tyrone Payne

Respondent: State of Tennessee

Petitioner's Claim: That allowing the jury to consider evidence of how his crimes affected his victims violated the Eighth Amendment.

Chief Lawyer for Petitioner: J. Brooke Lathram

Chief Lawyer for Respondent: Charles W. Burson, Attorney General of Tennessee

Justices for the Court: Anthony M. Kennedy, Sandra Day O'Connor, William H. Rehnquist, Antonin Scalia, David H. Souter, Byron R. White

Justices Dissenting: Harry A. Blackmun, Thurgood Marshall, John Paul Stevens

Date of Decision: June 27, 1991

Decision: The Supreme Court affirmed Payne's death sentence.

Significance: In *Payne,* the Supreme Court said prosecutors in death penalty cases may use victim impact evidence—evidence about how the crime affected the victim and her family. This decision overruled earlier decisions that the Supreme Court had made concerning victim impact evidence.

On Saturday, June 27, 1987, Pervis Tyrone Payne visited the apartment of his girlfriend, Bobbie Thomas, in Millington, Tennessee. Thomas was on her way home from her mother's house in Arkansas. While Payne waited for Thomas to arrive, he spent the morning and early afternoon injecting cocaine into his body and drinking beer. Then he and a friend drove around town while reading a pornographic magazine. Payne returned to Thomas's apartment complex around 3 p.m.

Across the hall from Thomas, twenty-eight year old Charisse Christopher lived with her three year old son Nicholas and two year old daughter Lacie. Payne entered Christopher's apartment and made sexual advances toward her. When Christopher resisted and screamed "get out," Payne grabbed a butcher's knife and stabbed her forty-one times, causing eighty-four separate wounds. Christopher died from massive bleeding. Payne also stabbed Christopher's children, Nicholas and Lacie. Nicholas survived by a miracle, but Lacie died with her mother.

When she heard the blood-curdling scream from Christopher's apartment, a neighbor called the police. The police officer who arrived saw Payne leaving the building soaked in blood and carrying an overnight bag. When the officer asked Payne what was happening, Payne hit him over the head with the bag and escaped. Later that day, the police found Payne hiding in the attic at a former girlfriend's home.

The Trial

The state of Tennessee charged Payne with two counts of murder and one count of assault with intent to commit murder. At trial, Payne said he had not hurt anyone. The evidence against him, however, was strong. At the murder scene, his baseball cap was strapped around Lacie's arm. There were cans of beer with Payne's fingerprints on them. The jury convicted Payne on all counts.

At the sentencing phase of the trial, the jury had to decide whether to give Payne the death penalty or life in prison. Payne presented evidence from his parents, his girlfriend, and a doctor. Payne's parents said he was a good person who did not use drugs or alcohol and who never had been arrested. Thomas called Payne a loving person who would not commit murder. The doctor testified that Payne was mentally handicapped.

The state presented victim impact evidence (evidence about how the crime affected one of the victims). Nicholas's grandmother testified that Nicholas cried for his mother and did not understand why she never came home. Nicholas also asked his grandmother if she missed his sister, Lacie, and said he was worried about Lacie.

During closing arguments to the jury, lawyers are allowed to explain the verdict if they want. The prosecutor for Tennessee said the jury should remember all the people who would miss Charisse Christopher and Lacie, especially Nicholas. He also said the jury should give Payne the death penalty so that when Nicholas grew up, he would know that his mother and sister's murderer received justice. The jury gave Payne the death penalty for both murders and a thirty year prison sentence for assaulting Nicholas.

Cruel and Unusual Evidence

The Eighth Amendment of the U.S. Constitution prevents the government from using cruel and unusual punishment. In **Booth v. Maryland** (1987) and *South Carolina v. Gathers* (1989), the Supreme Court said it is cruel and unusual to allow juries to hear victim impact evidence during a death penalty hearing and closing arguments. The Supreme Court said such evidence makes the jury focus on the victim instead of the defendant. Under the Eighth Amendment, the jury is supposed to decide whether a defendant deserves the death penalty by focusing on the defendant's crime, character, and background.

Payne appealed his death sentences. He said that under *Booth* and *Gathers,* it was illegal for the state of Tennessee to use evidence about how the crime affected Nicholas. The Supreme Court of Tennessee rejected Payne's argument. It said that when a man picks up a butcher's knife and stabs a mother and her two children, the effect on the child that survives helps the jury determine the criminal's punishment. Payne took his case to the U.S. Supreme Court.

Victims' Rights

With a 6–3 decision, the Supreme Court affirmed the death penalty for Payne. Writing for the Court, Chief Justice William H. Rehnquist said the Court decided to overrule its decisions in *Booth* and *Gathers.* When the Supreme Court overrules earlier decisions, it announces a new rule of law.

Rehnquist said that one of the goals of criminal justice in the United States is to make the punishment fit the crime. A jury cannot

VICTIMS' RIGHTS

The criminal justice system in the United States usually focuses on the criminal by asking who broke the law and what should be her punishment. Victims often are ignored in this process. That began to change, however, during the victims' rights movement.

Today, prosecutors' offices have entire units that keep victims informed about the progress of criminal cases. The federal government and most states allow juries to determine the punishment for a crime by using victim impact evidence—information about how the crime affected the victim and her family. Victims often present this evidence as a statement to the jury during the sentencing phase of a trial.

Some criminal justice systems use a practice called a victim-offender conference (VOC). At a VOC, the criminal and victim meet in a safe place to explore how the crime affected their lives. The criminal has a chance to apologize to the victim. The victim can ask questions and even forgive the criminal. Like other parts of the victims' rights movement, the VOC is supposed to help victims get on with their lives after suffering through crime.

do this if it does not know how the crime affected the victim and her family. In a murder case, victim impact evidence helps the jury determine how a family and community suffer and what they lose from the death of a loved one. As long as the evidence is not so unrelated to the crime as to become unfair, the Eighth Amendment allows victim impact evidence.

In the long run

As of 1999, forty-nine states and the federal government had laws allowing juries to hear victim impact evidence. After signing a victims' rights law in 1997, President William J. Clinton said, "when someone is a victim, he or she should be at the center of the criminal justice process, not on the outside looking in."

Suggestions for further reading

**Payne v.
Tennessee**

Almonte, Paul. *Capital Punishment.* New York: Crestwood House, 1991.

Gottfried, Ted. *Capital Punishment: The Death Penalty Debate.* Enslow Publishers, Inc., 1997.

Henson, Burt M., and Ross R. Olney. *Furman v. Georgia: The Death Penalty and the Constitution.* New York: Franklin Watts, Inc., 1996.

Herda, D.J. *Furman v. Georgia: The Death Penalty Case.* Enslow Publishers, Inc., 1994.

Lerman, David. "Restoring Dignity, Effecting Justice." *Human Rights,* Fall 1999.

Nardo, Don. *Death Penalty.* Lucent Books, 1992.

O'Sullivan, Carol. *The Death Penalty: Identifying Propaganda Techniques.* San Diego: Greenhaven Press, 1989.

Steins, Richard. *The Death Penalty: Is It Justice?* Twenty First Century Books, 1995.

Tushnet, Mark. *The Death Penalty.* New York: Facts on File, 1994.

Wawrose, Susan C. *The Death Penalty: Seeking Justice in a Civilized Society.* Millbrook Press, 2000.

Winters, Paul A., ed. *The Death Penalty: Opposing Viewpoints.* San Diego: Greenhaven Press, 1997.

Wolf, Robert V. *Capital Punishment.* Philadelphia: Chelsea House Publishers, 1997.

CRIMINAL LAW AND PROCEDURE

The American criminal justice system has two legal parts: law and procedure. Criminal law defines crime and punishment. It protects society by discouraging harmful conduct and punishing wrongdoers. Criminal procedure controls the process of investigating crime, arresting a suspected criminal, and convicting him in a court of law. Criminal procedure protects the rights of the accused, whether guilty or innocent.

Criminal Law

Criminal law in the United States has its roots in Great Britain. When the United States was born in 1776, criminal law in England existed in the common law. Under common law, judges developed definitions for crimes on a case-by-case basis. Criminal law in the United States originally came from the common law. Today the federal government and most states have statutes that define crime and punishment. Many of these definitions, however, come from the common law.

Under federal law and that of most states, crimes are categorized as felonies, misdemeanors, and petty offenses. A felony is a crime, such as murder, that is punishable by death or imprisonment for more than one year. Misdemeanors are less serious crimes, punishable by imprisonment for up to one year, a monetary fine, or both. Petty offenses are punishable by imprisonment for less than six months, a small fine, or both. Infractions, such as minor traffic and parking violations, are punishable only by a fine and are not considered crimes.

Most crimes are against either people or property. Crimes against people include murder, assault, battery, rape, and kidnapping. Crimes against property include arson, trespass, and burglary. The definitions for most crimes include both a bad act and a guilty mind. The bad act requirement makes sure people are not punished just for bad thoughts. The guilty mind requirement makes sure people are not punished when they do something bad accidentally. A person must intend to do something wrong to be guilty of a crime.

People charged with crimes can use many defenses to avoid being convicted and punished. Capacity defenses are for people who did not have the ability to control their behavior. Capacity defenses include insanity, infancy, and intoxication. Defenses such as duress, coercion, and necessity are for people who were forced to commit a crime. Entrapment is a defense for people whom the government tricks into committing a crime. Self defense is for people who respond to an attack with the force necessary to stop it and end up hurting or killing their attacker.

The U.S. Constitution says "No . . . *ex post facto* Law shall be passed." An *ex post facto* (after the fact) law makes a crime out of something a person did when it was not a crime. For example, imagine that it was legal in 1999 to protest outside an abortion clinic. If a state passed a law in 2000 that made it a crime to have protested outside abortion clinics in 1999, the law would be *ex post facto* and invalid under the Constitution.

Criminal Procedure Before Trial

Criminal procedure controls the process of investigating crime and convicting criminals. Supreme Court cases deal with criminal procedure more than criminal law. That is because the U.S. Constitution contains many provisions that make up the law of criminal procedure. The most general provision says "No Bill of Attainder . . . shall be passed." A bill of attainder is a law that convicts and punishes a person without a trial. The framers of the Constitution wanted to assure that people could only be convicted of crimes after fair, individual trials.

Criminal procedure, however, protects Americans well before a trial begins. When the police investigate a crime, the Fourth Amendment limits their investigation. Police may not search a private place without a warrant and probable cause. Probable cause means good reason to believe the place has evidence to be seized or criminals to be arrested. The Fourth Amendment also requires the police to have a warrant to arrest a criminal suspect.

There are exceptions to these rules. The police may arrest a person without a warrant when they have probable cause to believe she has committed a felony. Because felons can be dangerous to society, arresting them quickly is more important than making the police get a warrant. The police also may arrest a person without a warrant when he commits a crime in the officer's presence.

When the police arrest a suspect, the Fifth and Sixth Amendments protect the suspect's rights. One of those is the right not to be a witness against oneself. This is called the right against self-incrimination. It prevents the government from forcing a suspect to talk about a crime, make a confession, or share any evidence that could be used against him.

The Sixth Amendment gives all suspects the right to have an attorney. If the suspect cannot afford an attorney, the government must pay one to defend him. The suspect is allowed to have the attorney present during all police questioning. The attorney also must be allowed to watch if the police conduct a line-up. A line-up is when the suspect stands among a group of people to see if the victim can identify him. The suspect's attorney is allowed to be there to make sure the line-up is fair.

In *Miranda v. Arizona* (1966), the U.S. Supreme Court used the right against self-incrimination and the right to an attorney to create the famous warning that police officers must give when they arrest a suspect. It is called reading the suspect her rights. Police must tell the suspect she has the right to remain silent, and that anything she says will be used against her in court. The police also must tell the suspect she has the right to have an attorney, and that the government will appoint one if she cannot afford one. If the suspect says she wants to remain silent and get an attorney, the police cannot ask her any questions about the crime.

After the police arrest a suspect, the court conducts a preliminary hearing. There the government presents its evidence to a magistrate to show that it has probable cause to believe the defendant has committed a crime. It the magistrate agrees, she requires the suspect to enter a plea of guilty or not guilty. If the plea is guilty, the case goes right to the sentencing phase. If the plea is not guilty, the magistrate sets bail. Bail is an amount of money the defendant needs to pay the court to be released while waiting for a trial. The Eighth Amendment says bail may not be too high. If the defendant pays his bail and shows up for trial, he gets his money back. If he fails to show up for trial, he forfeits the money and the court issues a warrant for his arrest.

Before there is a trial in federal court for serious crimes, the Fifth Amendment requires a grand jury to indict the defendant. A grand jury is a large group of citizens, usually as many as twenty-three, that reviews the government's case to make sure it has enough evidence to charge the defendant with a crime. If the grand jury hands down an indictment, the defendant faces a trial on criminal charges.

Criminal Procedure During Trial

The Sixth Amendment gives the defendant many rights during a criminal trial. The defendant has a right to know the charges against him. The right to have an attorney continues through the trial. The trial must involve an impartial jury that determines whether or not the defendant is guilty. The Sixth Amendment says the trial must be speedy and open to the public.

The Sixth Amendment gives the defendant the right to see witnesses against him. In other words, witnesses must face the defendant when they testify against him. They cannot give their testimony in private. Courts sometimes make an exception when the witness is a young child whom the defendant is charged with sexually abusing. In any case, the defendant has a right to cross-examine all witnesses to challenge their testimony.

The defendant has the right to force witnesses in her favor to testify in court. The court accomplishes this with a subpoena (pronounced SUH-PEE-NUH), a document that orders the witness to appear in court to give testimony. The government also must give the defendant any evidence it has that suggests she is innocent. The defendant, however, need not share evidence that suggests he is guilty. In fact, the Fifth Amendment right against self-incrimination prevents the government from forcing the defendant to testify at all. The defendant cannot lie, but she can choose not to answer the government's questions.

The burden of proof is an important part of American criminal procedure. The burden of proof says a defendant is presumed innocent until proven guilty. The government has the burden of proving the defendant's guilt beyond a reasonable doubt. That does not mean there must be no doubt about the defendant's guilt. It means the government must present enough evidence of guilt so that no reasonable person would have any doubt that the defendant is guilty.

Criminal Procedure After Trial

If the jury finds the defendant guilty, the defendant receives a punishment, called a sentence. The judge usually determines the sentence. Sometimes the jury does so when it determines guilt. Sentences can include imprisonment, a fine, community service, and probation. Probation happens when the court allows the defendant to go free with orders to follow certain rules and obey all laws. If the defendant violates the terms of his probation by breaking a rule or law, the court can send the defendant back to jail.

Sometimes the court holds a separate hearing to determine a sentence. That is particularly true when the defendant faces the death penalty for first degree murder. In such cases, the defendant has a right to present evidence at the sentencing hearing about his character, background, and the circumstances of the crime to convince the jury he does not deserve the death penalty.

The Eighth Amendment limits the sentence a defendant can receive. It says the government may not impose "excessive fines" or "cruel and unusual punishments." The Eighth Amendment is supposed to make sure the punishment fits the crime. Applying the Eighth Amendment, the Supreme Court eliminated the death penalty for the crime of rape. As of 2000, most states restrict the death penalty to murder cases.

Sometimes a jury convicts a defendant and sends him to jail after a trial that was unfair. In such cases, the Constitution says the defendant may use a device called a writ of *habeas corpus.* The writ is a lawsuit the defendant files against his jailer. To win, the defendant must prove the government convicted him by violating one or more of his constitutional rights. If the defendant succeeds, the court orders the government to set him free.

Besides *habeas corpus,* most defendants can challenge their convictions by filing an appeal. In the federal system and most state systems, the first appeal to a court of appeals is a statutory right. The right to have an attorney still applies at this stage. If the defendant loses on appeal, her last hope is to appeal to the state supreme court or U.S. Supreme Court.

In most cases, the defendant does not have a right to file such an appeal. Instead, the supreme court must agree to hear the defendant's case. If the defendant loses all appeals, she must serve her sentence.

The Fifth Amendment contains an important protection called the Double Jeopardy Clause. It prevents the government from trying or punishing a person twice for the same crime. That means the government cannot hold another trial for burglary against the same defendant if it loses the first one. The Double Jeopardy Clause, however, does not prevent a different government from trying the defendant for the same crime. For example, if a federal court finds a defendant not guilty of murdering a federal law enforcement officer, the state in which the murder happened can hold a second murder trial.

Suggestions for further reading

Fireside, Harvey. *The Fifth Amendment: The Right to Remain Silent.* Enslow Publishers, Inc., 1998.

Force, Eden. *The Sixth Amendment.* Silver Burdett Press.

Franklin, Paula A. *The Fourth Amendment.* Englewood Cliffs: Silver Burdett Press, 1991.

Galloway, John. *The Supreme Court & the Rights of the Accused.* New York: Facts on File, 1973.

Holmes, Burnham. *The Fifth Amendment.* Silver Burdett Press, 1991.

Johnson, Joan. *Justice.* New York: Franklin Watts, 1985.

Karson, Jill, ed. *Criminal Justice: Opposing Viewpoints.* San Diego: Greenhaven Press, 1998.

Owens, Lois Smith, and Vivian Vedell Gordon. *Think about Prisons and the Criminal Justice System.* Walker & Co., 1992.

Wetterer, Charles M.*The Fourth Amendment: Search and Seizure.* Enslow Publishers, Inc., 1998.

Powell v. Alabama
1932

Petitioners: Ozzie Powell, Willie Roberson, Andy Wright, Olen Montgomery, Haywood Patterson, Charley Weems and Clarence Norris

Respondent: State of Alabama

Petitioner's Claim: The Sixth Amendment right to legal counsel for criminal defendants includes the effective help of counsel at the critical stages of investigation and preparation before the trial.

Chief Lawyer for Petitioner: Walter H. Pollack

Chief Lawyer for Respondents: Thomas E. Knight, Jr.

Justices for the Court: Louis D. Brandeis, Benjamin N. Cardozo, Charles Evans Hughes, Owen Josephus Roberts, Harlan Fiske Stone, George Sutherland Willis Van Devanter

Justices Dissenting: Pierce Butler, James Clark McReynolds

Date of Decision: November 7, 1932

Decision: That the right to the effective assistance of an attorney applies even before the trial.

Significance: The Scottsboro trials gave the American public insight into the prejudices and procedures of Southern courts in their treatment of blacks and other minorities. This case was the first time that the United States Supreme Court interpreted the Sixth Amendment of the Constitution and its guaranty to a criminal defendant of "the Assistance of Counsel for his defense". The Court decided this meant "effective" assistance of counsel.

On March 25, 1931, seven young white men entered a railroad station-master's office in northern Alabama. They claimed that while they were riding the rails, a "bunch of Negroes" picked a fight with them and threw them off the train. The stationmaster phoned ahead to the next station, near Scottsboro, Alabama. A Scottsboro deputy sheriff made deputies of every man in town with a gun. When the train stopped, the posse (group of people legally authorized keep the peace) rounded up nine young black men and two young white women. The women, Ruby Bates and Victoria Price, were dressed in men's caps and overalls.

The deputy sheriff tied the black youths together and started questioning them. All of them were from other states. Five of them were from Georgia. Twenty-year-old Charlie Weems was the oldest. Clarence Norris was nineteen. Ozie Powell was sixteen. Olin Montgomery, seventeen, was blind in one eye and had only 10 percent of his vision in the other eye. Willie Roberson, seventeen, suffered from the sexually-transmitted diseases syphilis and gonorrhea, which made him walk with a cane. The other four boys were from Chattanooga, Tennessee. Haywood Patterson and Andy Wright were nineteen. Eugene Williams was thirteen. Wright's brother, Roy, was twelve. None of them could read.

Accused of Rape

As the deputy sheriff loaded his prisoners onto an open truck, one of the women, Ruby Bates, spoke up. She told the deputy sheriff that she and her friend had been raped by the nine black youths.

In Scottsboro, the sheriff sent the women off to be examined by two doctors. Meanwhile, news of the rape had spread throughout the county. By nightfall, a mob of several hundred people stood before the Scottsboro jail, promising to lynch (hang) the prisoners. The sheriff, barricaded inside with twenty- one deputies, called the governor. The governor sent out twenty-five National Guardsmen, but by the time they arrived at the jail, the crowd had given up and drifted away.

The First Trial Begins

Only a few days after their arrest, their trial began on April 6, 1931, with the National Guard keeping a crowd of several thousand people at bay only 100 feet away from the courthouse. On the trial date, Judge Alfred E. Hawkins offered the job of defending the nine black youths to any attorney in the room who would take it. He selected Tennessee attorney Stephen R. Roddy, who volunteered but had not had an opportunity to prepare a defense and admitted he did not know much about Alabama law. A local attorney, Milo Moody offered to assist him with the trials. The defendants were tried in three separate trials.

Prosecutor H. G. Bailey tried Norris and Weems first. Victoria Price described how she and Ruby Bates had gone to Chattanooga to look for jobs. When they found none, they hopped freight trains to go home. After the black boys had thrown the whites off the train, Price said that the blacks turned on the women. She described how she was "beaten up" and "bruised up" as she was repeatedly raped until she lost consciousness.

Dr. R. R. Bridges examined the girls after the incident. He testified that he saw no evidence of violence when he examined the girls. A second doctor agreed and noted that both girls showed signs of having had sexual intercourse, it had occurred at least twelve hours before his physical examination.

Nonetheless, all of the defendants except twelve-year-old Roy Wright were found guilty and sentenced to die in the electric chair. Due to Roy Wright's age, the prosecution had asked for a life sentence for him rather than the death penalty. In spite of this request, seven of the jurors wanted to give Roy the death penalty. The judge was forced to declare a mistrial.

A Legal Lynching

A nationwide dispute arose as the news of the trials spread around the country. The Central Committee of the Communist Party of the United States called the sentences "legal lynching" and called the defendants the "victims of 'capitalist justice.'" Its International Labor Defense (ILD) section pushed the National Association for the Advancement of Colored People (NAACP) to push the case through the legal system to the U.S. Supreme Court. In Harlem (a part of New York City), 300,000 people marched in the streets with the slogan "The Scottsboro Boys Shall Not Die."

The ILD hired a famous Chattanooga lawyer George W. Chamlee. He and his co-counsel, Joseph Brodsky, asked for a new trial for the Scottsboro boys. To support this request, they showed the court sworn statements from Chattanooga blacks. These statements alleged that Victoria Price had been seen "embracing Negro men in dances in Negro houses," and that Ruby Bates had bragged that she could "take five Negroes in one night and that Victoria had rented a room for prostitution." The local press declared these statements false, but a Huntsville detective confirmed that both women were prostitutes.

"You Can't Mix Politics with Law"

The court refused to give the boys a new trial. Nationally celebrated attorney Clarence Darrow turned down the NAACP's request that he argue the appeal all the way up to the Supreme Court. "You can't mix politics with law," he said, adding that eventually the cases would have to be won in an Alabama trial. After that, the NAACP withdrew its support.

In March, the Alabama Supreme Court upheld the convictions of all but Eugene Williams. As a juvenile, he was granted a new trial. In November, the U.S. Supreme Court ruled that seven of the defendants had been denied due process of law under the Fourteenth Amendment due to the belated and casual treatment of the appointment of their attorneys by Judge Hawkins. The Court noted that until the very morning of trial no lawyer had been named to represent the defendants. The Court concluded that during the most critical time of the trial, from their arraignment to the start of the trial, the defendants were without the aid of any attorney. They were entitled to legal advice, a thorough investigation and most important preparation. The Supreme Court found that it was the duty of the trial court to give the defendants a reasonable time and chance to hire attorneys or to appoint counsel under such circumstances which prevents counsel from giving effective aid in the preparation and trial of the case. This failure of the trial court was a clear denial of their right to due process of law.

For the retrial, the ILD turned to noted New York criminal lawyer Samuel Leibowitz. Claiming that the defendants could not get a fair trial in Scottsboro, Leibowitz succeeded in having the trial transferred to Decatur, Alabama, before Judge James Edward Horton, Jr. Haywood Patterson was tried first. Leibowitz produced several surprises. Bates took back her earlier testimony, saying she had lied to avoid being arrested. The arresting posse had found the defendants in several different cars of the forty-two-car train. Willie Roberson's medical condition made it impossible for him to engage in sexual activity, and Olin Montgomery's blindness also made him an unlikely rapist. Victoria Price, who was married, had been convicted and served time for other sex related crimes.

Dr. Bridges repeated his testimony that neither girl had been raped. The second doctor, Marvin Lynch, privately told Judge Horton that he had confronted the girls with the fact that they knew they had not been raped "and they just laughed at me." But, he added, if he testified for the boys, "I'd never be able to go back into Jackson County." The judge believed the defense would prove Patterson innocent, so he said nothing.

Defense attorney Leibowitz now lived with National Guardsmen to protect him against threats of lynching. Prosecutor Wade Wright added to the tense atmosphere when he told the jury, "Show them that Alabama justice cannot be bought and sold with Jew money from New York."

The jury found Patterson guilty and he was sentenced to death. Judge Horton granted a new trial based on his review of the evidence. Then, under pressure from Attorney General Thomas Knight, he withdrew from the case.

Another New Trial

Opening the new trial, Judge William Washington Callahan, dismissed the National Guard and banned cameras from inside and outside the courtroom. He rejected Leibowitz's motion to dismiss Patterson's indictment because no blacks were on the jury list. He ran twelve-hour days in the courtroom. He refused to allow in testimony about Victoria Price's sexual activities in two nights before the train ride. When he gave the jury its instructions on the law, he told them that any intercourse between a black man and a white woman was rape. Until Leibowitz reminded him, Judge Callahan neglected to give the jury instructions on how to acquit the defendant if he was found not guilty.

Again Patterson was found guilty and sentenced to death. Next Clarence Norris was found guilty. Leibowitz discovered that two ILD attorneys were caught trying to bribe Price to change her testimony. The ILD attorneys told Leibowitz that a changed story would be "good for their cause." Furious, Leibowitz threatened to withdraw from the case "unless all Communists are removed from the defense." Attorney Brodsky withdrew.

Supreme Court Overturns
Convictions Again

The U.S. Supreme Court overturned all the convictions under the equal protection clause of the Constitution because the state of Alabama

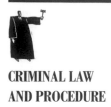
excluded African Americans from all juries at the time. In November 1935, a grand jury of thirteen whites and one black brought new indictments. At his fourth trial, in January 1936, a jury again found Patterson guilty. Sentenced this time to seventy-five years in jail, he said, "I'd rather die."

The next trial was delayed until July 1937. Clarence Norris was found guilty and sentenced him to death. Then Andy Wright was found guilty and received ninety-nine years in jail. Charlie Weems was declared guilty and given seventy-five years' imprisonment. The charges against Ozie Powell were dropped in exchange for his guilty plea to stabbing a deputy sheriff. He was sentenced to twenty years. After these convictions, prosecutor Thomas Lawson, suddenly dropped the charges against Olin Montgomery, Roy Wright, Willie Roberson, and Eugene Williams.

All Guilty or All Free

The U.S. Supreme Court refused to review Patterson's conviction. Alabama Governor Bibb Graves, asked to pardon the four convicted Scottsboro boys, agreed that "all were guilty or all should be freed." However, after setting a date for the pardon, he changed his mind.

Weems was freed in November 1943. Wright and Norris were released from jail in January 1944 on parole. They were sent back to prison after they broke the terms of their parole by moving north. Wright was paroled again in 1950. Patterson escaped from prison in 1948. He was arrested in Detroit, but Michigan Governor G. Mennen Williams refused a request to send him back to Alabama. Patterson was later convicted of manslaughter. He died of cancer in prison in 1952. Alabama Governor George Wallace pardoned Norris at the age of 64 in 1976.

Suggestions for Further Reading

Carter, Dan T. *Scottsboro: A Tragedy of the American South.* Baton Rouge: Louisiana State University Press, 1969.

Goodman, James. E. *Stories of Scottsboro.* New York: Vintage Books, 1995.

Haskins, James. *The Scottsboro Boys.* New York: Henry Holt, 1994.

Nash, Jay Robert. *Encyclopedia of World Crime.* Wilmette, IL: CrimeBooks, Inc., 1990.

Patterson, Haywood. *Scottsboro Boy.* Garden City, NY: Doubleday & Co., 1950.

Reynolds, Quentin. *Courtroom.* New York: Farrar, Straus and Cudahy, 1950.

Powell v. Alabama

Palko v. Connecticut
1937

Appellant: Frank Palko

Appellee: State of Connecticut

Appellant's Claim: That when Connecticut tried him a second time for murder, it violated the Double Jeopardy Clause of the Fifth Amendment.

Chief Lawyers for Appellant: David Goldstein and George A. Saden

Chief Lawyer for Appellee: William H. Comley

Justices for the Court: Hugo Lafayette Black, Louis D. Brandeis, Benjamin N. Cardozo, Charles Evans Hughes, James Clark McReynolds, Owen Josephus Roberts, Harlan Fiske Stone, George Sutherland

Justices Dissenting: Pierce Butler

Date of Decision: December 6, 1937

Decision: The Supreme Court affirmed Palko's second conviction for murder.

Significance: With *Palko,* the Supreme Court said the Bill of Rights does not automatically apply to the states. It took many cases over the next few decades for the Court to reverse this decision and apply most of the Bill of Rights to the states.

The Fifth Amendment of the U.S. Constitution says no person "shall . . . be twice put in jeopardy of life and limb" for the same crime. This is called the Double Jeopardy Clause. It prevents the federal government from trying or punishing a person twice for the same crime.

The Fifth Amendment is part of the Bill of Rights, which contains the first ten amendment to the Constitution. The United States adopted the Bill of Rights in 1791 to give American citizens rights against the federal government. State and local governments did not have to obey the Bill of Rights.

In 1868, after the American Civil War, the United States adopted the Fourteenth Amendment. The Fourteenth Amendment contains a phrase called the Due Process Clause. It says states may not "deprive any person of life, liberty, or property, without due process of law." Ever since 1868, the Supreme Court has struggled to define what is meant by "due process of law." In *Palko v. Connecticut* (1937), the Supreme Court had to decide whether "due process of law" means states must obey the Double Jeopardy Clause of the Fifth Amendment.

Associate Justice Benjamin N. Cardozo.
Courtesy of the Supreme Court of the United States.

Murder

Frank Palko was charged with first degree murder in Fairfield County, Connecticut, where he could get the death penalty. The jury found Palko guilty of second degree murder, a lesser crime that was punishable only with imprisonment. The court sentenced Palko to life in prison. A state law, however, allowed Connecticut to appeal the decision in a criminal case if there were errors during the trial. Connecticut appealed Palko's conviction.

The Supreme Court of Errors decided the trial judge made three errors during Palko's trial. The judge had refused to allow the jury to hear testimony about Palko's confession. He also refused to allow Connecticut to cross-examine Palko to impeach Palko's credibility, which means to challenge his truthfulness and believability. Finally, the trial judge erred when he instructed the jury about the difference between first and second degree murder. Based on these errors, the Supreme Court of Errors reversed Palko's conviction and ordered a new trial.

At the second trial, the jury found Palko guilty of first degree murder and the court sentenced him to death. Palko appealed his conviction. He said trying him twice for the same murder violated the Double Jeopardy Clause of the Fifth Amendment. Palko argued that the Due Process Clause of the Fourteenth Amendment required Connecticut to obey the entire Bill of Rights, including the Double Jeopardy Clause. The Connecticut Supreme Court of Errors rejected this argument and affirmed Palko's conviction, so he took his case to the U.S. Supreme Court.

Fundamental Justice

With an 8–1 decision, the Supreme Court affirmed Palko's conviction and death sentence. Writing for the Court, Justice Benjamin N. Cardozo rejected the argument that the Due Process Clause requires the states to obey the entire Bill of Rights. Cardozo said states only must obey those parts of the Bill of Rights that are fundamental. A right is fundamental when a system of justice would not be fair without it.

Cardozo said the First Amendment freedom of speech and the Sixth Amendment right to a jury trial in criminal cases are examples of fundamental rights. Without them, a fair system of justice would be impossible. In contrast, the Seventh Amendment right to jury a trial in civil cases—cases between private citizens—is not fundamental. A person cannot lose his life or freedom in a civil case.

The Supreme Court decided that in Palko's case, the rights under the Double Jeopardy Clause were not fundamental. Connecticut retried Palko because his first trial had serious errors. Defendants are allowed to get retrials when their first trials have errors. Cardozo said it made the system more fair to give both defendants and states the right to have error free trials.

BENTON v. MARYLAND

The Supreme Court overturned *Palko* in *Benton v. Maryland* (1969). In 1965, a jury in Maryland found John Benton guilty of burglary but not guilty of larceny. Afterwards, the Maryland Court of Appeals struck down a law that required jurors to swear to their belief in God. Maryland then gave Benton the chance to have a second trial. At that trial, the jury found Benton guilty of both larceny and burglary.

Benton took the case to the U.S. Supreme Court, arguing that two trials violated the Double Jeopardy Clause. The Supreme Court agreed and reversed Benton's larceny conviction. The Court overruled *Palko,* saying it no longer accepted the idea that the Fourteenth Amendment applied only a "watered down" version of the Bill of Rights to the states. After *Benton,* states must obey the Double Jeopardy Clause.

Impact

Thirty-two years later, the Supreme Court overturned *Palko* in **Benton v. Maryland** (1969). By then, the Supreme Court had decided that the Due Process Clause requires states to obey most of the Bill of Rights.

Suggestions for further reading

Galloway, John. *The Supreme Court & the Rights of the Accused.* New York: Facts on File, 1973.

Holmes, Burnham. *The Fifth Amendment.* Silver Burdett Press, 1991.

Johnson, Joan. *Justice.* New York: Franklin Watts, 1985.

Krull, Kathleen. *A Kids' Guide to America's Bill of Rights: Curfews, Censorship, and the 100-Pound Giant.* Avon Books, 1999.

Mikula, Mark, and L. Mpho Mabunda. *Great American Court Cases.* Detroit: The Gale Group, 1999.

Stein, Richard Conrad. *The Bill of Rights.* Children's Press, 1994.

Gideon v. Wainwright
1963

Petitioner: Clarence Earl Gideon

Respondent: Louie L. Wainwright

Petitioner's Claim: The Sixth Amendment right to legal counsel for defendants unable to afford an attorney should apply equally to the states.

Chief Lawyer for Petitioner: Abe Fortas

Chief Lawyer for Respondents: Bruce R. Jacob

Justices for the Court: Hugo Lafayette Black, William J. Brennan, Jr., Tom C. Clark, William O. Douglas, Arthur Goldberg, John Marshall Harlan II, Earl Warren, Byron R. White.

Justices Dissenting: None

Date of Decision: March 18, 1963

Decision: The Sixth Amendment applies to the states and they are required to provide defendants charged with serious crimes and unable to afford an attorney with legal counsel.

Significance: In taking his case to the United States Supreme Court, Clarence Gideon brought about an historic change in the way American criminal trials are conducted. Before this case, state courts only appointed attorneys for capital cases (cases with the possibility of the death penalty). Now all defendants charged with felony crimes (cases with the possibility of one year or more in prison) that cannot afford to pay for an attorney are entitled to court-appointed legal representation.

In The Supreme Court of The United States
Washington D.C.
clarence Earl Gideon
  Petitioner   *Petition for a writ*
 vs.   *of Certiorari Directed*
H.G. Cochran, Jr, as *to The Supreme Court*
Director, Divisions *State of Florida.*
of corrections State No. – 890 Misc.
of Florida.   OCT. TERM 1961

    U. S. Supreme Court

To The Honorable Earl Warren, Chief
 Justice of the United States
  Comes now The petitioner, Clarence
Earl Gideon, a citizen of The United states
of America, in proper person, and appearing
as his own counsel. Who petitions this
Honorable Court for a Writ of Certiorari
directed to The Supreme Court of The State
of Florida. To review the order and Judge-
ment of the court below denying The
petitioner a writ of Habeus Corpus.

*Clarence Earl
Gideon petitioned
the Supreme Court
himself to urge them
to consider his case.*
Courtesy of the
Supreme Court of the
United States.

At eight o'clock on the morning of June 3, 1961, a police officer in Panama City, Florida, noticed that the door of the Bay Harbor Poolroom was open. Stepping inside, he saw that someone had burglarized the pool hall, breaking into a cigarette machine and jukebox. The evidence gathered by police led to the arrest of Clarence Gideon, a fifty-one-year-old drifter who sometimes worked at the poolroom. Gideon declared that he was innocent. Nonetheless, two months later he faced trial in the Panama City courthouse. No one present had any idea that they were about to witness history in the making.

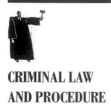

Clarence Earl Gideon, in court without money and without a lawyer, asked the judge to appoint an attorney. Judge Robert L. McCrary, Jr. denied his request as under Florida law, he could only appoint counsel in a capital case. Gideon argued that the United States Supreme Court said he had a right to counsel.

The First Trial

The judge was correct. At that time, Florida law did not allow for a court-appointed defense lawyer. A 1942 Supreme Court decision, *Betts v. Brady,* had extended this right only to those state court defendants facing a charge punishable with the death sentence. Many other states voluntarily provided all defendants accused of a felony with a lawyer. Florida did not. So at the start of the trial on August 4, 1961, Clarence Gideon was alone in defending himself. Gideon, a man of limited education, performed as well as he could, but he was not the equal of the Assistant State Attorney William E. Harris.

Prosecution witness Henry Cook claimed to have seen Gideon inside the poolroom at 5:30 on the morning of the robbery. He had watched Gideon for a few minutes through a window. When Gideon came out of the pool hall he had a pint of wine in his hand, he made a telephone call from a nearby booth. Soon afterward a cab arrived and Gideon left.

During cross-examination Gideon questioned Cook's reasons for being outside the bar at 5:30 in the morning. Cook replied that he had "just come from a dance, had been out all night." An attorney might have checked out this story further, but Gideon let it pass. Eight other witnesses testified on Gideons behalf. None proved helpful, and Gideon was found guilty. The whole trial had lasted less than a day. At the sentencing hearing three weeks later Judge McCrary sentenced Gideon to the maximum sentence of five years in prison.

Gideon Fights Back

Gideon was outraged at the verdict. He applied to the Florida Supreme Court for an order freeing him because he had been illegally imprisoned (a writ of *habeas corpus*). When this application was denied, Gideon hand-wrote a five page appeal of this denial to the United States Supreme Court.

Each year the United States Supreme Court receives thousands of petitions. Most are rejected without any hearing. Against the odds, the

HABEAS CORPUS:
A CONSTITUTIONAL RIGHT

Clarence Gideon claimed that he had not had a fair trial because he could not afford an attorney and the court refused to give him one. Based on that he argued he was being held illegally and he sought a writ of *habeas corpus*. The privilege of the writ of *habeas corpus* is guaranteed by Article I, Section 9 of the U.S. Constitution. *Habeas corpus* is a Latin term that means "you have the body." It refers to a prisoner's right not to be held except under circumstances outlined by law. In other words, the police cannot simply pick up someone and hold him or her in prison. To legally hold a person in jail, the person must either be legally arrested and awaiting trial or convicted of a crime and serving a sentence. Moreover, the Fifth Amendment guarantees that citizens cannot be "deprived of life, liberty, or property, without due process of law." So Gideon claimed that since he had not had an attorney for his trial, he had not received due process of law.

Supreme Court decided to hear Gideon's petition. The case was heard as *Gideon v. Wainwright* (the director of Florida's Division of Corrections). Bruce R. Jacob, Assistant Attorney General of Florida argued the case for the State of Florida. Abe Fortas, Gideon's appointed counsel for the appeal (and later a Supreme Court justice himself) argued Gideon's suit. The court heard the oral argument on January 14, 1963.

On March 18, 1963, the Supreme Court unanimously overruled the prior case law *Betts v. Brady,* saying that all felony defendants are entitled to legal representation and sent Gideon's case back to the Florida trial court for a second trial. Justice Hugo L. Black wrote the opinion that set aside Gideon's conviction:

> **Reason and reflection requires us to recognize that
> in our adversary system of criminal justice, any
> person haled [hauled] into court, who is too poor
> to hire a lawyer, cannot be assured a fair trial**

unless counsel is provided for him. This seems to us to be an obvious truth.

The Second Trial

On August 5, 1963, Clarence Gideon again appeared before Judge Robert L. McCrary in the Panama City courthouse, but at his new trial he had an experienced trial lawyer, W. Fred Turner, to defend him. Due to all of the publicity surrounding his Supreme Court victory there was an even stronger prosecution team against him at the second trial. State Attorney J. Frank Adams and J. Paul Griffith joined William Harris in an effort to convict Gideon a second time. Cook was again the main prosecution witness, Henry Cook, fell apart under Turner's expert questioning. Particularly damaging was Cook's admission that he had withheld details of his criminal record at the first trial. The jury found Gideon not guilty of all charges.

Clarence Earl Gideon died a free man in 1973 at age sixty-one.

Suggestions for further reading

Lewis, Anthony. *Gideons Trumpet.* New York: Random House, 1964.

Schwartz, Bernard. *History of the Law in America.* New York: American Heritage, 1974.

West Publishing Company Staff. *The Guide to American Law.* St. Paul, MN: West Publishing Co., 1985.

Robinson v. California
1962

Appellant: Lawrence Robinson

Appellee: State of California

Appellant's Claim: That convicting him for having a drug addiction was cruel and unusual punishment.

Chief Lawyer for Appellant: Samuel Carter McMorris

Chief Lawyer for Appellee: William E. Doran

Justices for the Court: Hugo Lafayette Black, William J. Brennan, Jr., William O. Douglas, John Marshall Harlan II, Potter Stewart, Earl Warren

Justices Dissenting: Tom C. Clark, Byron R. White (Felix Frankfurter did not participate)

Date of Decision: June 25, 1962

Decision: The Supreme Court reversed Robinson's conviction.

Significance: With *Robinson,* the Supreme Court said it is cruel and unusual to convict someone for having an illness, such as drug addiction. *Robinson* helped eliminate status crimes such as vagrancy and homelessness.

Lawrence Robinson was on the streets of Los Angeles one evening when Officer Brown confronted him. Although Robinson was not doing anything wrong, Officer Brown questioned and searched Robinson for evidence of a crime. Brown found needle marks, scar tissue, and discoloration on Robinson's arms. Under questioning, Robinson admitted that he occasionally used illegal drugs. Officer Brown arrested Robinson and took him to the Central Jail in Los Angeles.

The next morning, Officer Lindquist examined Robinson's arms, both in person and in photographs taken the night before. Based on ten years of experience in the Narcotics Division of the Los Angeles Police Department, Officer Lindquist concluded that Robinson was injecting illegal drugs into his arms. According to Lindquist, Robinson admitted this under questioning.

Despite the marks on Robinson's arms, there was no evidence that he was under the influence of illegal drugs or having withdrawal symptoms when he was arrested. California, however, had a law that made it a crime to be addicted to drugs. People convicted under the law got a minimum of ninety days in jail. California charged Robinson with being a drug addict.

At his trial, Robinson said the marks on his arms were an allergy condition he got from shots in the military. Two witnesses for Robinson said the same thing. Robinson denied that he ever used or admitted to using illegal drugs. Officers Brown and Lindquist, however, testified to what they saw on Robinson's arms. The judge instructed the jury that even if there was no evidence that Robinson had used drugs in California, it could convict Robinson for being addicted to drugs while in California. The court said the law made the "condition or status" of drug addiction a crime.

The jury convicted Robinson, so he appealed to the Appellate Department of the Los Angeles County Superior Court. When that court ruled against him too, Robinson appealed to the U.S. Supreme Court.

Cruel and Unusual Punishment

With a 6–2 decision, the Supreme Court reversed Robinson's conviction. Writing for the Court, Justice Potter Stewart said drug addiction is an illness, not a crime. Punishing someone for an illness violates the Eighth Amendment of the U.S. Constitution, which bans cruel and unusual punishments.

Justice Stewart said states can fight against America's serious drug problem by making it illegal to manufacture, sell, buy, use, or possess illegal drugs. States also may protect their citizens from criminal activity by drug addicts by requiring addicts to get medical treatment.

MANDATORY MINIMUM DRUG SENTENCES

When a jury convicts a criminal, the judge usually has the power to select a punishment, or sentence, to fit the crime. In the 1970s, however, America's war on drugs led to the enactment of mandatory minimum drug sentence laws. These laws forced judges to give drug offenders long prison sentences.

New York was the first state to enact a mandatory drug sentence law. Called the Rockefeller law after then Governor Nelson Rockefeller, it required a fifteen year sentence for anyone convicted of having at least four ounces or selling at least two ounces of an illegal drug. Thomas Eddy, one of the first to be convicted under New York's law, received 15 years to life in prison for selling two ounces of cocaine when he was a sophomore at State University of New York, Binghamton.

After over twenty-five years with such laws in the United States, many people call them a failure. The big drug dealers the laws were supposed to stop often escape punishment by turning in smaller dealers and users. America's jails are filled with first-time drug offenders serving stiff mandatory sentences. Meanwhile, overcrowded jails are forced to release rapists, robbers, and murderers to make room for drug users.

Supporters say mandatory minimum sentences are working. They say crime in the United States dropped in the 1990s because so many drug offenders were in jail. They also say tough mandatory sentences are the only way to fight drugs in the nation with the world's biggest drug problem.

California's law was different. It was meant to punish drug addicts, not cure them. Justice Stewart said punishing someone for having a drug addiction is like punishing someone for having a mental illness, leprosy, venereal disease, or the common cold. "Even one day in prison would be a cruel and unusual punishment for the 'crime' of having a common cold."

Losing the War on Drugs

Justices Tom C. Clark and Byron R. White dissented, which means they disagreed with the Court's decision. In a dissenting opinion, Justice Clark said California's law was not designed to punish people for drug addiction. It was designed to put them in jail for at least 90 days to help them break the addiction.

In addition, Justice Clark said there is no difference between a person who uses drugs and a person who is addicted to drugs. Both are dangerous to society because drug use leads to health problems and criminal behavior. Convicting someone for a drug addiction is the same as convicting an alcoholic for public drunkenness. They are not status crimes, they are crimes that endanger societal health and welfare. Justice Clark said California should be allowed to protect people from such dangers.

Impact

Robinson could have been used to eliminate all crimes resulting from a person's voluntary use of drugs and alcohol. In *Powell v. Texas* (1968), however, the Supreme Court said addiction to alcohol cannot be used as a defense the crime of public drunkenness. Instead, *Robinson* has been used to strike down other types of status crimes, such as vagrancy and homelessness.

Suggestions for further reading

Bernards, Neal. *The War on Drugs: Examining Cause and Effect Relationships.* San Diego: Greenhaven Press, 1991.

Brennan, Michael. "A Case for Discretion." *Newsweek,* November 13, 1995.

Gottfried, Ted. *Should Drugs Be Legalized?* Twenty First Century Books, 2000.

Hansen, Mark. "Mandatories Going, Going . . . Gone." *ABA J ournal,* April 1999.

Johnson, Joan. *America's War on Drugs.* New York: Franklin Watts, 1990.

Kronenwetter, Michael. *Drugs in America: The Users, the Suppliers, the War on Drugs.* Englewood Cliffs: Messner, 1990.

Marks, Alexandra. "Rolling Back Stiff Drug Sentences." *Christian Science Monitor,* December 8, 1998.

Powell, Jillian. *Drug Trafficking.* Copper Beach Books, 1997.

Santamaria, Peggy. *Drugs and Politics.* Rosen Publishing Group, 1994.

Stefoff, Rebecca. *The Drug Enforcement Administration.* New York: Chelsea House, 1989.

Terkel, Susan Neiburg. *Should Drugs Be Legalized?* New York: Franklin Watts, 1990.

Thompson, Stephen P., ed. *The War on Drugs: Opposing Viewpoints.* San Diego: Greenhaven Press, 1998.

Wier, William. *In the Shadow of the Dope Fiend: America's War on Drugs.* Archon, 1997.

Robinson v. California

Miranda v Arizona
1966

Petitioner: Ernesto Miranda

Respondent: State of Arizona

Petitioner's Claim: That the Fifth Amendment privilege against self-incrimination protects a suspect's right to be informed of his constitutional rights during police questioning and applies to the states through the Due Process Clause of the Fourteenth Amendment.

Chief Lawyer for Petitioner: John Flynn

Chief Lawyer for Respondents: Gary K. Nelson

Justices for the Court: Hugo Lafayette Black, William J. Brennan, Jr., William O. Douglas, Abe Fortas, Earl Warren

Justices Dissenting: Tom C. Clark, John Marshall Harlan II, Potter Stewart, Byron R. White

Date of Decision: June 13, 1966

Decision: The Fifth Amendment protection from self-incrimination requires that suspects be informed of their constitutional rights before questioning by the police when they are in police custody.

Significance: Few events have altered the course of American criminal law more than the events surrounding the 1963 rape conviction of Ernesto Miranda. The only strong evidence against him was a confession he made while in police custody. The events surrounding that confession captured the nations attention and prompted a landmark United States Supreme Court decision.

In Phoenix, Arizona, during the early hours of March 3, 1963, an eighteen-year-old movie theater attendant was kidnapped by a stranger while on her way home from work. The stranger dragged her into his car, drove out into the desert, and raped her. Afterwards, he dropped her off near her home.

The young woman's story of the events was vague and confusing. She described her attacker as a Mexican in his late twenties wearing glasses. He drove an early 1950s car, either a Ford or Chevrolet.

By chance, one week later, the woman and her brother-in-law saw what she believed was the car of her attacker, a 1953 Packard, license plate number DFL-312. License records showed that this plate was actually registered to a late model Oldsmobile. But plate number DFL-317 was a Packard, registered to a woman, Twila N. Hoffman. Further investigation showed that her boyfriend, Ernesto Miranda, age twenty-three, fit the attacker's description almost exactly.

Ernesto Miranda had a long history of criminal behavior. He had served a one-year jail term for attempted rape. Police put him into a line-up with three other Mexicans of similar height and build, though none wore glasses. The victim did not positively identify Miranda, but told detectives that he looked most like her attacker.

Detectives Carroll Cooley and Wilfred Young took Miranda into another room for questioning. They told him, incorrectly, that the victim had identified him as her attacker from the line-up. They asked him to make a statement. Two hours later, Ernesto Miranda signed a written confession. He was not forced to sign the statement. The detectives did not physically or verbally abuse him. The confession even included a section stating that he understood his rights.

Miranda was given a lawyer, appointed by the court, to represent him because he did not have enough money to hire his own attorney. His lawyer, Alvin Moore, studied the evidence against Miranda. The case against him was very strong, with the most damaging evidence being his confession to the crime. Moore found the events surrounding the statement troubling. Convinced it had been obtained improperly, he intended to ask the court suppress this evidence and not permit his admission of guilt to come into evidence and be heard by the jury.

Only four witnesses appeared to testify for the prosecution: the victim, her sister, and Detectives Cooley and Young. In his closing argument to the jury, the prosecutor, Deputy County Attorney Laurence Turoff, told the jury that Ernesto Miranda, by the use of force and violence, raped the victim.

CRIMINAL LAW AND PROCEDURE

In Miranda's defense, Attorney Moore was able to point out several inconsistencies in the victim's story, including the fact that she had no physical injuries after her supposed attack. In his cross-examination of Detective Cooley, Attorney Moore made his most important point:

> **Question: Officer Cooley, in the taking of this statement, what did you say to the defendant to get him to make this statement?**
>
> **Answer: I asked the defendant if he would . . . write the same story that he just told me, and he said that he would.**
>
> **Question: Did you warn him of his rights?**
>
> **Answer: Yes, sir, at the heading of the statement is a paragraph typed out, and I read this paragraph to him out loud.**
>
> **Question: I don't see in the statement that it says where he is entitled to the advice of an attorney before he made it.**
>
> **Answer: No, sir.**
>
> **Question: Is it not your practice to advise people you arrest that they are entitled to the services of an attorney before they make a statement?**
>
> **Answer: No, sir.**

Based on this testimony, Moore asked the judge to keep the jury from hearing Miranda's confession. Judge Yale McFate overruled him. The judge gave the jury a well-balanced and fair account of the law as it stood at the time and permitted them to hear the confession. In 1963, the law did not include a constitutional right to remain silent at any time before the beginning of a trial.

Consequently, on June 27, 1963, Ernesto Miranda was convicted of both crimes and sentenced to two concurrent sentences of twenty-to-thirty years imprisonment. Concurrent sentences run at the same time.

However, Alvin Moore's arguments about the confession touched off a legal debate. Miranda's conviction was appealed all the way to the U.S. Supreme Court. On June 13, 1966, Chief Justice Earl Warren, writing the decision for a 5–4 majority, established guidelines about what is and what is not acceptable police behavior in an interrogation:

INFLUENTIAL CHIEF JUSTICE

Earl Warren was Chief Justice of the U.S. Supreme Court from 1953 to 1969. During this time, the "Warren Court" made some of the most influential decisions in modern U.S. history, establishing many civil rights and individual liberties issues. No one expected such landmark decisions from Warren whose previous history was as a rather unremarkable Republican politician. Warren was California's attorney general from 1939 to 1943 and its governor from 1943 to 1953, involving himself in a shameful chapter in the state's history. As attorney general during World War II, he pressed for the internment of Japanese Americans in detention camps, based on the fear that they might be enemy agents and spies. As governor, he presided over the internment process. In 1948, he was an unsuccessful vice-presidential candidate, running with Republican Thomas Dewey against President Harry S Truman. Yet as Chief Justice, Warren led the court to establish new precedents that outlawed school segregation, established the right to court-appointed attorneys, and asserted the right of arrested men and women to know their rights. While serving as Chief Justice, Warren also headed the "Warren Commission," established by President Lyndon Johnson on November 29, 1963, to investigate the assassination of President John F. Kennedy.

> **Prior to any questioning, the person must be warned that he has a right to remain silent, that any statement he does make may be used as evidence against him, and that he has a right to the presence of an attorney, either retained or appointed . . .**

With Miranda's conviction overturned, the State of Arizona was forced to free its now famous prisoner. Without his confession, the state stood little chance of getting a second conviction.

It was Ernesto Miranda himself who brought about his own downfall. He expected to be released after the Supreme Court decision so he had begun a battle for custody of his daughter with Twila Hoffman, his common-law wife. A common-law marriage is an informal marriage where the couple has no license or ceremony but live together, with the intent to be married and tell others that they are married. Hoffman, angry and fearful, told authorities about a conversation with Miranda after his arrest, in which he had admitted the rape. This new evidence was all Arizona needed.

Miranda's second trial began February 15, 1967. Most of the arguments took place in the judge's private chambers. This time the main issue was whether Hoffman, his common-law wife could testify against Miranda, her common-law husband. Judge Lawrence K. Wren ruled that Hoffman's testimony could be allowed as evidence and Hoffman was allowed to tell her story to the jury. Miranda was convicted for a second time and sentenced him to twenty-to-thirty-years in jail.

On January 31, 1976, four years after his released from prison on parole, Ernesto Miranda was stabbed to death in a bar fight. The killer fled but his accomplice (helper) was caught. Before taking him to police headquarters for questioning, the arresting officers read the suspect his "Miranda rights."

The importance of this case cannot be overstated. Although presidents from Richard Nixon to Ronald Reagan have publicly disagreed with it, the *Miranda* decision remains law. Originally intended to protect the poor and the ignorant, the practice of "reading the defendant his rights" has become standard procedure in every police department in the country. The practice is seen so frequently in police movies and shows that the Miranda warnings are as familiar to most Americans as the Pledge of Allegiance.

Suggestions for further reading

Baker, Liva. *Miranda: Crime, Law and Politics.* New York: Atheneum, 1983.

Graham, Fred P. *The SelfInflicted Wound.* New York: Macmillan Co., 1970.

Skene, Neil. "The Miranda Ruling." *Congressional Quarterly* (June 6, 1991): 164.

Tucker, William. "The Long Road Back." *National Review* (October 18, 1985): 28–35.

Arizona v. Evans
1995

Petitioner: State of Arizona

Respondent: Issac Evans

Petitioner's Claim: That marijuana found during an illegal arrest caused by a computer error could be used to convict Evans.

Chief Lawyer for Petitioner: Gerald Grant

Chief Lawyer for Respondent: Carol Carrigan

Justices for the Court: Stephen Breyer, Anthony M. Kennedy, Sandra Day O'Connor, William H. Rehnquist, Antonin Scalia, David H. Souter, Clarence Thomas

Justices Dissenting: Ruth Bader Ginsburg, John Paul Stevens

Date of Decision: March 1, 1995

Decision: The Supreme Court said Arizona could use the evidence if the computer error was not the police department's fault.

Significance: *Evans* makes it easier for states to use evidence they get in violation of the Fourth Amendment.

The Fourth Amendment of the U.S. Constitution protects privacy. It requires federal law enforcement officers to get a warrant to arrest and search a suspected criminal. To get a warrant, law enforcement must have probable cause, which means good reason to believe the person to be arrested has committed a crime. State law enforcement officers must obey the Fourth Amendment under the Due Process Clause of the Fourteenth Amendment.

To enforce the Fourth Amendment, the U.S. Supreme Court created the exclusionary rule. This rule prevents the government from convicting a defendant with evidence found during an arrest or search that violates the Fourth Amendment. Without the exclusionary rule, the police would be encouraged to disobey the Fourth Amendment because they still could use any evidence they found.

Computer Glitch

Bryan Sargent was a police officer in Phoenix, Arizona. In January 1991, Sargent saw Issac Evans driving the wrong way on a one-way street in front of a police station. Sargent stopped Evans and asked to see his driver's license. Evans told Sargent he did not have a license because it had been suspended.

Sargent went back to his police car to enter Evans's name into a computer data terminal. The computer told Sargent that Evans's license had been suspended. It also said there was a warrant for Evans's arrest for failure to appear in court for traffic violations. On the strength of the warrant, Sargent returned to Evans's car and arrested him. While he was being handcuffed, Evans dropped a hand-rolled cigarette that smelled like marijuana, an illegal drug. The police searched Evans's car and found a whole bag of marijuana under the passenger seat.

The state of Arizona charged Evans with illegal possession of marijuana. It soon learned, however, that the warrant to arrest Evans did not exist when Sargent made the arrest. Evans had appeared in court seventeen days before the arrest to resolve his traffic violations. Unfortunately, the court clerk forgot to call the sheriff's office to tell it to erase the warrant from its computer system. When the computer told Sargent there was a warrant for Evans's arrest, the computer was wrong. That made the arrest illegal under the Fourth Amendment.

Without the arrest, the police never would have found Evans's marijuana. At Evans's trial, his lawyer made a motion to enforce the exclusionary rule by getting rid of the marijuana evidence. Without that evidence, the court would have to dismiss Arizona's case against Evans. The trial court granted the motion, so Arizona took the case all the way up to the U.S. Supreme Court.

Good Faith Exception

With a 7–2 decision, the Supreme Court ruled in favor of Arizona. Writing for the Court, Chief Justice William H. Rehnquist said the exclusionary rule does not apply to every violation of the Fourth Amendment. The Supreme Court designed the exclusionary rule to discourage police misconduct. If the police believe in good faith that they are obeying the Fourth Amendment, there is no reason to apply the exclusionary rule.

Officer Sargent thought he had a valid warrant to arrest Issac Evans. The fact that there was a computer error was the court clerk's fault. The clerk was the one who failed to tell the sheriff's office to erase the warrant for Evans's arrest. Since Officer Sargent thought he was obeying the Fourth Amendment when he arrested Evans, there was no reason to apply the exclusionary rule. Arizona was allowed to proceed with its case against Evans for illegal possession of marijuana.

Big Brother

Two justices dissented, which means they disagreed with the Court's decision. Justice John Paul Stevens did not think the Fourth Amendment and the exclusionary rule were designed to discourage police misconduct alone. He said they were designed to prevent all state actors, including courts, from violating the Fourth Amendment.

In her own dissent, Justice Ruth Bader Ginsburg cautioned against allowing the police to rely on new computer systems that might contain lots of errors. Quoting the Arizona Supreme Court, Ginsburg said, "It is repugnant to the principles of a free society that a person should ever be taken into custody because of a computer error [caused] by government carelessness."

Impact

When the Supreme Court created the exclusionary rule for the federal government in *Weeks v. United States* (1914), it strengthened the Fourth Amendment for American citizens. The Court strengthened the amendment even further when it applied the exclusionary rule to state governments in ***Mapp v. Ohio*** (1961). Since then, the Court has weakened the Fourth Amendment by creating exceptions such as the "good faith" exception in *Arizona v. Evans*. Some think the exceptions are necessary to help law enforcement protect society from dangerous criminals. Others think the exceptions allow law enforcement officers to harass American citizens with warrantless searches and illegal arrests.

RUTH BADER GINSBURG

Justice Ruth Bader Ginsburg, who dissented in *Arizona v. Evans,* set an example of excellence for women and men in the legal profession. Born on March 15, 1933 in Brooklyn, New York, Ginsburg grew up in a middle class family. Along with the opportunity that brought, Ginsburg fought through gender discrimination to work her way to the nation's highest court.

When Ginsburg attended Harvard Law School in 1956, she was told that she and her eight female classmates were taking places away from qualified men. After transferring to Columbia Law School and graduating top in her class, Ginsburg failed to receive a job offer from any law firm. Even Supreme Court Justice Felix Frankfurter refused to hire Ginsburg as a law clerk because he was not ready to hire a woman.

Ginsburg did not let the discrimination stop her. After working for a district court judge in New York, Ginsburg taught law at Rutgers University, Harvard, and then Columbia. From 1973 to 1980, she worked as an attorney on the Women's Rights Project for the American Civil Liberties Union. In that role, Ginsburg surprised people by taking on cases supporting equal rights for both men and women. Ginsburg did not think equal rights meant greater rights for women than for men.

Ginsburg served as a judge on the U.S. Court of Appeals for the District of Columbia from 1980 to 1993. As a judge, Ginsburg again surprised many people by being more conservative than she was as a lawyer. Still, President William J. Clinton appointed Ginsburg to the U.S. Supreme Court in 1993. In 1996, Justice Ginsburg wrote an opinion that ended gender discrimination by all-male state military colleges in the United States.

Suggestions for further reading

Franklin, Paula A. *The Fourth Amendment.* Englewood Cliffs: Silver
   Burdett Press, 1991.

Mooney, Louise, ed. *Newsmakers: The People Behind Today's Headlines.* Detroit: Gale Research Inc., 1993.

Persico, Deborah A. *Mapp v. Ohio: Evidence and Search Warrants.* Enslow Publishers, Inc., 1997.

—-*New Jersey v. T.L.O: Drug Searches in Schools.* Enslow Publishers, Inc., 1998.

Shattuck, John H.F. *Rights of Privacy.* Skokie: National Textbook Co., 1977.

Wetterer, Charles M.*The Fourth Amendment: Search and Seizure.* Enslow Publishers, Inc., 1998.

United States v. Ursery
1996

Petitioner: United States

Respondent: Guy Ursery

Petitioner's Claim: That convicting Ursery for growing marijuana and then taking the house in which he grew the marijuana did not violate the Double Jeopardy Clause of the Fifth Amendment.

Chief Lawyer for Petitioner: Drew S. Days III, U.S. Solicitor General

Chief Lawyers for Respondent: Lawrence Robbins, David Michael, Jeffry K. Finer

Justices for the Court: Stephen Breyer, Ruth Bader Ginsburg, Anthony M. Kennedy, Sandra Day O'Connor, William H. Rehnquist, Antonin Scalia, David H. Souter, Clarence Thomas

Justices Dissenting: John Paul Stevens

Date of Decision: June 24, 1996

Decision: The Supreme Court affirmed Ursery's conviction and approved the forfeiture proceeding against his house.

Significance: On one level, *Ursery* said a civil forfeiture that is not punitive does not raise Double Jeopardy concerns. On another level, the case indicated the Supreme Court would give Congress as much power as possible to fight the war on drugs.

Guy Ursery grew marijuana in his home in Flint, Michigan. Marijuana is an illegal drug that people smoke to get "high." Ursery grew the marijuana for himself and his family and friends. He worked as an autoworker, however, not a drug dealer.

Double Trouble

Based on a tip from Ursery's former girlfriend, Michigan police raided Ursery's home and found marijuana seeds, stems, stalks, and a light for growing the plants. Under federal law, the government is allowed to take away personal property that is used to make illegal drugs. This is called forfeiture because it makes a person forfeit his property. The federal government began a forfeiture proceeding against Ursery's home. Ursery eventually settled the case by paying the government $13,250.

Federal law also makes it a crime to make illegal drugs. Before the forfeiture proceeding was over, the United States charged Ursery with

People are often caught and prosecuted for growing marijuana, an illegal drug, on thier property.
Reproduced by permission of AP/Wide World Photos.

violating the law by growing marijuana. A jury found Ursery guilty and the judge sentenced him to five years and three months in prison.

The Double Jeopardy Clause of the Fifth Amendment says no person "shall . . . be twice put in jeopardy of life and limb" for the same crime. This means the government cannot prosecute or punish a person twice for the same crime. Ursery appealed his conviction to the U.S. Court of Appeals for the Sixth Circuit. He argued that the forfeiture proceeding and criminal conviction were double punishment that violated the Double Jeopardy Clause. The Sixth Circuit agreed and reversed Ursery's conviction, so the United States took the case to the U.S. Supreme Court.

Forfeiture Not Punishment

With an 8–1 decision, the Supreme Court ruled in favor of the United States and affirmed Ursery's conviction. Writing for the Court, Chief Justice William H. Rehnquist said the Double Jeopardy Clause forbids successive punishments for the same crime. Imprisonment after a criminal conviction is certainly punishment. The question, then, was whether the forfeiture proceeding was punishment.

Rehnquist said there are two types of civil forfeitures. "In personam" forfeitures are cases in which the government fines a person for unlawful behavior. Rehnquist said these fines can be a form of punishment, meaning they count as punishment under the Double Jeopardy Clause.

"In rem" forfeitures are cases in which the government directly sues the property to be forfeited. The government punishes the property that was being used for criminal activity by taking it away from the criminal. In such cases, the government does not punish the criminal. "In rem" forfeiture cases, then, do not usually count as punishment under the Double Jeopardy Clause.

Rehnquist analyzed the history of Supreme Court forfeiture cases. The most important example was *Various Items of Personal Property v. United States* (1931). In that case, a corporation was using property to make alcohol during Prohibition in the 1920s, when making alcohol was illegal. After convicting the corporation on criminal charges, the government sued the property in a forfeiture action. The Supreme Court said that did not violate the Double Jeopardy Clause. It said, "the forfeiture is not part of the punishment for the criminal offense."

DRUG ENFORCEMENT ADMINISTRATION

The Drug Enforcement Administration (DEA) is an office in the U.S. Department of Justice. Formed in 1973, the DEA enforces federal drug laws in the United States. Its primary goal is to prevent criminals from making, smuggling, and transporting illegal drugs in the country. The DEA works with individual states and foreign countries to stop drugs at their source in the United States and around the world. It also works to enforce regulations on prescription drugs.

Asset forfeiture is an important tool for the DEA. Federal laws allow the DEA to seize valuable property that is used to violate drug laws. The DEA sells most of the property at auctions and puts the money into an Asset Forfeiture Fund. That fund helps victims and crime fighting programs across the nation.

The DEA also uses seized property to help communities with drug problems. In Philadelphia, Pennsylvania, for example, the DEA gave two drug stash houses to an organization called United Neighbors Against Drugs. The organization uses the homes to run drug abuse prevention, job training, and education programs for neighborhood adults and children.

For the same reasons, the Court decided that Ursery's conviction and the forfeiture proceeding against his home did not violate the Double Jeopardy Clause. The forfeiture proceeding was not designed to punish Ursery for growing marijuana. It was designed to take away property that was being used to commit a crime. In effect, the government punished Ursery once with imprisonment and his property once with forfeiture. The government punished nobody twice, so it did not violate the Double Jeopardy Clause.

Taking Property is Punishment

Justice John Paul Stevens wrote a dissenting opinion, which means he disagreed with the Court's decision. Stevens said there was no way to

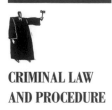

CRIMINAL LAW AND PROCEDURE

characterize forfeiture of Ursery's home as anything other than punishment. The house was neither illegal by itself nor bought with illegal money. It was not harming society. The only reason to take it was to punish Ursery and discourage others from breaking the law. Stevens said such forfeitures should count as punishment under the Double Jeopardy Clause.

Impact

Forfeiture laws are a weapon in the war on drugs in the United States. *Ursery* was a sign the Supreme Court would give Congress all the power it could to fight that war. In another case the same year, *Bennis v. Michigan* (1996), the Supreme Court said the government could seize a car that was used for illegal sex with a prostitute even when the car's co-owner did not know about the illegal activity. With forfeiture laws, then, the government hopes to take a bite out of crime.

Suggestions for further reading

Bernards, Neal. *The War on Drugs: Examining Cause and Effect Relationships.* San Diego: Greenhaven Press, 1991.

Drug Enforcement Administration website, [Online] http://www.usdoj.gov/dea/programs/af.htm (Accessed August 8, 2000).

Gottfried, Ted. *Should Drugs Be Legalized?* Twenty First Century Books, 2000.

Holmes, Burnham. *The Fifth Amendment.* Silver Burdett Press, 1991.

Jaffe, Jerome H., ed. *Encyclopedia of Drugs and Alcohol.* 1995 ed., s.v. "U.S. Government."

Johnson, Joan. *America's War on Drugs.* New York: Franklin Watts, 1990.

Kronenwetter, Michael. *Drugs in America: The Users, the Suppliers, the War on Drugs.* Englewood Cliffs: Messner, 1990.

Powell, Jillian. *Drug Trafficking.* Copper Beach Books, 1997.

Santamaria, Peggy. *Drugs and Politics.* Rosen Publishing Group, 1994.

Stefoff, Rebecca. *The Drug Enforcement Administration.* New York: Chelsea House, 1989.

Terkel, Susan Neiburg. *Should Drugs Be Legalized?* New York: Franklin Watts, 1990.

Thompson, Stephen P., ed. *The War on Drugs: Opposing Viewpoints.* San Diego: Greenhaven Press, 1998.

Wier, William. *In the Shadow of the Dope Fiend: America's War on Drugs.* Archon, 1997.

United
States v.
Ursery

FAMILY LAW

"Not so many years ago, the law considered a man's wife and children as little more than his property, and he was free to treat them accordingly. Few areas of the law have undergone as much change in the past half century as the area known as family law, and few areas of the law affect so many people." (From *The 21st Century Family Legal Guide,* p. 19)

The importance of families to maintaining order in society has long been recognized. However, throughout much of history, most domestic (within the household) family matters were considered separate from general public law and not subject to government regulation. Family issues, including finances and disputes between family members, were almost always left for the family to resolve. Exceptions would include criminal cases of murder or assault, or other severe occurrences.

By the late twentieth century, fears were growing that a decline in "family values" was occurring. A greater desire to regulate family grew. In addition, medical advances in the 1980s and 1990s opened new avenues for both creating life and extending life. These advances led to new legal issues no one imagined only a few decades earlier. To further complicate matters, the character of American families was radically changing as well. Family law developed as a mix of diverse legal issues.

History of Family Law

Dating back to early historic times of the European feudal period and later English common law, the husband was legally considered the dominant person in a family. He owned all property and held certain rights not enjoyed by the wife. The husband controlled all of the wife's property after the marriage, but was obligated to provide support for the wife and children. Marriage and divorce were considered private matters. In fact, the biggest issue prior to 1900 was the recognition by one state of marriages performed in another.

By the middle of the nineteenth century, the Industrial Revolution led to many fathers working away from the household during a large part of the day. Wives assumed larger roles in raising children and taking care of the home. As a result, various states began passing laws giving wives greater legal standing. The earliest laws, like the Married Women's Property Acts, allowed wives to own and sell the property they held before marriage, to enter into contracts, and to sue others and be sued. A wife had become more of a person before the law. Then, by outlawing polygamy (having two or more marriage partners at the same time) in **Reynolds v. United States** (1879), the Court began to create national standards for marital (marriage) rights.

The American Family

Traditionally, many Americans normally thought of families as consisting of a husband, wife, and one or two children. However, by 1970 only half of American households met that idea. A later University of Chicago study showed that by 1998 only one-fourth of households had a husband, wife, and child. The study also showed that only fifty-six percent of adults were married in 1998, a dramatic drop from seventy-five percent in 1972. Similarly, the percentage of children living in a household with two parents had dropped from seventy-three percent in 1972 to just over half by 1998. The number of children living with single parents in the same time span rose from less than five percent to over eighteen percent. And finally, the number of households composed of two unmarried adults with no children had more than doubled from 1972 to 1998 to thirty-three percent of American homes, actually outnumbering households meeting the earlier ideal family model.

One contributing factor to these statistics is the aging U.S. population. Grown children of married couples of the post-World War II (1939–1945) "baby-boom" generation had left home. However, this study and others clearly showed that the character of the American family had indeed changed significantly.

Marriage

Various aspects of marriage are addressed by family law. Known also as a "consortium," a marital relationship is a contract through which both partners have a right to support, cooperation, and companionship. Marriages require both governmental and public recognition. A governmental license to marry must be obtained and advanced public notice given to the community, commonly through local newspaper notices. These are followed by a public wedding overseen by an governmentally authorized person and one additional witness. Specific legal rights and duties are then established.

Increasingly looking at marriage as a public contract between two individuals, states sought to regulate most conditions of marriage. The Supreme Court affirmed this right of the states. State laws commonly set minimum ages for marriage, identifies duties and obligations of the husband and wife, how property is controlled including inheritance, limits who one may marry regarding incest and mental illness, and how a marriage may be ended. For example, bigamy (marrying a second time while still married) is considered a crime. A decreasing number of states legally recognize common law marriages in which a couple has lived together for a certain length of time and have consistently represented themselves as married to others.

Historically, husbands held the right to have physical control over wives, including physical punishment. Courts traditionally avoided involvement in such matters until the concern over domestic violence came to the forefront as a national issue in the 1980s. States made domestic violence a criminal offense. In 1994 Congress passed the Violence Against Women Act increasing penalties for domestic violence and making such gender-related crimes violations of constitutional civil rights laws.

The sexual relationship between spouses (marriage partners) has also come under family law. Historically, if one partner was unable to engage in sexual relations, it was grounds for divorce. In a birth control case, the Supreme Court ruled in **Griswold v. Connecticut** (1965) that state laws could not unreasonably intrude in sexual relationships of marriage. Marriage, they ruled, is protected by Constitutional rights of privacy. Similarly, in **Loving v. Virginia** (1967) the Court ruled that state laws prohibiting interracial marriages was unconstitutional, violating equal protection of the laws.

As late as 1953 the Supreme Court in *McGuire v. McGuire* was unwilling to define minimum living standards. It is a matter of the family. Adequacy of support by one spouse for the other and their children, however, began to be addressed in courts through the "doctrine of necessities." Under this doctrine, the state can hold one or the other spouse, or both, responsible for providing essential support, such as clothing, shelter, food, education, and medical care. In many states it became a criminal offense to not provide minimum support.

When the death or severe injury of a spouse occurs such as a car accident or doctor's error, the other spouse can sue those responsible for the death or injury. These suits are called wrongful injury or death lawsuits. The spouse can win money awards to cover expenses for the care of the injured spouse as well as for loss of love, affection, companionship, and future income.

Neither the husband or wife may be forced to testify in court against the other. This privileged communication is recognized as part of the constitutionally protected privacy. The Court did rule in *Trammel v. United States* (1980) that one can testify against the other in a federal criminal trial if they so choose.

Property

Property issues related to marriage are also controlled by state laws. Therefore, disputes over property is handled differently around the nation. Types of property often involved in disputes include real estate, bank savings, stocks and bonds, retirement benefits, personal items, and savings plans. Usually, courts are reluctant to get involved in family property disputes except in divorce cases.

Two legal standards are used. Some states use a "title" standard which connects ownership of each piece of property to the spouse who controls it. Often it is the spouse who earned the money to purchase it unless given as a gift to the other. At death, the deceased (dead) spouse may have willed their property to someone other than the surviving (still living) spouse. However, to promote fairness under the title standard, state laws have established that the surviving spouse is entitled to some portion of the deceased spouse's property, often one-third, depending on the state.

Other states apply a "community property" standard which considers marriage to be a partnership of equal partners. This second standard assumes each spouse contributed equally to the accumulation of the property and, therefore, it is equally owned. The husband and wife can also have separate property including gifts from others and inheritance prior to marriage. In an important development, a new approach to fairly distribute property at divorce under community property law considers the non-economic as well as economic contributions of the spouses to the marriage. Non-economic contributions would include maintaining a home and tending to the children while the other spouse works.

Divorce

Divorce (the ending of marriage) creates a new legal relationship between previous spouses, leading to different rights and responsibilities particularly when children are involved. Divorce was rare in eighteenth century colonial times. In the new nation, divorce actually required action by a state legislature, a difficult process. The only exception was Massachusetts which had passed a law in 1780 allowing court justices to grant divorces rather than state legislature. The U.S. Constitution, adopted in 1789, did not address divorce, leaving it to the states to regulate. By 1900 all states except South Carolina had passed laws like Massachusetts, greatly changing the way in which divorces could be granted. Special divorce courts were established to deal with the cases.

However, divorce was still strongly discouraged by religious groups. To seek divorce, the husband or wife commonly had to charge the other with some wrong doing, such as adultery (having sexual relations with someone other than spouse), desertion (walking out), or cruelty. The California Family Law Act of 1969 introduced yet another important change to divorce law with creation of "no-fault" divorces. Marriages could be ended through mutual agreement rather than one having to accuse the other of a wrong doing. Consideration of wrong doing was reserved for child custody and support and alimony (allowance to the former spouse) decisions. By the late 1980s all states had adopted no-fault divorce. Many critics charged that divorce had become too easy, not forcing couples to work hard enough to solve their problems and hurting many more children.

In 1970 Congress passed the Uniform Marriage and Divorce Act establishing national standards for marriage, divorce, property, and child custody and support. Still, the individual states vary considerably in regard to divorce law. As with marriages, states are required by the Constitution to recognize divorces granted in other states.

The Family's Children

Issues surrounding child custody and support are central to divorce law. Until the nineteenth century, fathers commonly retained custody of their children following divorce. In the early agricultural societies, fathers, owning the family property, needed the children to help with the farm he retained. However, during the nineteenth century the courts established two principles leading to mothers having the primary right to retain custody: the "best-interests-of-the-child" and the "tender years" doctrines. Such custody decisions at the time of divorce have important influence on a child's future. The parent retaining custody holds almost complete control over key decisions affecting the child's life. In contrast, the parent having visitation rights holds almost no control. @p:Responding to calls for custody reform, in 1980 Congress amended the Judiciary Act to establish greater governmental oversight of custody disputes. With each state having different divorce laws, parents would sometimes move to another state where they might get a more favorable custody decision. Sometimes the actual kidnaping of the child to another state might occur. To address this growing problem Congress passed the Parental Kidnapping Prevention Act of 1980 to stop the trend. Also, all states passed various forms of the Uniform Child Custody Jurisdiction Act to help resolve interstate (between different states) custody disputes.

Regarding child support, the divorced parent not having custody usually must provide financial support to help with expenses in the raising the children. With concerns over the rising incidents of non-payment and the effects on state government budgets because of growing welfare roles, the states and federal government have taken several measures to help locate parents (often referred to as deadbeat dads) that have not provided the court-ordered support. To enhance cooperation in tracking deadbeat dads, all states have adopted various versions of the Uniform Reciprocal Enforcement of Support Act. In 1975 Congress also established the Office of Child Support Enforcement to oversee collection of overdue child support. By the 1990s family law allowed for various collection methods, including employers withholding money from paychecks, taking away drivers licenses, placing liens (ownership claims) on property and bank accounts, withhold welfare and retirement benefits, and make deductions from tax refunds. The Welfare Reform Act of 1996 also provided for more aggressive child support collection.

In the late twentieth century women increasingly pursued careers outside the home and many families had both the father and mother working. The father became more involved in child rearing. As a result, a joint custody option arose in which both parents keep decision-making powers. Actual physical custody can go with either parent, or shared as well. By the close of the twentieth century, women, however, still predominately retained custody of children at divorce.

The rights of children also expanded late in the twentieth century. Historically considered as property, by the 1990s the courts recognized the right of children to end their relationship with parents in *Kingsley v. Kingsley* (1992). Children could now sue parents for lack of support, property loss, and personal injury. They could also sue to maintain a relationship with foster parents when challenged by the biological parents as recognized in *Mays v. Twigg* (1993). Some states have taken measures to protect parents against lawsuits, establishing "reasonable parent" standards.

Family Issues Multiply

By the late twentieth century, various means of conceiving babies had developed. These included artificial insemination in which sperm of a father are medically placed in the mother and in vitro fertilization which involves fertilizing an egg outside the womb then medically placing the resulting embryo in the mother. Use of surrogate (substitute) mothers also emerged. All of these medical advances brought with them new legal issues in family law. Who are the legal parents of children conceived with donated sperm or eggs, or given birth by a surrogate (substitute) mother? Family law normally does not recognize donors as legal parents. The famous case of "Baby M" known as *In re Baby M* (1988) involved the custody dispute between the surrogate mother and a married couple who had paid her to be artificially inseminated and give birth to a child for them. The New Jersey Supreme Court ruled that such financial arrangements are improper. But, using the "best interests of the child" doctrine, the court awarded custody to the couple and visitation rights to the surrogate mother.

In addition, efforts to legally recognize same-sex marriages grew. Key issues involved protection of such benefits as inheritance, property rights, and tax and social security benefits. The Minnesota Supreme Court in *Baker v. Nelson* (1971) ruled that marriage could only be legally recognized between people of the opposite sex. In 1996 Congress passed the Defense of Marriage Act defining marriage as only being between people of opposite sex. Same-sex marriage advocates argued the Fourteenth Amendment's "equal protection of the laws" was violated due to discrimination based on sex by denying the same protections and benefits to gays and lesbians. The issue rose to the Hawaii Supreme Court in 1999 which denied the legality of same-sex marriages. However, in December of 1999 the Vermont Supreme Court ruled that the state constitution guarantees the same rights to gay and lesbian couples as to opposite-sex couples.

Saving the Family

Though studies indicate Americans have become increasingly accepting of the many social changes and although these opinions are being reflected in family law applications, efforts are still popular to promote the traditional family idea and look for ways it could work in the twenty-first century. Child care, family leave programs under the Family and Medical Leave Act of 1993, non-traditional workweek arrangements, and "telecommuting" from home in the electronic age have raised new family legal issues.

Suggestions for further reading

Battle, Carl W. *Legal-Wise: Self-Help Legal Guide for Everyone.* New York: Allworth Press, 1996.

Binder, Julee, Harvey Loomis, and Nancy Nicholas, eds. *Know Your Rights and How to Make Them Work for You.* Pleasantville, NY: The Reader's Digest Association, Inc., 1995.

Gregory, John De Witt, Peter N. Swisher, and Sheryl L. Scheible. *Understanding Family Law.* New York: Matthew Bender, 1993.

Mierzwa, Joseph W. *The 21st Century Family Legal Guide.* Highlands Ranch, CO: Prose Associates, Ince., 1994.

Very, Donald L. *The Legal Guide for the Family.* Chicago: J. G. Ferguson Publishing Co., 1989.

Moore v. East Cleveland
1977

Appellant: Inez Moore

Appellee: City of East Cleveland, Ohio

Appellant's Claim: That restrictions in an East Cleveland housing ordinance concerning which family members could occupy the same household violates a basic liberty of choice protected by the Fourteenth Amendment of the U.S. Constitution.

Chief Lawyers for Appellant: Edward R. Stege, Jr.

Chief Lawyers for Appellee: Leonard Young

Justices for the Court: Harry A. Blackmun, William J. Brennan, Jr., Thurgood Marshall, Lewis F. Powell, Jr., Potter Stewart,

Justices Dissenting: Chief Justice Warren E. Burger, William H. Rehnquist, John Paul Stevens, Byron R. White

Date of Decision: May 31, 1977

Decision: Ruled in favor of Moore by finding that government through zoning restrictions cannot prohibit an extended family from living together merely to prevent traffic problems and overcrowding.

Significance: The Court determined that the protection of the "sanctity of the family" guaranteed by the U.S. Constitution extended beyond the nuclear family consisting of a married couple and dependent children. Also protected are extended families that can include various other related family members. The right of relatives to live under the same roof was recognized.

FAMILY LAW

"This Court has long recognized that freedom of personal choice in matters of marriage and family life is one of the liberties protected by the Due Process Clause of the Fourteenth Amendment." Written by the U.S. Supreme Court in *Cleveland Board of Education v. LaFleur* (1974).

Families

The family is one of the oldest and most basic aspects of human societies. The family provides protection and training for children. It also provides emotional and economic support for all its members. Most families are based on kinship ties established through birth, marriage, or adoption. About sixty-six million families lived in the United States in the 1990s.

Various types of families exist. Extended families have been historically common in many societies through time. These families include various combinations of grandparents, aunts, uncles, cousins, or grandchildren sharing the same household with a married couple and their dependent children. However, the industrial revolution of the nineteenth

century dramatically changed patterns of family life. Americans began to think of families being restricted to a husband, wife, and one or two children, known as the nuclear family.

Faced with scientific, economic, and social changes in the 1960s and 1970s, family relationships began to once more change away from the ideal nuclear family pattern, to a much more diverse grouping including many single parent families. By 1970 only half of American households met the earlier twentieth century ideal. By 1998 only one-fourth of households had a husband, wife, and child.

The East Cleveland Housing Ordinance

Concerned about the livability of their community as its population increased, the city of East Cleveland, a suburb of Cleveland, Ohio, passed a zoning ordinance (city law) in 1966 describing who may occupy individual residences. Rather than drawing a line simply to include only persons related by blood, marriage, or adoption, the city chose to draw a tighter, more complicated line. The city established that only certain combinations of relatives could occupy a residence. Besides a husband and wife, the household could also include unmarried dependent children, but only one dependent child having a spouse and dependent children themselves, and only one parent of either the husband or wife. The ordinance gave the city's Board of Building Code Appeals authority (power) to grant variances (deviations) "where practical difficulties and unnecessary hardships shall result from the strict compliance with or the enforcement of the . . . ordinance." Violation of the ordinance was a misdemeanor criminal offense subject to a maximum of six months in prison and a fine not to exceed $1,000. Each day the ordinance was violated could be considered a separate offense. The ordinance essentially selected what types of kin could live together.

Inez Moore

In the early 1970s Inez Moore owned a two and a half story wood frame house in East Cleveland. The house was split into two residences in which Moore lived in one side with an unmarried son, Dale Moore, Sr., and his son Dale, Jr., and John Moore, Jr., another grandson of Inez. John had joined the household following the death of his mother. John and Dale, Jr., were, therefore, cousins. In January of 1973 a city housing inspector issued a violation notice to Inez Moore for occupying the resi-

FAMILY LAW

dence with a combination of family members not allowed by the city ordinance. John could not legally live in his grandmother's household as long as his uncle and cousin lived there. The notice directed Moore to correct the situation.

As the city continued to complain of the violation, Moore resisted changing the situation or applying for a variance. Sixteen months after the notice was first issued, Moore was brought before a city court. She filed a motion to dismiss the charge claiming the restrictions on family choice in the city ordinance violated the U.S. Constitution. The city court rejected her claim and found Moore guilty. She was sentenced to five days in jail and fined $25. Moore appealed to the Ohio Court of Appeals which ruled in favor of the city. After the Ohio Supreme Court refused to hear the case, Moore appealed to the U.S. Supreme Court which accepted her case.

Freedom to Make Family Decisions

Before the Court in November of 1976, East Cleveland claimed its housing ordinance was designed to protect the city's quality of life by preventing overcrowding, minimizing traffic and parking congestion, and limiting the financial burden on the city's school system. The city argued that the Court had supported a similar ordinance in *Village of Belle Terre v. Boraas* (1974). Moore argued that the ordinance deprived her of a basic liberty (freedom) without due process of law (fair legal hearing). The Fourteenth Amendment specifically states that no state may "deprive any person of life, liberty, or property, without due process of law." More specifically, the zoning ordinance denied her the right to make important family choices about where and with whom her grandson could live.

First, the Court sought to determine if such a family choice is a constitutionally protected liberty. Justice Lewis F. Powell, Jr., in writing for the Court, reviewed the history and tradition of family life in American society. Powell noted that extended families, ordinarily consisting of close relatives and family friends, would come together to raise children and care for the elderly and disabled. This tradition, strongly founded in America's agricultural society in its early history, was reinforced by the waves of immigrants in the late nineteenth century. Powell noted that such a drawing together has been "virtually a means of survival . . . for large numbers of the poor and deprived minorities of our society (involving the) . . . pooling of scant resources" and has been critical "to maintain or rebuild a secure home life." Powell concluded,

> **Ours is by no means a tradition limited to respect for the bonds uniting the members of the nuclear family. The tradition of uncles, aunts, cousins, and especially grandparents sharing a household along with parents and children has roots equally venerable [ancient] and equally deserving of constitutional recognition.**

Powell concluded the right to live in an extended family household is recognized in the Fourteenth Amendment's freedom of personal choices. Other private family life freedom include the right to marry, to bear and raise children, and the right to education. Extended families were entitled to the same constitutional protections as nuclear families. Inez's choice to raise John, Jr. was a private family matter.

Finding that indeed living in extended families is a constitutional right, Lewis next examined the ordinance to determine if it served an important government purpose. If so, then the ban on certain family households would be valid. Powell quickly concluded the ordinance was ineffective in achieving its goals. If John and Dale had been brothers they both could have lived in the residence, but as cousins they could not. East Cleveland did not show a substantial relationship of the ordinance to protecting public health, safety, or general welfare. Powell added that the ordinance supported in the *Belle Terre* decision affected only unrelated individuals, not kinship ties.

By a 5–4 decision, the Court ruled the housing ordinance unconstitutional. The Court concluded,

> **the zoning power is not a license for local communities to enact senseless and arbitrary restrictions which cut deeply into private areas of protected family life . . . [T]his ordinance displays a depressing insensitivity toward the economic and emotional needs of a very large part of our society.**

A Closer Look

The decision expanded the liberties enjoyed under the Fourteenth Amendment. The government could not unreasonably intrude in decisions concerning family living arrangements. This meant family choices would come under closer review (strict scrutiny) in future cases involving such issues. A family of any type would be protected by the right to due process of law.

MAKING FAMILY CHOICES

Interpretation of the Fourteenth Amendment's Due Process Clause has expanded through the years to include fundamental rights and liberties not specifically identified in the U.S. Constitution and Bill of Rights but considered essential to freedom in a democracy. Deeply rooted in U.S. legal and social traditions, these include the right to privacy in maintaining certain family relations. The 1977 decision in *Moore v. East Cleveland* expanded on these liberties. Earlier, the Court recognized a right to an education in *Meyer v. Nebraska* (1923) and a right to bear children in *Skinner v. Oklahoma* (1942). Later, in **Griswold v. Connecticut** (1965) the Court described "zones of privacy" created by these liberties. In **Loving v. Virginia** (1967) the Court upheld the right to freely choose a marriage partner. The landmark case of **Roe v. Wade** (1973) extended the zone of privacy to include the right to abortions. Shortly after the *Moore* decision, the Court ruled parents had the right to commit children to mental hospitals without a hearing in *Parham v. J.R.* (1979). Later in 1990 the Court ruled in **Cruzan v. Director, Missouri Department of Health** that competent individuals could refuse medical treatment, even if their death might result.

In sum, the Court has determined that personal choice in almost all family matters is a fundamental right. The Due Process Clause serves to protect these basic liberties. Consequently, any law or regulation that limits such choices must be shown to have a highly important (compelling) government purpose and be designed to affect as few people as need be (narrowly tailored).

Suggestions for further reading

Coontz, Stephanie. *The Way We Never Were: American Families and the Nostalgia Trap.* New York: Basic Books, 1992.

Eshleman, J. Ross. *The Family: An Introduction.* Boston: Allyn and Bacon, 1997.

Skolnick, Arlene. *Embattled Paradise: The American Family in an Age of Uncertainty.* New York: Basic Books, 1991.

Stacey, Judith. *Brave New Families: Stories of Domestic Upheaval in Late Twentieth Century America.* Berkeley, CA: University of California Press, 1998.

Moore v. East Cleveland

Orr v. Orr
1979

Appellant: William H. Orr

Appellee: Lillian M. Orr

Appellant's Claim: That Alabama's alimony law requiring only husbands, not wives, to pay alimony violated the Equal Protection Clause of the Fourteenth Amendment.

Chief Lawyers for Appellant: John L. Capell III

Chief Lawyers for Appellee: W. F. Horsley

Justices for the Court: Harry A. Blackmun, William J. Brennan, Thurgood Marshall, John Paul Stevens, Potter Stewart, Byron R. White

Justices Dissenting: Chief Justice Warren E. Burger, Lewis F. Powell, Jr., William H. Rehnquist

Date of Decision: March 5, 1979

Decision: Ruled in favor of William Orr by agreeing that Alabama's alimony law fostered unconstitutional sex discrimination by requiring only husbands, not wives, to pay alimony.

Significance: The decision changed the way in which family court judges determine alimony payments during divorce proceedings. Both the husband's and wife's circumstances must be considered, rather than only the wife's situation, as before.

"No longer is the female destined solely for the home and the rearing of the family, and only the male for the marketplace [employment] and the world of ideas [important decision-making roles]." Statement by the U.S. Supreme Court in *Stanton v. Stanton* (1975).

Alimony is regular payments of money that a family court judge determines one spouse (husband or wife) owes the other after divorce. The purpose of the payments is to make divorce more fair for the spouse who is most economically affected. Alimony is different from property settlements or child support. Alimony payments are not considered punishment by the courts.

Alimony and Divorce Through Time

In early English history, divorce between a married couple was not permitted. Unhappy married couples would often live apart with the husband still responsible for providing ongoing financial (money) support for the wife. As divorce became more acceptable through time, the traditional responsibility of the husband providing support continued. This monetary support became known as alimony.

Traditionally in America, husbands and wives took on certain set roles in the family that society expected of them. The wife was responsible for taking care of the home and raising the kids. College educations and professional careers were discouraged. The husband was expected to provide the primary source of income supporting the family. Some states wrote their alimony laws to match this expected family norm.

During proceedings divorce judges would often follow general state guidelines in determining the amount of financial support (alimony) needed by the wife, if any. The divorce judges exercised a great deal of flexibility to determine what was fair. If the ex-husband failed to make the alimony payments, one of the few options the former wife had available to her to correct the situation was to file contempt-of-court charges against the former husband.

An example of state laws reflecting these family norms was the Alabama gender-based (based on sex of the person) alimony law. The law read, "If the wife has no separate estate [possessions] or if it be insufficient for her maintenance, the judge, upon granting a divorce, at his discretion, may order to the wife an allowance out of the estate of the husband, taking into consideration the value thereof and the condition of his family." The law assumes that the wife is always dependent on the husband's income, and never the reverse. The husband's needs were not important. The Alabama Supreme Court had noted in 1966 that for situations where the wife had been the primary source of family income "there is no authority in this state for awarding alimony to the husband."

Gender Discrimination and Equal Protection

Such gender-based state laws began to increasingly reach the attention of the U.S. Supreme Court in the 1970s. In *Reed v. Reed* (1971) the Court for the first time struck down a state law by extending the Equal Protection Clause of the Fourteenth Amendment to gender discrimination. The clause requires equal treatment of all citizens by state laws unless sufficient reasons support otherwise. In *Craig v. Boren* (1976) the Court expressed a more modern vision of the American woman having her own political and economic identity in striking down an Oklahoma law. Importantly, the Court ruled that gender discrimination cases must be more closely examined (scrutiny) by the Court than in the past. The government must now prove that the challenged law serves an important government objective (goal) and the law must substantially (significantly) relate to reaching that objective.

The Orrs

In February of 1974, Lillian and William Orr obtained a divorce in the Lee County Circuit Court of Alabama. As part of the divorce settlement, the court ordered William to pay Lillian $1,240 each month in alimony. After a couple of years William stopped making the required payments. In July of 1976 Lillian went back to the Circuit Court and filed contempt of court charges. She demanded he begin making the payments again, plus provide missing payments. The court responded by ordering William to begin making payments again. The court also told him to pay back payments and Lillian's court expenses, a total of over $5,500.

William appealed the decision to the Alabama's Court of Civil Appeals claiming Alabama's alimony law was not valid. He asserted that because the law only required husbands to pay alimony and not wives, the law violated the Equal Protection Clause of the Fourteenth Amendment. In March of 1977, the appeals court rejected William's

argument and agreed with the circuit court's decision. William appealed
again, first to the Alabama Supreme Court which declined to accept the
case, and then to the U.S. Supreme Court which agreed to hear it.

An Important Government Purpose

As in the lower courts, Lillian Orr simply argued that the Alabama law
was indeed constitutionally valid under the Equal Protection Clause.
Because the state law treated males and females differently therefore not
equally protecting the two groups, it must serve some important government purpose to be considered constitutionally valid. Lillian asserted the
alimony law served three important government purposes, she contended: (1) to support the traditional structure of families by making the husband always economically responsible for the family; (2) to lessen the
cost of divorce for needy wives; and, (3) to repay women for past economic discrimination within traditional American marriages. In arguing
against the law's constitutionality, William Orr did not claim that Lillian
should pay him alimony. He did argue, however, that if the circuit court
was required to consider his circumstances too, then the amount of
alimony payments might have been less. He contended the law was
unconstitutional based on lack of equal protection.

Justice William J. Brennan, writing for the Court, noted that previous Supreme Court rulings had established that "classifications by gender must serve important governmental objectives and must be substantially related to achievement of those objectives." In reviewing the
Alabama law, Brennan disagreed with the first government purpose of
supporting traditional family structure. He asserted that the ideas of what
the state thought a family should be did not apply to many families in
modern America. Though agreeing the law's other two purposes had
some merit, the law's approach requiring only husbands to pay alimony
was clearly not valid.

Brennan pointed out that the process of review by a family law judge
in determining alimony makes the process very personalized. The Alabama
law need not be gender-based. The Alabama law more likely served to
uphold outdated role models than correct past social injustices. Brennan
concluded, "it would cost the State nothing more, if it were to treat men and
women equally by making alimony burdens independent of sex."

In the 6–3 decision, the Court ruled the Alabama law unconstitutional in violation of the Equal Protection Clause of the Fourteenth

ALIMONY FACTORS

A key effect of the Supreme Court decision in *Orr v. Orr* was how judges determine alimony payments in divorce proceedings. The amount and length of payment can be determined through a court-approved agreement between the former husband and wife, or it could be set by the court, especially when agreement was not possible.

The amount a husband or wife owes usually depends on several complex factors. These include the person's financial needs who is requesting alimony whether it be the husband or wife, the ability of the other person to pay alimony, the standard of living they had been use to in marriage, their age and health, how long they were married, and how long it would take the person requesting alimony to become more self-sufficient through education or job-training. Court decisions often consider the non-monetary contributions of both husband and wife to the marriage, including neglecting their own careers to support the spouse's.

Alimony payments end if the former wife dies or remarries. However, alimony payments could continue from the estate of a former husband, even after his death, through trusts or insurance policies. Payments can always been changed, as well, if basic conditions of either person changes.

Amendment. The Court also sent William Orr back to the lower courts to determine his alimony situation.

Who Was Injured?

In dissent, Justice William Rehnquist asserted that there was no case existed because no one was wronged by the Alabama law in this instance. William Orr is "a divorced male who has never sought alimony, who is . . . not entitled to alimony even if he had, and who contractually bound himself to pay alimony to his former wife and did so without objection for over two years." The case would have been more appropriate if brought by a man deserving support, but denied alimony by the state gender-based law. Orr had little to gain from the decision.

Changing Alimony Standards

The decision provided a major change in how American marriages were legally viewed. Factors concerning both the husband and wife would have to be equally considered in divorce settlements. Sometimes the woman might have to pay alimony to the man if she was the primary income provider. Though the procedures actually changed greatly, the results of alimony decisions changed far less. Despite making alimony laws not gender-oriented, still by the mid-1990s few women were ordered to pay alimony to former husbands.

Suggestions for further reading

Horgan, Timothy J. *Winning Your Divorce: A Man's Survival Guide.* New York: Dutton, 1994.

Miller, Kathleen A. *Fair Share Divorce for Women.* Bellevue, WA: Miller, Bird Advisors, Inc., 1995.

Pistotnik, Bradley A. *Divorce War! 50 Strategies Every Woman Needs to Know to Win.* Holbrook, MA: Adams Media, 1996.

Woodhouse, Violet, Victoria F. Collins, and M. C. Blakeman. *Divorce and Money: How to Make the Best Financial Decisions During Divorce.* Berkeley, CA: Nolo.com, 2000.

DeShaney v. Winnebago County Department of Social Services 1989

Petitioner: Melody DeShaney for her son, Joshua DeShaney

Respondent: Winnebago County Department of Social Services

Petitioner's Claim: That Winnebago County in Wisconsin violated the due process clause of the Fourteenth Amendment by failing to protect Joshua DeShaney from the violent abuse of his father.

Chief Lawyer for Petitioner: Donald J. Sullivan

Chief Lawyer for Respondent: Mark J. Mingo

Justices for the Court: Anthony M. Kennedy, Sandra Day O'Connor, Chief Justice William H. Rehnquist, Antonin Scalia, John Paul Stevens, Byron R. White

Justices Dissenting: Harry A. Blackmun, William J. Brennan, Jr., Thurgood Marshall

Date of Decision: February 22, 1989

Decision: Ruled in favor of Winnebago County by finding the county was not responsible for Joshua's severe beating.

Significance: The ruling raised considerable concern among advocates for protecting children from abusive parents. The Court's decision approved the inaction of a government welfare agency, even when aware of ongoing abuse.

Winnebago
County
Department
of Social
Services

Well into the nineteenth century, children were considered property of the father. However, later in the century concern increased over the well-being of the nation's children. The relationship between child and parent received more special legal attention. Cases of neglect or abuse attracted particular public interest.

In the United States, state laws primarily govern the parent-child relationship, protecting the relationship as well as the rights of both. Ordinarily, the parent holds a constitutional right to custody (making key life decisions for another) of their child as well as the duty to care for the child. A child has the right to receive sufficient care, including food, clothing, shelter, medical care, and presumably love and affection. Through time states have assumed greater responsibility for making sure children are receiving this proper care. The growing responsibilities include greater powers to intervene (come in to settle) in family matters, particularly in cases of neglect or abuse. Parents not adequately performing their duties may be criminally charged. In determining custody of children, a rule known as the "best interest of the child" is often used by the court for cases that come before them.

Joshua's Plight

Joshua was born to Randy and Melody DeShaney in 1979 in Wyoming. Soon after, in 1980, the DeShaneys divorced with Randy receiving custody of Joshua. Randy and Joshua moved to Wisconsin and before long Randy remarried. With a break up of the second marriage soon occurring, a pattern of child abuse began to emerge. In 1982 the second wife, shortly before divorce, reported regular physical abuse of Joshua to Wisconsin child welfare agencies. The Winnebago County Department of Social Services (DSS) began to investigate. However, denials of the accusations by Randy DeShaney led to the county taking no action at the time.

In January of 1983, Joshua arrived at a hospital emergency with bruises that an attending physician believed resulted from abuse. The doctor notified DSS and a team of child care workers were assembled to tackle the case. Joshua was temporarily placed in custody of the hospital for three days. However, no charges against Randy were made and Joshua was returned to him. The county did make several recommendations, including that Joshua be enrolled in a pre-school program and Randy attend counseling. Also, a social worker, Ann Kemmeter, was assigned to the case to watch over Joshua through regular visits to his home.

CHILD ABUSE: SIGNS AND SYMPTOMS

Although these signs do not necessarily indicate that a child has been abused, they may help adults recognize that something is wrong. The possibility of abuse should be investigated if a child shows a number of these symptoms, or any of them to a marked degree:

Sexual Abuse

Being overly affectionate or knowledgeable in a sexual way inappropriate to the child's age
Medical problems such as chronic itching, pain in the genitals, venereal diseases
Other extreme reactions, such as depression, self-mutilation, suicide attempts, running away, overdoses, anorexia
Personality changes such as becoming insecure or clinging
Regressing to younger behavior patterns such as thumb sucking or bringing out discarded cuddly toys
Sudden loss of appetite or compulsive eating
Being isolated or withdrawn
Inability to concentrate
Lack of trust or fear someone they know well, such as not wanting to be alone with a babysitter
Starting to wet again, day or night/nightmares
Become worried about clothing being removed
Suddenly drawing sexually explicit pictures
Trying to be "ultra-good" or perfect; overreacting to criticism

Physical Abuse

Unexplained recurrent injuries or burns
Improbable excuses or refusal to explain injuries
Wearing clothes to cover injuries, even in hot weather
Refusal to undress for gym
Bald patches
Chronic running away
Fear of medical help or examination
Self-destructive tendencies
Aggression towards others
Fear of physical contact—shrinking back if touched
Admitting that they are punished, but the punishment is excessive (such as a child being beaten every night to "make him/her study")
Fear of suspected abuser being contacted

Emotional Abuse

Physical, mental, and emotional development lags
Sudden speech disorders
Continual self-depreciation ("I'm stupid, ugly, worthless, etc.")
Overreaction to mistakes
Extreme fear of any new situation
Inappropriate response to pain ("I deserve this")
Neurotic behavior (rocking, hair twisting, self-mutilation)
Extremes of passivity or aggression

Neglect

Constant hunger	Poor personal hygiene	No social relationships
Constant tiredness	Poor state of clothing	Compulsive scavenging
Emaciation	Untreated medical problems	Destructive tendencies

A child may be subjected to a combination of different kinds of abuse. It is also possible that a child may show no outward signs and hide what is happening from everyone.

Source: Kidscape, http://www.solnet.co.uk/kidscape/kids5.htm. Reprinted by permission.

Through the following year Kemmeter visited the DeShaneys approximately twenty times. She made notes of bumps and bruises on occasion including injuries to the head. She also noted that Randy never enrolled Joshua in pre-school or attended counseling sessions. During this time period Joshua visited emergency rooms twice more where doctors observed more suspicious injuries. Despite Kemmeter later admitting she feared for Joshua's life, the state still took no action to intervene in the father and child relationship.

Finally, in March of 1984, one day after yet another visit by Kemmeter, the four year old boy fell into a coma after a severe beating. Joshua came out of his coma, but was suffering from severe brain damage leaving him permanently paralyzed and mentally retarded. Joshua had to be placed in an institution for full-time care for the rest of his life at public expense.

**DeShaney v.
Winnebago
County
Department
of Social
Services**

Mother Sues the Child Welfare Agency

Randy DeShaney was charged with child abuse and found guilty. He was sentenced for up to four years in prison, but actually served less than two years before receiving parole. Disappointed with the conviction and sentencing, Joshua's mother, Melody, filed suit against DSS for not rescuing Joshua from his father before the fateful beating. Melody charged that Winnebago County and its social workers had violated Joshua's due process rights under the Fourteenth Amendment to the Constitution by not taking action.

The due process clause of the Fourteenth Amendment declares that states shall not "deprive any person of life, liberty, or property, without due process of law." Melody DeShaney charged the state had denied Joshua his rights to liberty by not taking action when it was fully aware of the situation. The federal district court, however, ruled in favor of Winnebago County. Melody DeShaney appealed the decision to the federal court of appeals which affirmed the district court's decision. DeShaney next appealed to the U.S. Supreme Court which agreed to hear the case. DeShaney again argued that the county had a responsibility to protect the child since it not only knew of the situation and had even held custody of Joshua for three days. She claimed the state had established a "special relationship" with Joshua and that relationship created a responsibility to protect him from known dangers.

OPPOSITE PAGE:

There are many signs that may indicate child abuse. Reproduced by permission of Kidscape.

State Not Constitutionally Responsible

Chief Justice William Rehnquist delivered the opinion of the Court. Rehnquist found that the due process clause of the Fourteenth Amendment only applies to states, not private citizens. Rehnquist wrote that the purpose of the due process clause "was to protect the people from the State, not to ensure that the State protected them from each other." He found neither "guarantee of certain minimal levels of safety and security" for the nation's citizens through the clause nor did he find a "right to governmental aid." Therefore, "the State cannot be held liable under the Clause for the injuries" that might have been prevented if it had more fully used its protective services.

Rehnquist further explained that the due process clause would only apply in cases where the state had assumed custody of a person against their will and then had not adequately provided for their "safety and general well-being." Then a deprivation (withholding) of liberty by the state would have occurred.

In summary, the Court concluded the state had neither played any part in directly causing the injuries nor had made him more vulnerable. Rehnquist wrote, "Under these circumstances, the State had no constitutional duty to protect Joshua." In fact, if the state had acted to take custody of Joshua away from Randy DeShaney, it may have been charged with "improperly intruding into the parent-child relationship" under the same due process clause. Rehnquist did add, however, that the state may have been guilty of some duty under Wisconsin law, but that was not the subject of DeShaney's charges.

State Has Responsibility By Its Very Existence

Three of the Court justices dissented (disagreed) with the majority's decision. Justice Brennan, writing for the other two, asserted that the very existence of the Wisconsin child-welfare system means that its citizens have a certain level of dependence on the services in provides. Public expectations create a state responsibility to act when conditions come to its attention, such as with Joshua. If the services did not exist, then those concerned with Joshua might have taken other action to help which might have made a major difference in his life.

As Justice Blackmun, also dissenting, added,

DeShaney v.
Winnebago
County
Department
of Social
Services

BEST INTEREST OF THE CHILD

Well into the nineteenth century, fathers normally received custody of children following divorce. Then, following the American Civil War (1861–1865), the "tender years" standard began to be applied by the courts in justifying awarding custody to the mother who was believed to provide better nurturing to the child during its earliest years. However, before long another standard was adopted, known as "best interests of the child." This second standard which weighs the right of the mother to custody against the needs of the child became the most important standard used by the courts to determine child custody.

Among the factors considered by judges in determining the best interest of the child are: (1) which parent can best provide daily care; (2) what special needs might the child have; (3) what is the health and fitness of each parent; (4) where are their brothers or sisters; (5) is one parent keeping the home or staying in the community the child is used to living in; and, (6) what does the child herself want. Still, most often the mother has been the child's primary caretaker and is awarded custody. But, increasingly fathers have been granted custody in certain situations.

Poor Joshua! Victim of repeated attacks by an irresponsible, bullying, cowardly, and intemperate father, and abandoned by respondents who placed him in a dangerous predicament and who knew or learned what was going on, and yet did essentially nothing except . . . 'dutifully recorded these incidents in [their] files.'

Concern for Children's Safety Raised

The Court's ruling raised considerable concern among child welfare advocates. They claimed the rights of the child to a safe, nurturing home environment were ignored. The decision, they believed, set a dangerous

FAMILY LAW

precedent for future rulings in similar cases of abuse. They reasoned, what if the police knew of a murder about to happen, but chose to do nothing to stop it? Similar to the county's inaction to help Joshua, the police would not have caused the death directly, nor made the victim worse off. Yet many would consider the police negligent (failing to do take the required action) in their duties to protect the citizens in their jurisdiction.

Suggestions for further reading

Helfer, Mary Edna, Ruth S. Kempe, and Richard D. Krugman, eds. *The Battered Child.* Chicago: University of Chicago Press, 1997.

Pelzer, David J. *A Child Called "It:" An Abused Child's Journey from Victim to Victor.* Deefield Beach, FL: Health Communications, 1995.

Trickett, Penelope K., and Cynthia D. Schellenbach, eds. *Violence Against Children in the Family and the Community.* Washington, DC: American Psychological Association, 1998.

Besharov, Douglas. *Recognizing Child Abuse: A Guide for the Concerned.* New York: Free Press, 1990.

Haskins, James. *The Child Abuse Help Book.* Reading, MA: Addison-Wesley, 1982. (for adolescent readers)

Troxel v. Granville
2000

Petiotioners: Jenifer and Gary Troxel

Respondent: Tommie Granville

Petitioner's Claim: That the Washington Supreme Court's denial of their petition for visitation of their grandchildren was in error.

Chief Lawyer for Petitioner: Mark D. Olson

Chief Lawyer for Respondent: Catherine W. Smith

Justices for the Court: Stephen Breyer, Ruth Bader Ginsburg, Sandra Day O'Connor, Chief Justice William Rehnquist, David H. Souter, Clarence Thomas.

Justices Dissenting: Anthony M. Kennedy, Antonin Scalia, John Paul Stevens

Date of Decision: June 5, 2000

Decision: Ruled in favor of Granville by stating that Washington statute, as applied to the case at hand, unconstitutionally infringed upon her right to care for her children.

Significance: Reaffirmed the constitutionally protected right to raise one's children free from overly evasive interference from government.

In today's society, it is difficult to describe the "average" American family. "While many children may have two married parents and grandparents who visit regularly, many other children are raised in single-parent households." In the latter case, both maternal (the parents of the mother)

Custody is a matter that concerns not only parents, but grandparents as well.
Reproduced by permission of Stock Boston, Inc.

and paternal (the parents of the father) grandparents of the children may desire to have visitation. On June 5, 2000, the United States Supreme Court decided *Troxel v. Granville,* a case involving paternal grandparents seeking visitation of their two grandchildren.

Troxel involved an unmarried couple, Tommie Granville and Brad Troxel, who had two children together, Isabelle and Natalie. In 1991, Tommie and Brad's relationship ended. Two years later, Brad committed suicide. After Brad's death, his parents, Jenifer and Gary, desired to visit their grandchildren. They sought two weekends of overnight visitation per month and two weeks of visitation each summer. Though Tommie allowed some visitation, she did not allow visitation in the amount that Isabelle and Natalie's grandparents wanted. She preferred that the Troxels have only one night of visitation a month with no overnight stays. Because of the differences in opinion, Jenifer and Gary sued Tommie in Washington state court to obtain visitaiton of their grandchildren.

The Troxels sued Tommie under a Washington Revised Code, which permitted "any person," including grandparents, to petition a superior court for visitation rights "at any time." The statute also allowed a court to grant visitation whenever it might "serve the best interest of the child" regardless

of whether there had been a change in circumstances of the children. The Troxels won their initial suit against Tommie in Washington Superior Court, and the judge entered an oral ruling (which was later put into writing). In finding for the Troxels, the superior court judge determined that visitation was in the best interest of Isabelle and Natalie. In particular, the court noted that "[t]he Petitioners [the Troxels] are part of a large, central, loving family, all located in this area, and the Petitioners can provide opportunities for the children in the areas of cousins and music." The court "took into consideration all factors regarding the best interest of the children and considered all the testimony."

Though the court decided that the children would benefit from spending time with their grandparents, it also determined that the children would benefit from spending time with their mother and stepfather's other six children. Thus, the court ordered visitation in the amount of one weekend per month, one week in the summer, and four hours on both of the grandparents birthdays. Tommie appealed from this decision to the Washington Court of Appeals. During this time, Tommie married Kelly Wynn, who eventually adopted both Isabelle and Natalie.

The Washington Court of Appeals reversed the lower court's decision and dismissed the Troxels' petition for visitation. The court determined that the Washington statute only allowed people to sue for visitation when there was a custody action pending. Since this was no such action, the court opined, the Troxels did not have standing (permission) to sue for visitation.

The Washington Supreme Court disagreed with the court of appeals' determination that the statute did not give the Troxels standing to sue. Instead, the Washington Supreme Court said, the statute's plain language authorized "any person" to petition a superior court for visitation rights "at any time." The Washington Supreme Court, however, agreed with the appellate court's ultimate conclusion that the Troxels could not obtain visitation of Isabelle and Natalie, as it violated the Constitution's fundamental right of parents to rear their children.

The Washington Supreme Court found two problems with the statute. First, the Constitution permitted a State to interfere with the right of parents to rear their children only to prevent harm or potential harm to a child. Since the statute provided no requirement that a petitioner show harm, it violated the Constitution. Second, the statute was too broad because it allowed "'any person' to petition for forced visitation of a child at 'any time' with the only requirement being that the visitation serve the best interest of the child." The Washington Supreme Court felt that a parent had the right to limit visitation with their children of third parties. In that court's opinion, parents, not judges, "should be the ones to choose whether to expose their children to certain people or ideas."

The Troxels appealed the Washington Supreme Court's decision to the United States Supreme Court. The Supreme Court granted certiorari (agreed to hear the case), and affirmed the Washington Supreme Court's decision. Announcing the judgment of the Court, Justice O'Connor first pointed out that the government cannot interfere "with certain fundamental rights and liberty interests." Included in these rights and interests is a parent's ability to care for and control her children. According to Justice O'Connor, Supreme Court decisions such as *Meyer v. Nebraska, Pierce v. Society of Sisters,* and *Prince v. Massachusetts,* had long established the right of parents to "establish a home and bring up children" and "to direct the upbringing and education of children under their control." Indeed, Justice O'Connor added, "the custody, care and nurture of the child reside[s] first in the parents."

Given these facts, the Supreme Court decided that the Washington statute was too intrusive on a parent's right to determine what was in the best interest of her child. Specifically, the Supreme Court concluded that the statute "placed the best-interest determination solely in the hands of the [court]." Thus, if a judge merely disagreed with a parent as to whether visitation by a third party was in the best interest of a child, she could simply order that it occur. This, the Supreme Court opined, exceeded the bounds of the Constitution.

Moreover, the Superior Court Judge gave no "special weight at all to Granville's determination of her daughters' best interst." Instead, the judge "applied exactly the opposite presumption." He presummed that the grandparents' request for visitation should be granted "unless the children would be 'impact[ed] adversely.'" Indicative of this fact was the judge's statement: "I think [visitation with the Troxels] would be in the best interst of the children and I haven't been shown it is not in [the] best interest of the children."

Thus, the Supreme Court concluded that the visitation order in this case was an unconstitutional infringment of Tommie's fundamental right to make decisions concerning the care, custody and control of her children, Isabelle and Natalie. The Supreme Court, however, did not decide whether all visitation statutes were unconstitutional. Instead, it decided to allow state courts to determine, on a case-by-case basis, whether or not a visitation staute unconstitutionally infringed upon the parental right.

OTHER TYPES OF THIRD-PARTY VISITATION STATUTES

All fifty states have third-party visitation statutes. The statutes primarily allow petitions from persons who are: (1) stepparent; (2) grandparent - death of their child; (3) grandparent - child divorce; (4) (grand)parent of child born out of wedlock; and (5) any interested party. Only three states allow all of the above to petition the court for visitation. Twelve states allow only grandparents of either type to petition. Twelve additional states allow grandparents of either type and relatives of babies born out of wedlock to petition for visitation. The remaining allow various combinations of third parties to petition a court for visitation. In light of *Troxel,* the status of each of these statutes is uncertain.

Only three other Supreme Court Justices agreed with Justice O'Connor: Justice Rehnquist, Justice Ginsburg and Justice Breyer. Justices Souter and Thomas filed opinions concurring (agreeing) in the judgment. Both of these Justices felt that the ultimate decision of the Court was correct, but that the logic was incorrect. Justices Stevens, Scalia and Kennedy, however, dissented (disagreed), and filed separate opinions. Each of these Justices outlined why they felt the Court had come to the wrong conclusion, and laid out what he felt the correct outcome should be. Regardless of the split in the Court, one this is apparant from this decision, a parent's right to raise his children and to make decision for them can be violated by the government only with caution.

Suggestions for further reading

American Bar Association, *Grandparent visitation disputes: A legal resource manual*, June 1998.

Boland, Mary, *Your right to child custody, visitation and support (Legal survival guide),* Sphinx Publication, February 2000.

Truly, Traci, *Grandparent rights,* Sphinx Publication, March 1999.

JURIES

A jury is a group of ordinary citizens that hears and decides a legal case. The jury's decision is called a verdict. Juries base their verdicts on testimony from witnesses and other evidence. A jury's verdict represents a community's opinion about who should win a legal case. Jurors, then, play an important role in the American system of justice.

History of the Jury

Historians have traced the jury system back to Athens, Greece, around 400 BC. Aristotle, a Greek philosopher, recorded that juries decided cases based on their understanding of general justice. The ancient Roman Empire, however, did not use juries. A professional court system decided cases without ordinary citizens. The Dark Ages that followed the fall of the Roman Empire had little law and no use for juries.

Great Britain did not use a jury system until the twelfth century AD. Prior to then, the Catholic Church's courts controlled the legal system. The ordeal was a popular way of deciding criminal cases. If the accused could survive physical torture, the court declared him innocent.

Compurgation was a method of resolving civil cases, those between individual citizens. The person who brought the most friends to support his side of the case won.

In the twelfth century AD, King Henry II gave Great Britain its first jury system for deciding disputes over land. Later, his son King John was a ruthless monarch who regularly seized the land and families of landowners who could not pay their debts on time. In 1215, a group of landowners confronted King John at knifepoint and forced him to sign the Magna Carta. That historic document gave British citizens the right to have a jury trial before being "imprisoned or seized or exiled or in any way destroyed."

The Right to Jury Trials in the United States

The English jury system migrated to the American colonies. Great Britain, however, did not allow jury trials in all cases in the colonies. Some cases were bench trials, which means a judge decided them from his bench. Because colonial judges depended on the British monarch for their jobs and the amount of their salaries, they often were unfair to the colonists. When Thomas Jefferson and the Second Continental Congress wrote the Declaration of Independence in 1776, they listed unfair judges and the lack of jury trials among their reasons for breaking ties with Great Britain.

The U.S. Constitution mentions jury trials in three places. Article III says that all criminal trials, except for impeachment, must be jury trials. The Sixth Amendment repeats this right and adds that juries must be impartial, which means fair, neutral, and open-minded. In *Duncan v. Louisiana* (1968), the Supreme Court said the right to a jury trial applies in all criminal cases in which the penalty can be imprisonment for more than six months.

The Seventh Amendment guarantees a jury trial in all civil cases in which the amount in dispute is greater than twenty dollars. This amendment applies only to the federal government and not to the states. Most state constitutions, however, give citizens the right to jury trials in both criminal and civil cases.

Jury Selection

Choosing a jury for a case happens in two stages. The first stage is called assembling the venire. The venire is a large group of citizens selected from voting, tax, driving, or address records. This group acts as a pool from which the court selects juries for individual cases. To be selected for the venire, citizens must satisfy certain requirements. For example, many states require jurors to be over eighteen, able to read, and without any serious criminal convictions.

Federal and state courts used to restrict jury service to white males. The U.S. Supreme Court ended that with two important cases. In **Strauder v. West Virginia** (1879), the Court said the Fourteenth Amendment makes it illegal to exclude African Americans from jury service. In **Taylor v. Louisiana** (1975), the Court struck down a law that tended to exclude women from jury service in Louisiana. With the Federal Jury Service and Selection Act of 1968, Congress required federal jury venires to contain a fair cross section of the community.

The second stage in jury selection is called voir dire. Judges conduct voir dire by asking the members of the venire questions to make sure they can consider a case impartially and deliver a fair verdict. Under the jury system in England, jurors usually were selected because of their knowledge of the case. The American system of impartiality requires that jurors know as little as possible about a case before serving on a jury. That way they can render a verdict based on the evidence in court rather than what they have learned on the outside.

Attorneys also participate in voir dire. Sometimes they ask questions through the judge, while other times they pose questions directly to potential jurors. After questioning, the parties can strike people from the jury using jury challenges. Attorneys can make an unlimited number of challenges "for cause." A challenge is for cause when the attorney has a good reason to excuse a potential juror from service. For example, if a potential juror is the defendant's brother, the prosecutor can challenge him for cause and dismiss him from service on the case.

Attorneys also get a limited number of peremptory challenges. Attorneys do not have to explain their reason for using a peremptory challenge. It gives them a chance to get rid of jurors they think will be against their clients' case. The U.S. Supreme Court, however, has limited the use of peremptory challenges. In **Batson v. Kentucky** (1986), the Court said prosecutors cannot use peremptory challenges to dismiss potential jurors because of their race. In **J.E.B. v. Alabama** (1994), the

Court said attorneys may not use peremptory challenges to dismiss potential jurors because of their gender.

Voir dire ends when the court finds the right number of jurors who can render a fair decision and are not challenged by the attorneys. The English jury system typically used twelve jurors. Legend says this number came from the number of Jesus Christ's apostles in the Bible's New Testament. Most juries in America have twelve jurors. Some states use as few as six jurors. In *Ballew v. Georgia* (1978), the U.S. Supreme Court said a five member jury is too small to decide a case fairly.

Jury Verdicts

After the jury hears the evidence in a case, the judge instructs the jury on what law to apply. The jury then retires to the jury room to deliberate, which means to discuss the case and reach a verdict. The jury reaches a verdict by deciding what really happened in the case, called determining the facts, and then applying the law to those facts to determine who wins.

At the federal level and in most states, a jury verdict must be unanimous. That means all twelve jurors must agree on the verdict. Some states allow jury verdicts by super majorities of ten or eleven out of the twelve jurors. If the jury cannot agree on a verdict, it is called a hung jury. A hung jury requires the judge to dismiss the entire case without a decision.

The jury's verdict is not always the final decision in the case. If the judge thinks the verdict is wrong, she can either order a new trial or enter the verdict she thinks is correct. There is one important exception. When a jury finds a defendant not guilty in a criminal case, the judge must accept the verdict.

When the jury reaches a verdict in a civil case, it also decides how much money the winning party receives. In a criminal case, the jury usually only decides guilt or innocence. If the verdict is guilty, the judge determines the criminal's sentence. Many southern states allow the jury to determine the sentence within certain guidelines. In cases in which the defendant faces the death penalty, however, the federal government and most states allow the jury to determine the sentence or at least make a recommendation.

Suggestions for further reading

Guinther, John. *The Jury in America.* New York: Facts on File
     Publications, 1988.

Summer, Lila E. *The American Heritage History of the Bill of Rights: The Seventh Amendment.* New Jersey: Silver Burdett Press, Inc., 1991.

Wolf, Robert V. *The Jury System.* Philadelphia: Chelsea House Publishers, 1999.

Zerman, Melvyn Bernard. *Beyond a Reasonable Doubt: Inside the American Jury System.* New York: Crowell, 1981.

Strauder v. West Virginia
1879

Appellant: Taylor Strauder

Appellee: State of West Virginia

Appellant's Claim: That West Virginia violated his constitutional rights by excluding African Americans from the jury selection process.

Chief Lawyers for Appellant: Charles Devans and George O. Davenport

Chief Lawyers for Appellee: Robert White, Attorney General of West Virginia, and James W. Green

Justices for the Court: Joseph P. Bradley, John Marshall Harlan, Ward Hunt, Samuel Freeman Miller, William Strong, Noah Haynes Swayne, Morrison Remick Waite

Justices Dissenting: Nathan Clifford, Stephen Johnson Field

Date of Decision: March 1, 1880

Decision: The Supreme Court reversed Strauder's murder conviction.

Significance: With *Strauder,* the Supreme Court said African American men have the same right as white men to serve on juries.

The American Declaration of Independence, written in 1776, says all men are created equal. Shamefully, the United States of America did not treat all men equally when it was born that year. White men owned

African Americans as slaves, forcing them to work on plantations to make the white men wealthy.

The United States finally outlawed slavery with the Thirteenth Amendment in 1865. Prejudice against African Americans remained high, however, in the former slave states. There was concern that these states would discriminate against newly freed slaves by treating them differently under the law. To prevent that, the United States adopted the Fourteenth Amendment in 1868.

The Equal Protection Clause is an important part of the Fourteenth Amendment. It says states may not deny anyone "the equal protection of the laws." This means states must apply their laws equally to all citizens. In *Strauder v. West Virginia,* the U.S. Supreme Court had to decide whether a law that prevented African Americans from serving on juries violated the Equal Protection Clause.

White Men Only

Taylor Strauder was an African American who was charged with murder in Ohio County, West Virginia, on 20 October 1874. A West Virginia law said only white men could serve as jurors. Strauder did not think he could get a fair trial in a state that did not allow African Americans to serve on juries. In fact, he thought West Virginia's law violated the Equal Protection Clause by treating African Americans unequally.

A federal law said a defendant could have his case moved from state court to federal court whenever the state court was violating its citizens' equal rights. Strauder used this law to ask the state court to move his trial to a federal court. The state court refused and forced Strauder to stand trial in West Virginia. After he was convicted, Strauder appealed his case to the Supreme Court of West Virginia. When he lost there too, Strauder appealed to the U.S. Supreme Court.

Jury of His Peers

With a 7-2 decision, the Supreme Court reversed Strauder's conviction. Writing for the Court, Justice William Strong said West Virginia violated the Equal Protection Clause by preventing African Americans from serving as jurors. Strong said under the Equal Protection Clause, "the law in the States shall be the same for the black as for the white; that all persons, whether colored or white, shall stand equal before the laws of the

JURIES AND RACE

Selecting a jury is a two-stage process. In the first stage, a court uses local records to create a pool of people from the community. This pool is called a venire. The venire must contain a cross-section of the community. That means all races of Americans must be eligible to be selected for the venire. In the second stage, the judge and lawyers select twelve people from the venire to be the jury for a specific case. The jury does not have to contain a cross-section of the community. That means juries often are dominated by people from one race. When that happens, the public sometimes wonders whether race affected a jury's decision.

For example, in 1991, four white Los Angeles police officers beat an African American motorist named Rodney G. King. In 1992, the officers faced criminal charges in the mostly white Los Angeles suburb of Simi Valley. The jury, which contained no African Americans, found the officers not guilty of almost all charges against them. Many Americans thought racial prejudice affected the jury's verdict.

Two years later, football star O.J. Simpson's ex-wife, Nicole Brown Simpson, was murdered in Los Angeles along with her boyfriend, Ronald L. Goldman. Simpson, an African American, faced murder charges for the crime in 1995. At his trial, nine of the twelve jurors were African American. When the jury found Simpson not guilty, many Americans again believed racial prejudice affected the verdict. Some even thought the verdict was payback for the King verdict three years earlier.

States, and . . . that no discrimination shall be made against [African Americans] because of their color."

A law that allows only whites to be jurors treats citizens unequally. Justice Strong asked what white men would think about a law that allowed only African Americans to be jurors, or that excluded Irish Americans from being jurors. Such laws would defeat the very purpose of a criminal trial, which is to allow a man to be judged by a jury of his peers-his neighbors, fellows, and associates.

Justice Strong made it clear that Strauder did not have a right to have a certain number of African Americans on his jury. He only had the right to have the jury selected from a group of citizens that included African Americans. Moreover, West Virginia was free to apply non-racial requirements for jurors. For example, West Virginia could require jurors to be men who had reached a certain age and received an education. It simply could not exclude entire races of people from ever serving as jurors.

Impact

With *Strauder,* the Supreme Court gave African Americans the right to serve as jurors in the United States. States, however, often got around this by requiring jurors to have a certain education and reading ability. Newly freed slaves in the late 1800s usually could not afford a good education. African Americans spent many more decades fighting through such prejudice to enjoy their right to serve as jurors. Moreover, it was not until 1975 in **Taylor v. Louisiana** that the Supreme Court struck down all laws that made it difficult for women to serve as jurors.

Suggestions for further reading

Claireborne, William. "Acquitted, O.J. Simpson Goes Home." *Washington Post,* October 4, 1995.

Guinther, John. *The Jury in America.* New York: Facts on File Publications, 1988.

Morin, Richard. "Polls Uncover Much Common Ground on L.A. Verdict." *Washington Post,* May 11, 1992

Summer, Lila E. *The American Heritage History of the Bill of Rights: The Seventh Amendment.* New Jersey: Silver Burdett Press, Inc., 1991.

Wolf, Robert V. *The Jury System.* Philadelphia: Chelsea House Publishers, 1999.

Zerman, Melvyn Bernard. *Beyond a Reasonable Doubt: Inside the American Jury System.* New York: Crowell, 1981.

Taylor v. Louisiana
1975

Appellant: Billy Jean Taylor

Appellee: State of Louisiana

Appellant's Claim: That by excluding women, Louisiana's jury selection system violated his Sixth Amendment right to have an impartial jury.

Chief Lawyer for Appellant: William M. King

Chief Lawyer for Appellee: Kendall L. Vick

Justices for the Court: Harry A. Blackmun, William J. Brennan, Jr., Warren E. Burger, William O. Douglas, Thurgood Marshall, Lewis F. Powell, Jr., Potter Stewart, Byron R. White (writing for the Court)

Justices Dissenting: William H. Rehnquist

Date of Decision: January 21, 1975

Decision: The Supreme Court reversed Taylor's conviction.

Significance: With *Taylor,* the Supreme Court said juries must be selected from a fair cross section of the community, including both men and women.

The Sixth Amendment of the U.S. Constitution gives every American the right to be tried by an impartial jury when accused of a crime. An impartial jury is one that is fair, neutral, and open-minded. The use of juries in criminal trials allows defendants to be judged by their peers from the community.

Selecting a jury for a case is a two-stage process. In the first stage, the court creates a large pool of people from the community to serve as jurors. This pool is called a venire. In the second stage, the court selects twelve people from the venire to be the jury for a specific case. In *Taylor v. Louisiana,* the U.S. Supreme Court had to decide whether Louisiana's jury selection system violated the Sixth Amendment.

Mostly Men

On September 28, 1971, police arrested Billy Jean Taylor, a twenty-five year old convict in St. Tammany parish, Louisiana. (In Louisiana, a parish is a county.) The police charged Taylor with aggravated kidnapping, armed robbery, and rape. Taylor's trial was scheduled to begin on April 13, 1972.

Louisiana had a law that said women could not be selected for jury service unless they registered with the court. Men did not have to register to serve as jurors. The law had the effect of making women a rare sight on juries in St. Tammany parish. Only one out of every five women registered for jury service. Although women made up fifty-three percent of the people eligible for jury service in St. Tammany, the venire of one hundred seventy-five people selected before Taylor's trial contained no women.

The day before his trial, Taylor filed a motion to get rid of the venire. He argued that excluding women from jury service violated his Sixth Amendment right to have an impartial jury. Taylor said a venire without women did not represent the community of his peers.

The trial court rejected Taylor's motion and selected an all-male jury to try his case. The jury convicted Taylor and the court sentenced him to death. Taylor appealed, but the Supreme Court of Louisiana affirmed his conviction. As his last resort, Taylor appealed to the U.S. Supreme Court.

Fair Cross Sections

With an 8–1 decision, the Supreme Court reversed Taylor's conviction. Writing for the Court, Justice Byron R. White said Louisiana violated the Sixth Amendment by excluding women from juries. Louisiana and all states must obey the Sixth Amendment under the Due Process Clause of the Fourteenth Amendment.

Before the Supreme Court, Louisiana argued that as a man, Taylor had no right to complain about the lack of women on his jury. Justice

FEDERAL JURY SELECTION AND SERVICE ACT OF 1968

In the Civil Rights Act of 1957, Congress gave most Americans the right to serve on juries in federal court cases. In the Federal Jury Selection and Service Act of 1968, Congress went one step further. It said federal courts must select juries from a fair cross section of the community. The Act specifically prevents federal courts from excluding citizens from jury service based on their race, color, religion, sex, national origin, or economic status.

The Act has some qualifications. Federal jurors must be American citizens, eighteen years of age or older, and able to read, write, and speak English. If a federal court selects a citizen as a possible juror, he must fill out a form to allow the court to decide whether he satisfies these requirements. An American who refuses to fill out a juror qualification form or fails to appear as a juror when called can be fined $one-hundred and imprisoned for three days.

White rejected this argument. He said all Americans, male and female, have a right under the Sixth Amendment to be tried by an impartial jury. An impartial jury is one that is "drawn from a fair cross section of the community." A venire with no women in a parish that is half female does not represent the community.

White explained the importance of impartial juries. They make sure a defendant is judged by his peers. If a prosecutor wants to convict an innocent man, the jury can prevent that. Juries also can prevent a biased judge from doing injustice. A jury cannot properly do its job unless it is the voice of the entire community. Jury service by all members of a community also creates public confidence in the criminal justice system.

Louisiana said it was protecting women from having to leave the important position of taking care of families at home. Justice White pointed out that as of 1974, fifty-two percent of all women between eighteen and sixty-four worked outside the home. It no longer was right to assume that women cannot be interrupted from taking care of a home. The courts would have to handle each person individually to determine if jury service would be too much of a burden.

Justice White closed by emphasizing that individual juries do not have to contain a cross section of the community. That would be impossible to do with every jury of twelve people. Juries, however, must be selected from venires that fairly represent the community. Only then can defendants be fairly judged by their peers.

Suggestions for further reading

Guinther, John. *The Jury in America.* New York: Facts on File Publications, 1988.

Summer, Lila E. *The American Heritage History of the Bill of Rights: The Seventh Amendment.* New Jersey: Silver Burdett Press, Inc., 1991.

Wolf, Robert V. *The Jury System.* Philadelphia: Chelsea House Publishers, 1999.

Zerman, Melvyn Bernard. *Beyond a Reasonable Doubt: Inside the American Jury System.* New York: Crowell, 1981.

Batson v. Kentucky
1986

Petitioner: James Kirkland Batson

Respondent: State of Kentucky

Petitioner's Claim: That by striking African Americans from his jury, the prosecutor violated his constitutional rights.

Chief Lawyer for Petitioner: J. David Niehaus

Chief Lawyer for Respondent: Rickie L. Pearson, Assistant Attorney General of Kentucky

Justices for the Court: Harry A. Blackmun, William J. Brennan, Jr., Thurgood Marshall, Sandra Day O'Connor, Lewis F. Powell, Jr., John Paul Stevens, Byron R. White

Justices Dissenting: Warren E. Burger, William H. Rehnquist

Date of Decision: April 30, 1986

Decision: The Supreme Court sent Batson's case back to the trial court to determine whether the prosecutor had race-neutral reasons for striking African Americans from the jury.

Significance: With *Batson,* the Supreme Court said striking jurors because of their race violates the Equal Protection Clause of the Fourteenth Amendment.

The Sixth Amendment of the U.S. Constitution gives every American the right to be tried by an impartial jury when accused of a crime. An impartial jury is one that is fair, neutral, and open-minded. The use of impartial juries allow defendants to be judged fairly by their peers from the community.

Associate Justice Lewis F. Powell.
Courtesy of the Supreme Court of the United States.

Selecting a jury for a case is a two-stage process. In the first stage, the court creates a large pool of people from the community to serve as jurors. This pool is called a venire. In the second stage, the court and lawyers select twelve people from the venire to be the jury for a specific case. During this stage the lawyers for both parties get to make jury challenges. A jury challenge allows the parties to exclude specific people from the jury.

There are two kinds of jury challenges. A challenge "for cause" happens when a party has a good reason to believe a potential juror might not be able to decide a case fairly. For example, if a potential juror is the defendant's brother, the prosecutor can use a for cause challenge to prevent the brother from serving on the jury. There is no limit to the number of for cause challenges a party can make during jury selection.

The second kind of challenge is called a peremptory challenge. Each party gets a limited number of peremptory challenges. They allow the parties to exclude potential jurors who the lawyers feel will be against their cases. Traditionally, a lawyer could use peremptory challenges without giving a good reason. All he needed was a hunch that a potential juror would rule against his client. Peremptory challenges were one way for defendants to make sure they got an impartial jury.

Jury of His White Peers

In 1981, James Kirkland Batson stood trial in Jefferson county, Kentucky, on charges of second-degree burglary and receipt of stolen goods. Batson was an African American. During jury selection, the prosecutor used his peremptory challenges to strike the only four African Americans from the jury venire. The resulting jury had only white people.

Batson made a motion to dismiss the jury and get a new one. (When a party makes a motion, he asks the court to do something.) Batson argued that the prosecutor violated his right to an impartial jury by eliminating African Americans. Batson also argued that using peremptory challenges to get rid of jurors based on race violates the Equal Protection Clause of the Fourteenth Amendment. The Equal Protection Clause says states may not discriminate against citizens because of race.

The trial court denied Batson's motion and the jury convicted him on both counts. Batson appealed to the Supreme Court of Kentucky, but it affirmed his conviction. As his last resort, Batson took his case to the U.S. Supreme Court. There he got help from the Legal Defense and Education Fund of the National Association for the Advancement of Colored People.

Discrimination Disallowed

With a 7-2 decision, the Supreme Court ruled in favor of Batson. Writing for the Court, Justice Lewis F. Powell, Jr., said dismissing African American jurors because of their race suggests that African Americans are incapable of being jurors or deciding a case fairly. The Supreme Court could not allow prosecutors to reinforce such ignorant, old-fashioned ideas.

The Equal Protection Clause prevents Kentucky and all states from discriminating against races of people. When a prosecutor uses a peremptory challenge to strike an African American from a jury, he hurts the defendant, the potential juror, and society. The defendant loses the right to have a jury free from discrimination. The potential juror loses the right to serve on a jury. Society loses confidence in the fairness of the criminal justice system.

The Supreme Court sent Batson's case back to the trial court in Kentucky. That court had to determine whether the prosecutor had race-neutral reasons for striking the four African Americans from the jury. If not, the court would have to reverse Batson's conviction.

Justice Thurgood Marshall filed a concurring opinion, which means he agreed with the Court's decision. Justice Marshall said, however, that he would go one step further by eliminating peremptory challenges entirely. He thought it would be too difficult to determine whether a pros-

NORRIS V. ALABAMA

In March 1931, Clarence Norris and eight other African American boys were indicted in Scottsboro, Alabama, for raping two white girls. The case of the Scottsboro boys drew national attention. Locals bent on revenge were determined to see the nine boys convicted. Evidence of the boys' innocence, however, led people around the work, including scientist Albert Einstein, to sign a petition requesting Alabama to release the boys.

Alabama rejected the petition and tried the Scottsboro boys in court. The U.S. Supreme Court overturned the first trial because Alabama failed to appoint a good lawyer for the boys. Clarence Norris was convicted and sentenced to death in a second trial. Norris appealed the conviction because the grand jury that indicted him and the jury that convicted him had no African Americans.

The U.S. Supreme Court reversed Norris's second conviction. If found that Morgan and Jackson counties in Alabama, where Norris was indicted and tried, regularly excluded African Americans from jury service. There even was evidence that local authorities were tampering with jury lists to make it look like they were considering African Americans for jury service when in fact they were not. The evidence proved that in a generation, no African Americans had served on a grand or petit jury in Morgan and Jackson counties. For that reason, Norris deserved a new trial.

ecutor used a peremptory challenge for a race-neutral reason. Marshall said the only way to get rid of the evil of discrimination is to get rid of peremptory challenges.

Leaving Long Traditions Behind

Chief Justice Warren E. Burger and Justice William H Rehnquist filed dissenting opinions, which means they disagreed with the Court's decision. Burger and Rehnquist said peremptory challenges were one of the most important parts of America's criminal justice system. They stated very frankly that people tend to favor other people of their own race, religion, age, and ethnicity. Peremptory challenges make sure such favoritism does not affect a jury's decision. Making prosecutors use these challenges for race-neutral reasons would force them to keep biased people on juries.

Impact

Batson only applied to prosecutors in criminal cases. Eventually, however, the courts extended the decision to civil cases, which are between individual citizens. Eight years later in ***J.E.B. v. Alabama*** (1994), the Supreme Court said lawyers may not use peremptory challenges to exclude jurors based on their sex either. As of 1999, however, the Court has declined to prevent religious discrimination in the selection of jurors.

Suggestions for further reading

Guinther, John. *The Jury in America.* New York: Facts on File Publications, 1988.

Mikula, Mark, and L. Mpho Mabunda, eds. *Great American Court Cases.* Detroit: The Gale Group, 1999.

Summer, Lila E. *The American Heritage History of the Bill of Rights: The Seventh Amendment.* New Jersey: Silver Burdett Press, Inc., 1991.

Wolf, Robert V. *The Jury System.* Philadelphia: Chelsea House Publishers, 1999.

Zerman, Melvyn Bernard. *Beyond a Reasonable Doubt: Inside the American Jury System.* New York: Crowell, 1981.

Lockhart v. McCree
1986

Petitioner: A.L. Lockhart

Respondent: Ardia V. McCree

Petitioner's Claim: That Arkansas did not violate the constitution in death penalty cases by removing prospective jurors who could not vote for death under any circumstances.

Chief Lawyer for Petitioner: John Steven Clark, Attorney General of Arkansas

Chief Lawyer for Respondent: Samuel R. Gross

Justices for the Court: Harry A. Blackmun, Warren E. Burger, Sandra Day O'Connor, Lewis F. Powell, Jr., William H. Rehnquist, Byron R. White

Justices Dissenting: William J. Brennan, Jr., Thurgood Marshall, John Paul Stevens

Date of Decision: May 5, 1986

Decision: The Supreme Court said Arkansas did not violate the constitution.

Significance: *Lockhart* allows states to use death-qualified juries during the guilt phase of death penalty cases even though evidence suggests that death-qualified juries are more likely to convict defendants.

The Sixth Amendment of the U.S. Constitution gives every American the right to be tried by an impartial jury when accused of a crime. An impartial jury is one that is fair, neutral, and open-minded. A jury cannot be fair unless it is selected from a fair cross-section of the community. Using impartial juries allow defendants to be judged fairly by their peers from the community.

Selecting a jury for a case is a two-stage process. In the first stage, the court creates a large pool of people to serve as jurors. This pool is called a venire. It is supposed to contain a cross-section of the community. In the second stage, the court and lawyers select twelve people from the venire to be the jury for a specific case.

During the second stage, lawyers for both parties get to make jury challenges. A jury challenge allows the parties to exclude specific people from the jury. One kind of jury challenge is called "for cause." Parties use for cause challenges to strike jurors who might not be able to decide a case fairly. For example, if a potential juror is the defendant's brother, the prosecutor can use a for cause challenge to prevent the brother from serving on the jury.

Jurors take an oath promising to apply the law when deciding a case. In states that use the death penalty, that means jurors must be able to impose the death penalty if the defendant deserves it. Often a juror says she opposes the death penalty and could not sentence a person to die under any circumstances. In *Witherspoon v. Illinois* (1968), the U.S. Supreme Court said prosecutors may use for cause challenges to exclude such jurors. This is called selecting a death-qualified jury. In *Lockhart v. McCree,* the Supreme Court had to decide whether death-qualified juries violate the defendant's Sixth Amendment right to have an impartial jury.

Bloody Valentine

Evelyn Boughton owned and operated a service station with a gift shop in Camden, Arkansas. On Valentine's Day in 1978, Boughton was murdered during a robbery. Eyewitnesses said the getaway car was a maroon and white Lincoln Continental.

Later that afternoon, police in Hot Springs, Arkansas, arrested Ardia McCree, who was driving a maroon and white Lincoln Continental. McCree admitted to being at Boughton's shop during the murder. He claimed, however, that he had given a ride to a tall black stranger who was wearing an overcoat. McCree said the stranger took McCree's rifle from the back seat of the car and used it to kill Boughton, then rode with McCree to a nearby dirt road and got out of the car with the rifle.

Two eyewitnesses disputed McCree's story. They saw McCree's car with only one person in it between Boughton's shop and the place where McCree said the black man got out. The police found McCree's rifle and a bank bag from Boughton's shop alongside the dirt road. The Federal Bureau of Investigation determined that the bullet that killed Boughton came from McCree's rifle.

Life in Prison

Arkansas charged McCree with capital felony murder. Felony murder is a murder committed in the course of a felony, such as a robbery. At McCree's trial, the prosecutor used jury challenges to remove eight prospective jurors who said they could not impose the death penalty under any circumstances. The jury convicted McCree but gave him life in prison instead of the death penalty.

McCree filed a habeas corpus lawsuit against his jailer, the Arkansas Department of Corrections. A habeas corpus lawsuit is for people who are in jail because their constitutional rights have been violated. McCree said Arkansas violated his Sixth Amendment right to an impartial jury by excluding jurors who would not impose the death penalty. He said it also violated his Sixth Amendment right to have the jury selected from a fair cross-section of the community.

At a hearing, McCree presented evidence that people who favor the death penalty are more likely to convict than are people who oppose it. By excluding people who oppose the death penalty, Arkansas increased the chance that the jury would find McCree guilty of murder. McCree said that violated the Sixth Amendment. The federal trial court and court of appeals both agreed and ordered Arkansas to release McCree from prison. Arkansas thought the courts were wrong, so it took the case to the U.S. Supreme Court.

Juries Must Apply the Law

With a 6–3 decision, the Supreme Court reversed and ruled in favor of the Arkansas Department of Corrections. Writing for the Court, Justice

William H. Rehnquist rejected the evidence that death-qualified juries are more likely to convict defendants. Rehnquist said the evidence was faulty and did not prove anything. Rehnquist, however, did not base the Court's decision on the evidence alone. Even assuming that death-qualified juries are more likely to convict, Rehnquist said they do not violate the Sixth Amendment.

Rehnquist gave two reasons for the Court's decision. First, he said the Sixth Amendment only guarantees that a jury will be drawn from a fair cross-section of the community. That means the venire from which a jury is selected must be a cross-section of the community. The Sixth Amendment does not require each jury to represent the entire community. Rehnquist said it would be impossible to make sure that every jury of twelve people represented the various viewpoints of all members of the community.

Second, Rehnquist said the Sixth Amendment requires juries to be impartial. There was no evidence that any member of McCree's jury did not decide his case fairly and impartially. Indeed, there was no reason to believe that death-qualified juries cannot be impartial when deciding whether defendants are guilty. Because death-qualified juries can be impartial, they do not violate the Sixth Amendment.

In the end, Rehnquist said states have a good reason for using death-qualified juries. Jurors must apply the law. In death penalty states, jurors must be able to impose the death penalty if the defendant deserves it. Excluding jurors who cannot ensures that all jurors in death penalty cases can obey their oaths. McCree's conviction did not violate the Sixth Amendment, so he had to serve his sentence of life in prison.

Organized to Convict

Three justices dissented, which means they disagreed with the Court's decision. Justice Thurgood Marshall wrote a dissenting opinion. He believed the evidence was overwhelming that death-qualified juries are more likely to convict defendants. Marshall said that means death-qualified juries are "organized to return a verdict of guilty." Marshall did not understand how such juries satisfy the Sixth Amendment guarantee of a fair, impartial jury.

Marshall even proposed a solution to the whole problem. In death penalty cases, states can use two juries. The first jury can decide guilt or innocence. Citizens can serve on that jury even if they oppose the death

WITHERSPOON V. ILLINOIS

In 1960, Illinois had a law that allowed prosecutors to exclude jurors who had conscientious, religious, or other general objections to the death penalty. William C. Witherspoon was convicted and sentenced to death by such a death-qualified jury. When Witherspoon appealed his case, the Supreme Court affirmed his conviction but reversed his death sentence. The Court said prosecutors may exclude jurors who say they could never vote for the death penalty. But a juror who simply is opposed to the death penalty may serve as a juror if he promises to apply the law as instructed by the judge. According to the Court, "A man who opposes the death penalty, no less than one who favors it, can … obey the oath he takes as a juror."

penalty. If the first jury decides the defendant is guilty, a second jury can determine the sentence. Only citizens who are able to impose the death penalty can serve on the second jury. Marshall criticized the Court for rejecting this solution in favor of allowing death-qualified juries to convict defendants.

Suggestions for further reading

Guinther, John. *The Jury in America.* New York: Facts on File Publications, 1988.

Mikula, Mark, and L. Mpho Mabunda, eds. *Great American Court Cases.* Detroit: The Gale Group, 1999.

Wolf, Robert V. *The Jury System.* Philadelphia: Chelsea House Publishers, 1999.

Zerman, Melvyn Bernard. *Beyond a Reasonable Doubt: Inside the American Jury System.* New York: Crowell, 1981.

J.E.B. v. Alabama ex rel. T.B.
1994

Petitioner: J.E.B.

Respondent: Alabama ex rel. T.B.

Petitioner's Claim: That by striking men from his jury, Alabama violated his constitutional rights.

Chief Lawyer for Petitioner: John F. Porter III

Chief Lawyer for Respondent: Lois B. Brasfield

Justices for the Court: Harry A. Blackmun, Ruth Bader Ginsburg, Anthony M. Kennedy, Sandra Day O'Connor, David H. Souter, John Paul Stevens

Justices Dissenting: William H. Rehnquist, Antonin Scalia, Clarence Thomas

Date of Decision: April 19, 1994

Decision: The Supreme Court sent J.E.B.'s case back to the trial court to determine whether Alabama had gender-neutral reasons for striking men from the jury.

Significance: With *J.E.B.,* the Supreme Court said striking jurors because of their gender violates the Equal Protection Clause of the Fourteenth Amendment.

The American system of justice uses jury trials. A jury is a group of citizens, usually numbering twelve, that hears and decides a legal case. Juries are supposed to be impartial, which means fair, neutral, and open-minded. The use of impartial juries allows parties to be judged fairly by their peers from the community.

J.E.B. v.
Alabama ex
rel. T.B.

Selecting a jury for a case is a two-stage process. In the first stage, the court creates a large pool of people from the community to serve as jurors. This pool is called a venire. In the second stage, the court and lawyers select twelve people from the venire to be the jury for a specific case. During this stage the lawyers for both parties get to make jury challenges. A jury challenge allows the parties to exclude specific people from the jury.

There are two kinds of jury challenges. A challenge "for cause" happens when a party has a good reason to believe a juror might not be able to decide a case fairly. For example, if a juror is one litigant's brother, the other side can use a for cause challenge to strike the juror from the jury. There is no limit to the number of for cause challenges a party can make during jury selection.

The second kind of challenge is called a peremptory challenge. Each party gets a limited number of peremptory challenges. They allow the parties to exclude jurors who the lawyers feel will be against their cases. Traditionally, a lawyer could use peremptory challenges without giving a good reason. All he needed was a hunch that a potential juror would rule against his client. Peremptory challenges were one way for parties to make sure they got an impartial jury.

In **Batson v. Kentucky** (1986), the Supreme Court decided that lawyers are not allowed to use peremptory challenges to strike jurors just because of their race. For example, a lawyer who represents an African American cannot strike white jurors because he thinks white people will be against his client. That violates the Equal Protection Clause of the Fourteenth Amendment, which prevents states from allowing discrimination based on race. In *J.E.B. v. Alabama ex rel. T.B.,* the Supreme Court had to decide whether the Equal Protection Clause prevents lawyers from using peremptory challenges to strike jurors because of their gender.

Jury of His Female Peers

T.B. was the mother of a young child in Alabama. She believed that J.E.B. was the child's father. (The courts used the parents' initials to protect their privacy.) J.E.B. denied that he was the father, so Alabama sued J.E.B. for T.B. Alabama wanted to prove that J.E.B. was the father and then force him to pay child support, which is money to take care his child.

JURIES

On 21 October 1991, the case went to trial and the parties began jury selection. They had to pick a jury of twelve from thirty-six people in the venire. Alabama believed women would be better for its case against J.E.B., so it used its peremptory challenges to strike nine male jurors. The resulting jury had no men on it.

J.E.B. believed Alabama violated the Equal Protection Clause by eliminating men from the jury. He urged the court to extend *Batson,* which prohibited race-based peremptory challenges, to gender-based challenges too. The trial court denied J.E.B.'s request and held the trial with the all-female jury. The jury decided J.E.B. was the father of T.B.'s child, and the court ordered J.E.B. to pay child support. J.E.B. appealed the decision, but the Alabama Court of Civil Appeals affirmed and the Supreme Court of Alabama refused to review the case. J.E.B. finally took the case to the U.S. Supreme Court.

Equal Protection Includes Men and Women

With a 6–3 decision, the Supreme Court ruled in favor of J.E.B. Writing for the Court, Justice Harry A. Blackmun said gender-based peremptory challenges violate the Equal Protection Clause.

Although the case involved peremptory challenges against men, lawyers in other cases used challenges to strike women from juries. Blackmun said striking women reinforces the old-fashioned idea that women are less capable than men. In fact, it sends America back to the 1800s, when laws prevented women from serving on juries. Men made such laws because they thought trials were too ugly for ladies, who belonged at home taking care of their families.

The Supreme Court refused to support such "outdated misconceptions concerning the roles of females in the home rather than in the marketplace and world of ideas." Women, like African Americans, went too long in the United States without equal rights. Women were not allowed to vote until 1920, when the United States adopted the Nineteenth Amendment. Women were not allowed to serve on juries in some states until the 1960s.

In American history, then, women suffered discrimination just like African Americans. The United States adopted the Equal Protection Clause of the Fourteenth Amendment in 1868 to prevent

HESTER VAUGHAN TRIAL

Hester Vaughan was a housekeeper in Philadelphia, Pennsylvania, in the mid-1800s. When she became pregnant from being raped by a member of the household, Vaughan left to rent a small, unheated room where she waited for her child to be born. Because she had little money, Vaughan became malnourished. She gave birth around February 8, 1868.

Two days later, Vaughan asked a neighbor to give her a box in which to put her baby, who was dead. The neighbor reported this to the police, who arrested Vaughan and charged her with murder. At the time, women were not allowed to be jurors in Pennsylvania. Vaughan's all-male jury convicted her of murder and the court sentenced her to death.

Prominent women leaders stepped in to ask Pennsylvania Governor John W. Geary to pardon Vaughan, which means to forgive her and get rid of her death sentence. Dr. Susan A. Smith told Governor Geary that she believed Vaughan's baby died during childbirth. Women's rights leaders Susan B. Anthony and Elizabeth Cady Stanton objected to convicting Vaughan with a jury that contained no women. In the summer of 1869, Governor Geary pardoned Vaughan on the condition that she return to England, which she did.

discrimination against African Americans. Likewise, the Equal Protection Clause must protect women too. Gender-based peremptory challenges could not survive in a society that wanted to end illegal discrimination.

Justice White said ending gender-based peremptory challenges would benefit litigants, jurors, and society. Litigants get impartial juries that contain a fair cross section of the community. Jurors get the right to participate in the justice system regardless of sex. Society gains confidence in a system that does not discriminate against men or women.

JURIES

Suggestions for further reading

Frost-Knappman, Elizabeth, Edward W. Knappman, and Lisa Paddock, eds. *Courtroom Drama: 120 of the World's Most Notable Trials.* Detroit: Gale Research, 1998.

Guinther, John. *The Jury in America.* New York: Facts on File Publications, 1988.

Summer, Lila E. *The American Heritage History of the Bill of Rights: The Seventh Amendment.* New Jersey: Silver Burdett Press, Inc., 1991.

Wolf, Robert V. *The Jury System.* Philadelphia: Chelsea House Publishers, 1999.

Zerman, Melvyn Bernard. *Beyond a Reasonable Doubt: Inside the American Jury System.* New York: Crowell, 1981.

JUVENILE COURTS AND LAW

Juvenile law is the body of law that applies to young people who are not yet adults. These people are called juveniles or minors. In most states, a person is a juvenile until eighteen years old. Juvenile cases are handled in a special court, usually called a juvenile court. Before the American juvenile justice system was created in the late 1800s, juveniles who broke the law were treated like adult criminals.

Historical Background

When the United States was born in 1776, children under seven years of age were exempt from the criminal laws. Courts, however, treated juveniles seven years and older like miniature adults. Juveniles could be arrested, tried, and convicted of crimes. If convicted, they received prison sentences just like adults. Children convicted of minor crimes found themselves in jails with adult murderers and rapists, where children learned the ways of these criminals.

In the early 1800s, immigrants from Europe filled American cities such as New York. Neglected immigrant children often roamed city streets and got into trouble while their parents looked for work. In 1818, the Society for the Prevention of Pauperism created the term "juvenile delinquents" to describe these children.

Social awareness led people to search for a better way to handle young people who broke the law. In the 1820s, the Society for the Prevention of Juvenile Delinquency suggested separating adult and juvenile criminals. The Society for the Reformation of Juvenile Delinquents worked to reform juvenile delinquents instead of punishing them. It sent them to live in dormitories and to go to school to learn to work in factories. Unfortunately, these programs often did more harm than good. Manufacturers overworked the young children while school directors kept the children's wages.

In the late 1800s, Americans decided it was time to treat juvenile criminals differently than adult criminals. As one man put it, "Children need care, not harsh punishment." Many people believed that if cared for properly, juvenile criminals could become law-abiding citizens. In 1872, Massachusetts became the first state to hold separate court sessions for children. In the 1890s, the Chicago Women's Club urged Illinois to create an entirely separate justice system for juveniles. Illinois did so by creating the world's first juvenile court in 1899.

By 1925, all but two states had juvenile justice systems. As of 1999, all states have such systems. The federal government even has a juvenile justice system for people under eighteen who violate federal law. The goal of all juvenile justice systems is to protect society from young people who break the law while reforming them into lawful adults.

Juvenile Law

Juvenile courts handle cases involving three kinds of problems: crimes, status offenses, and child abuse or neglect. Criminal cases involve the same kinds of crimes that adults commit, such as burglary, robbery, and murder. For serious cases such as murder, some states allow juveniles over a certain age, often fourteen, to be tried as adults. In such cases, if the court decides a juvenile cannot be reformed by the juvenile justice system, it sends him to the regular court system to be tried as an adult.

Status offenses are things that are illegal for juveniles but not for adults. Truancy (missing school), running away from home, smoking cigarettes, and drinking alcohol are status offenses. Abuse and neglect cases are lawsuits by states against parents or guardians who are abusing or not taking care of their children. In these cases, the parent or guardian is on trial, not the child. States can order parents and guardians to stop abusing children and to care for them properly with food, shelter, and clothing. States also can take children away from abusive parents and place them with loving relatives or in child care centers and foster homes.

Juvenile Courts

A juvenile case usually begins with a police investigation in response to a complaint by a citizen, parent, or victim of juvenile crime. In many cases, the police resolve the problem themselves by talking to the juvenile, his parents, and the victim. The police can give the juvenile a warning, arrange for him to pay for any damage he caused, make him promise not to break the law again, and make sure the victim is alright.

If the police think a juvenile case needs to go to court, they arrest the juvenile and take him to the police station. If the juvenile committed a serious crime, such as rape or murder, the police may keep him in jail until the juvenile court decides how to handle the case. After the police arrest a juvenile, an intake officer in the juvenile court decides whether there really is a case against the juvenile. If not, the police give the juvenile back to his parents or guardians.

If there is a case, the intake officer may arrange an informal solution. If the intake officer thinks the state needs to file a case against the juvenile, she makes this recommendation to the state district attorney. The district attorney then files a petition against the juvenile, charging him with specific violations. While a juvenile waits for his hearing to begin, the state prepares a social investigation report about the juvenile's background and the circumstances of his offense.

In court, a juvenile case is called a hearing or adjudication instead of a trial. Most hearings are closed to the public to protect the juvenile's privacy. The judge decides the case instead of a jury. As in a regular trial, the judge listens to testimony from witnesses for both the state and the juvenile. If the state has charged the juvenile with a crime, it must prove its case beyond a reasonable doubt. That means the case must be so strong that no reasonable person would doubt that the juvenile committed the crime.

After the judge hears all the evidence, she decides whether the juvenile has committed the offense charged. If so, the juvenile is called delinquent instead of guilty of a crime. The judge next holds a dispositional hearing instead of a sentencing. At the dispositional hearing, the judge uses the state's social investigation report to decide how to reform the juvenile while protecting society from him. The judge may require probation, community service, a fine, restitution, or confinement in a juvenile detention center. Probation allows the juvenile to go home but requires him to obey certain rules under court supervision. Restitution requires the juvenile to pay for any damage he caused. Juveniles who commit the most serious crimes find themselves in juvenile detention centers. Although they resemble jails, detention centers are supposed to rehabilitate juvenile delinquents, not punish them.

Constitutional Rights

The U.S. Constitution gives adult defendants many rights in criminal cases. For example, defendants have the right to know the charges against them, to be represented by an attorney, and to have a jury trial in cases in which they face imprisonment for more than six months. When states created juvenile justice systems in the early 1900s, they did not give these same rights to juvenile defendants. Juvenile justice systems were supposed to help juveniles rather than punish them, so people did not think juveniles needed constitutional rights.

As the century passed, people began to question whether juveniles need constitutional protection. The Fourteenth Amendment says states may not deprive a person of liberty, meaning freedom, without due process of law. Due process of law means a fair trial. Juveniles who are found delinquent and either placed on probation or confined in juvenile detention centers lose their freedom.

In a series of cases beginning in the 1960s, the U.S. Supreme Court decided that the Fourteenth Amendment requires states to give juveniles many of the constitutional rights that criminal defendants have. In the first case, *Kent v. United States* (1966), the Supreme Court said the due process clause of the Fourteenth Amendment applies to juveniles. One year later in *In re Gault* (1967), the Court said juveniles have the right to know the charges against them and to be represented by an attorney. Juveniles also have the right to cross-examine witnesses against them and the right not to testify against themselves. Three years later in *In re Winship* (1970), the Court said states must prove criminal charges against juveniles beyond a reasonable doubt.

In *McKeiver v. Pennsylvania* (1973), the Supreme Court decided that juveniles do not have the right to jury trials. The Court said jury trials would turn the juvenile justice system into the criminal justice system, making it senseless to run two systems. The trend in favor of juveniles continued, however, in *Breed v. Jones* (1975). There the Court said juveniles who are found delinquent cannot be tried again for the same offense as adults. Then in *Thompson v. Oklahoma* (1988), the Supreme Court said states may not execute a defendant who is younger than sixteen at the time of his offense.

The Future

At the end of the twentieth century, the American juvenile justice system received low marks from many critics. Extending constitutional rights to juveniles made hearings seem more like criminal trials. That made it harder to use the system to reform delinquents instead of treating them like adult criminals. The availability of drugs and weapons led to increased juvenile crime. According to *Congressional Quarterly,* "Between 1985 and 1995, the juvenile arrest rate for violent crimes rose 69 percent. For murders it rose 96 percent." Finally, some say the juvenile justice system is racist because minority youths are more likely to find themselves in detention centers.

Many people wonder whether the juvenile justice system is doing, or can do, its job of helping juvenile delinquents. A rash of juvenile shootings in schools across the country forced Americans to look at whether families are taking care of their children. Frustrated and scared, Americans looked to the future of juvenile justice with more questions and concerns than solutions.

Suggestions for further reading

Berry, Joy. *Every Kid's Guide to Laws that Relate to Parents and Children.* Chicago: Children's Press, 1987.

——. *Every Kid's Guide to the Juvenile Justice System.* Chicago: Children's Press, 1987.

Burns, Marilyn. *I Am Not a Short Adult: Getting Good at Being a Kid.* Boston: Little, Brown, & Co. 1977.

Greenberg, Keith Elliot, and Jeanne Vestal. *Adolescent Rights: Are Young People Equal under the Law?* Twenty First Century Books, 1995.

Hyde, Margaret O. *Juvenile Justice and Injustice.* New York: Franklin Watts, 1977.

Kowalski, Kathiann M. *Teen Rights: At Home, at School, Online.* Enslow Publishers Inc., 2000.

Landau, Elaine. *Your Legal Rights: From Custody Battles to School Searches, the Headline-Making Cases That Affect Your Life.* Walker & Co., 1995.

Marx, Trish, and Sandra Joseph Nunez. *And Justice for All: The Legal Rights of Young People.* Millbrook Press, 1997.

Olney, Ross R., and Patricia J. Olney. *Up against the Law: Your Legal Rights as a Minor.* New York: E.P. Dutton, 1985.

Riekes, Linda, Steve Jenkins, and Armentha Russell. *Juvenile Responsibility and Law.* St. Paul: West Publishing Co., 1990.

In Re Gault
1967

Appellants: Paul L. Gault and Marjorie Gault, parents of Gerald Francis Gault, a minor

Appellee: State of Arizona

Appellants' Claim: That states must give juvenile defendants the same constitutional rights as adult criminal defendants.

Chief Lawyer for Appellants: Norman Dorsen

Chief Lawyer for Appellee: Frank A. Parks, Assistant Attorney General of Arizona

Justices for the Court: Hugo Lafayette Black, William J. Brennan, Jr., Tom C. Clark, William O. Douglas, Abe Fortas, John Marshall Harlan II, Earl Warren, Byron R. White.

Justices Dissenting: Potter Stewart

Date of Decision: May 15, 1967

Decision: The Supreme Court held that Arizona violated Gault's constitutional rights.

Significance: With *Gault,* the Supreme Court said juvenile defendants must have notice of the charges against them, notice of their right to have an attorney, the right to confront and cross-examine witnesses against them, and the right not to testify against themselves.

Gerald Francis Gault was a boy who lived in Gila County, Arizona. Early in 1964, police arrested him for being with a friend who stole a wallet from a woman's purse. For that offense, the juvenile court ordered Gault to be on probation for six months. Probation lets the court supervise someone who has broken the law.

On June 8, 1964, while Gault was still on probation, a neighbor named Mrs. Cook complained to the police that Gault and a friend made an obscene telephone call to her. Police arrested Gault while his parents were at work and took him to the Children's Detention Home. When Gault's mother arrived

Associate Justice Abe Fortas.
Reproduced by permission of Archive Photos, Inc.

home, she had to search to find her son in the detention home. There Superintendent Flagg told Mrs. Gault that there would be a hearing the next day in juvenile court.

The juvenile court held two hearings for Gault's case, one on June 9 and one on June 15. The police and the court never told Gault what law he was accused of breaking. They did not explain that he could have an attorney represent him in court. The court did not even require Mrs. Cook to testify against Gault. Instead, it relied on testimony by Superintendent Flagg that Gault admitted to making an obscene telephone call to Mrs. Cook. According to Judge McGhee, Gault even confessed during the second hearing to making obscene comments on the telephone. Gault's parents denied this, saying that Gault only dialed Mrs. Cook's number and then handed the telephone to his friend.

Based on the testimony, Judge McGhee decided that Gault was a juvenile delinquent. He ordered Gault to be confined in the State Industrial School, a juvenile detention center, until he was twenty-one. Gault was only fifteen at the time, so he faced six years in detention. If Gault had been an adult, his crime would have been punishable by only two months in prison.

The Rights of the Accused

The Fourteenth Amendment of the U.S. Constitution says states may not take away a person's liberty, meaning freedom, without due process of law. Due process means a fair trial. Under the Sixth Amendment, a trial is not fair unless the defendant has notice of the charges against him, the right to have an attorney, and the chance to face and cross-examine witnesses against him. Under the Fifth Amendment, the right against self-incrimination says defendants cannot be forced to make confessions or to testify against themselves.

Juvenile courts are not supposed to be run like criminal courts. They are supposed to help juvenile delinquents become lawful adults by reforming them, not punishing them. For this reason, Arizona's juvenile courts did not give juvenile defendants the same constitutional rights as criminal defendants.

Arizona, however, sent Gault to a detention center for six years for making an obscene telephone call. Gault's parents did not think the state should be allowed to do that without giving their son the same rights as criminal defendants. The Gaults filed a lawsuit against Arizona for holding their son in detention without giving him a fair trial. The Arizona Superior Court dismissed the case and the Arizona Supreme Court affirmed, so the Gaults appealed to the U.S. Supreme Court.

Justice for All

With an 8–1 decision, the Supreme Court ruled in favor of the Gaults, releasing their son from detention. Writing for the Court, Justice Abe Fortas said "neither the Fourteenth Amendment nor the Bill of Rights is for adults alone." Even though a juvenile case is not a criminal case, sending a juvenile to a detention center takes away his liberty and freedom. "Instead of mother and father and sisters and brothers and friends and classmates, his world is peopled by guards, custodians, state employ-

JUVENILE MURDER

On February 29, 2000, a six-year-old boy in Michigan shot and killed his classmate with a .32 caliber semi-automatic handgun. The victim, Kayla Rolland, died from a single gunshot wound to her chest. Both children attended Theo J. Buell Elementary School in Mount Morris Township, where they had an argument the day before the shooting. The boy said Kayla slapped him on the arm during the argument and that he brought the gun to school to scare her.

Investigators learned that the boy was living with his uncle and a nineteen-year-old man named Jamelle Andrew James in a house where drug deals were common. The boy, whose mother had been evicted from her home and whose father was in jail, slept in the house without a bed. Police arrested James for allegedly letting the boy get the stolen gun to take to school. James faced a charge of involuntary manslaughter for Kayla's death, a crime punishable by up to fifteen years in prison.

Because the law says children under seven cannot intend to commit a crime, the boy probably will not face criminal charges. Prosecutor Arthur A. Busch said the boy "is a victim in many ways and we need to put our arms around him and love him." Sadly, friends and family can no longer put their arms around Kayla, who a relative described as a "very well-behaved little girl, loved by everybody."

ees, and 'delinquents' confined with him for anything from waywardness to rape and homicide."

The state cannot deprive a person, even a juvenile delinquent, of liberty without a fair trial. Fortas said Gault's trial was not fair because he did not know which crime he was accused of breaking. Without such notice and an attorney to help him, Gault could not defend himself properly. Without the right to confront and cross-examine witnesses, Gault could not test whether Mrs. Cook had told the truth. Without the right against self-incrimination, Gault may have been pressured to admit to a crime he did not commit. Justice Fortas said that when a juvenile faces detention, he must have these rights and protections during his hearing.

The End of an Era

Justice Potter Stewart filed a dissenting opinion, which means he disagreed with the Court's decision. Justice Stewart agreed that juveniles deserve rights during their hearings. He disagreed, however, that they need the same rights as criminal defendants. The whole purpose of the juvenile justice system is to treat juveniles differently than adult criminals. Stewart feared the Court's decision would turn juvenile cases into criminal trials, sending America back to the days when twelve-year-old boys were sentenced to death like adults.

Suggestions for further reading

Berry, Joy. *Every Kid's Guide to the Juvenile Justice System.* Chicago: Children's Press, 1987.

Claiborne, William. "A 'Life in Chaos' Shaped Young Shooter." *Washington Post,* March 2, 2000.

Claiborne, William. "Man Charged in Schoolgirl's Slaying." *Washington Post,* March 3, 2000.

Gora, Joel M. *Due Process of Law.* National Textbook Co., 1982.

Greenberg, Keith Elliot, and Jeanne Vestal. *Adolescent Rights: Are Young People Equal under the Law?* Twenty First Century Books, 1995.

Hyde, Margaret O. *Juvenile Justice and Injustice.* New York: Franklin Watts, 1977.

Johnson, Joan. *Justice.* New York: Franklin Watts, 1985.

Kowalski, Kathiann M. *Teen Rights: At Home, at School, Online.* Enslow Publishers Inc., 2000.

Landau, Elaine. *Your Legal Rights: From Custody Battles to School Searches, the Headline-Making Cases That Affect Your Life.* Walker & Co., 1995.

Marx, Trish, and Sandra Joseph Nunez. *And Justice for All: The Legal Rights of Young People.* Millbrook Press, 1997.

**JUVENILE
COURTS AND LAW**

Olney, Ross R., and Patricia J. Olney. *Up against the Law: Your Legal Rights as a Minor.* New York: E.P. Dutton, 1985.

"Pupils Return to Site of Child's Slaying." *Washington Post,* March 7, 2000.

Riekes, Linda, Steve Jenkins, and Armentha Russell. *Juvenile Responsibility and Law.* St. Paul: West Publishing Co., 1990.

Goss v. Lopez
1975

Appellants: Norval Goss, et al.

Appellees: Dwight Lopez, et al.

Appellants' Claim: That Ohio schools did not violate the Due Process Clause of the Fourteenth Amendment by suspending public school students without a hearing.

Chief Lawyer for Appellants: Thomas A. Bustin

Chief Lawyer for Appellees: Peter D. Roos

Justices for the Court: William J. Brennan, Jr., William O. Douglas, Thurgood Marshall, Potter Stewart, Byron R. White

Justices Dissenting: Harry A. Blackmun, Warren E. Burger, Lewis F. Powell, Jr., William H. Rehnquist

Date of Decision: January 22, 1975

Decision: The Supreme Court decided that the Ohio schools did violate the Due Process Clause.

Significance: *Goss* requires public schools to give students a chance to explain their conduct before or soon after suspending them from school.

The American justice system is supposed to be fair. When a person is accused of breaking a law, fairness means giving him notice of the charges against him. Fairness also means holding a hearing or trial to give the accused a chance to defend himself. Punishing a person without notice and a hearing is very un-American.

The Due Process Clause of the Fourteenth Amendment protects Americans from unfair treatment by state governments. It says states may not take away life, liberty, or property without "due process of law." Due process usually means notice and a hearing. In *Goss v. Lopez,* the U.S. Supreme Court had to decide whether public schools may suspend students for up to ten days without notice or a hearing.

School Riot

In the early 1970s, an Ohio law allowed public school principals to suspend students for up to ten days without a hearing. Demonstrations related to the Vietnam War and other public issues of the day resulted in a lot of suspensions. Dwight Lopez was a student at Central High School in Columbus, Ohio. Lopez was suspended along with 75 other students after a lunchroom disturbance that damaged school property. Although Lopez said he did not destroy anything, the school suspended him without a hearing and without explaining what he did wrong.

Betty Crome, who attended McGuffey Junior High School in Columbus, attended a demonstration at another high school. The police arrested Crome and many others during the demonstration, but released Crome without charges at the police station. The next day, Crome learned that she had been suspended from school for ten days. Crome also did not get a hearing or an explanation of what she had done wrong.

Lopez and Crome joined a group of other students to sue the Columbus Board of Education and the Columbus Public School System. They wanted the court to strike down the Ohio law that allowed principals to suspend students without a hearing. Lopez and the students said the law violated the Due Process Clause of the Fourteenth Amendment. When the trial court ruled in favor of the students and ordered the schools to remove the suspensions from the students' records, the school system and school board appealed to the U.S. Supreme Court.

High Court Rules

With a 5–4 decision, the Supreme Court ruled in favor of the students. Writing for the Court, Justice Byron R. White said public schools must obey the Due Process Clause. "The Fourteenth Amendment, as now

CALIFORNIA JUSTICE

In the late 1990s, statistics said crime by juveniles was declining. In spite of this trend, violent juvenile crime captured headlines and horrified the nation. In April 1999, two teenagers shot and killed classmates and a teacher at Columbine High School in Colorado before killing themselves. In early 2000, a thirteen-year-old boy in Michigan was convicted for a murder he committed at age eleven. On February 29, 2000, a six-year-old boy in Michigan shot and killed Kayla Rolland, his six-year-old classmate.

On March 7, 2000, voters in California went to the polls to take a stand against juvenile crime. Voting that day in the presidential primary, Californians approved a new law called Proposition 21. The new law toughened California's laws for juvenile crime.

Most juveniles charged with crimes face delinquency proceedings in juvenile court instead of trials in criminal court. For serious crimes, Proposition 21 allowed prosecutors to try teenagers as young as fourteen like adults in criminal courts. Convicted juveniles could receive long sentences in adult prisons. The law also created mandatory jail sentences for minor crimes committed by gang members.

A spokesman for California governor Gray Davis called the new laws necessary. "Just because you're fourteen doesn't mean you're immune to picking up a gun and shooting someone anymore." State Senator Tom Hayden, however, questioned whether the law was a good idea. "If [juveniles] aren't antisocial when they go into prison, that's what they are going to be when they come out."

applied to the States, protects the citizen against the State itself and all of its creatures—Boards of Education not excepted." Students are citizens just like adults, so the Fourteenth Amendment protects them at school.

The Court said the right to attend public school is a property right because it is something valuable that the state provides all students.

When a school suspends a student, it takes away her property right for a certain number of days. Suspension also harms a student's reputation, which is a part of liberty and freedom. Because suspension takes away both a property right and liberty, schools may not suspend students without "due process of law."

Due process usually requires notice and a hearing. The Court decided, however, that it would be impossible to conduct a full hearing for every suspension. It would take too much time and money, both of which are scarce resources in public schools.

The Court decided that schools cannot suspend students without notifying them of the charges, explaining the evidence against them, and giving them an informal hearing. Without notice, a student may not know why he is being suspended. Without a hearing, he cannot explain his conduct or convince the school that he did nothing wrong. The Court said, "Fairness can rarely be obtained by secret, onesided determination of facts decisive of rights."

In most cases, the hearing can be a discussion with the principal before the student is suspended. Something more formal may be appropriate in serious cases. If the student is endangering other students, the hearing may happen soon after the school dismisses the student. In any event, students must get notice of the charges against them and a chance to explain why they should not be suspended. Otherwise, students may not learn the procedures that are supposed to make American justice fair.

Suggestions for further reading

Berry, Joy. *Every Kid's Guide to the Juvenile Justice System.* Chicago: Children's Press, 1987.

Gora, Joel M. *Due Process of Law.* National Textbook Co., 1982.

Greenberg, Keith Elliot, and Jeanne Vestal. *Adolescent Rights: Are Young People Equal under the Law?* Twenty First Century Books, 1995.

Hyde, Margaret O. *Juvenile Justice and Injustice.* New York: Franklin Watts, 1977.

Johnson, Joan. *Justice.* New York: Franklin Watts, 1985.

Kowalski, Kathiann M. *Teen Rights: At Home, at School, Online.* Enslow Publishers Inc., 2000.

Landau, Elaine. *Your Legal Rights: From Custody Battles to School Searches, the Headline-Making Cases That Affect Your Life.* Walker & Co., 1995.

Marx, Trish, and Sandra Joseph Nunez. *And Justice for All: The Legal Rights of Young People.* Millbrook Press, 1997.

Olney, Ross R., and Patricia J. Olney. *Up against the Law: Your Legal Rights as a Minor.* New York: E.P. Dutton, 1985.

Riekes, Linda, Steve Jenkins, and Armentha Russell. *Juvenile Responsibility and Law.* St. Paul: West Publishing Co., 1990.

Sanchez, Rene, and William Booth. "California Toughens Juvenile Crime Laws." *Washington Post,* March 13, 2000.

Goss v. Lopez

Ingraham v. Wright
1977

Petitioners: James Ingraham and Roosevelt Andrews

Respondents: Willie J. Wright, et al.

Petitioners' Claim: That officials at Drew Junior High School violated the Eighth and Fourteenth Amendments by spanking them.

Chief Lawyer for Petitioners: Bruce S. Rogow

Chief Lawyer for Respondents: Frank A. Howard, Jr.

Justices for the Court: Harry A. Blackmun, Warren E. Burger, Lewis F. Powell, Jr., William H. Rehnquist, Potter Stewart

Justices Dissenting: William J. Brennan, Jr., Thurgood Marshall, John Paul Stevens, Byron R. White

Date of Decision: April 19, 1977

Decision: The Supreme Court dismissed the case against Drew Junior High School, saying the school did not violate the students' constitutional rights.

Significance: With *Ingraham,* the Court said corporal punishment, or spanking, is not cruel and unusual punishment. It also said schools can use corporal punishment without giving students a chance to explain their conduct or otherwise defend themselves. If a student is injured by corporal punishment, he may file civil or criminal charges against the school.

The American justice system is supposed to be fair. When a person is accused of breaking a law, fairness means giving him notice of the charges against him. Fairness also means holding a hearing or trial to give the accused a chance to defend himself. Notice and a hearing are part of "due process of law." The Fourteenth Amendment requires states to use due process of law before taking away a person's liberty or freedom.

When a defendant is found guilty after a criminal trial, the Eighth Amendment prevents the government from using cruel and unusual punishments—punishments that are barbaric in a civilized society. Under the Due Process Clause of the Fourteenth Amendment, states must obey the Eighth Amendment and avoid cruel and unusual punishments.

Public schools often punish students who misbehave in school. The punishment can be detention, suspension, expulsion, or corporal punishment. Corporal punishment is punishment inflicted on a student's body, such as spanking. In *Ingraham v. Wright,* the Supreme Court had to decide whether corporal punishment is cruel and unusual under the Eighth Amendment. The Court also had to decide whether schools must give students notice and a hearing before using corporal punishment.

Ingraham
v. Wright

Paddle Licks

In the early 1970s, a Florida law allowed public schools to use corporal punishment to maintain discipline. In Dade County, Florida, a local law said teachers could punish students using a flat wooden paddle measuring less than two feet long, three to four inches wide, and one-half inch thick. Teachers were supposed to get permission from the principal before paddling a student, and then were supposed to limit the paddling to one to five licks on the student's buttocks. Teachers, however, paddled students without getting permission and used more than five licks.

During the 1970-71 school year, James Ingraham and Roosevelt Andrews were students at Drew Junior High School in Dade County. On one occasion in October 1970, Ingraham was slow to respond to his teacher's instructions. As punishment, Ingraham received twenty licks with a paddle while being held over a table in the principal's office. The paddling was so severe that Ingraham missed several days of school with a hematoma, a pool of blood in his buttocks.

That same month, school officials paddled Andrews several times for breaking minor school rules. On two occasions the school paddled

Corporal
punishment, such
as spanking, was
an acceptable form
of discipline in the
United States for
a long time.
AP/Wide World Photos.

Andrews on his arms. One paddling was so bad that Andrews lost full use of his arm for a week. Other students also received severe paddlings. One student got fifty licks for making an obscene telephone call.

Ingraham and Roosevelt filed a lawsuit against the principals of Drew Junior High and the superintendent of the Dade County School System. Ingraham and Roosevelt thought the school violated the Eighth Amendment by using cruel and unusual punishment and the Fourteenth Amendment by paddling them without a hearing. Ingraham and Roosevelt wanted to recover damages and to prevent the school from using corporal punishment in the future. The trial court dismissed the lawsuit, however, and the court of appeals affirmed, so the students took their case to the U.S. Supreme Court.

Corporal Punishment Approved

With a 5–4 decision, the Supreme Court ruled in favor of Drew Junior High. Writing for the Court, Justice Lewis F. Powell, Jr., first addressed whether the Eighth Amendment applies to public schools. The Eighth Amendment says, "Excessive bail shall not be required, nor excessive fines imposed, nor cruel and unusual punishments inflicted." Powell said bail, fines, and punishment are part of the criminal justice system. Public schools are not part of that system, so they do not have to obey the Eighth Amendment.

Bruce S. Rogow, Ingraham and Roosevelt's lawyer, urged the court to apply the Eighth Amendment to corporal punishment in public schools. He said there were few public schools when the United States adopted the amendment in 1791 because most children were educated privately. Americans did not know that someday students would be forced to attend public schools in which corporal punishment would be used. Rogow said it would be absurd to protect criminals but not school children from cruel and unusual punishment.

The Court rejected Rogow's argument. It said public schools are different from prisons. Public schools are open environments where children are free to go home at the end of each day. That means parents are likely to learn if schools are beating their children too severely. That alone is enough to protect the students in most cases.

Attorney Rogow also argued that schools should have to give students a hearing and a chance to defend themselves before using corporal punishment. After all, in *Goss v. Lopez* (1975), the Supreme Court said schools must give students notice and a hearing before suspending them from school for up to ten days. Students should get the same due process rights before being paddled.

The Supreme Court also rejected this argument. Florida laws allowed students who were injured by severe beatings to sue school officials to recover their damages. School officials also could face criminal charges in such cases. Justice Powell said civil and criminal charges are enough to protect students who receive beatings that are unfair or too harsh. Forcing schools to hold a hearing in every case would make cor-

CRUEL AND UNUSUAL MUSIC?

When the Supreme Court decided *Ingraham v. Wright,* only two states outlawed corporal punishment in schools. In the 1990s, twenty-one states banned the practice. As opposition to corporal punishment grew, schools were forced to become more creative with their punishments.

Bruce Janu, a teacher at Riverside High School near Chicago, Illinois, made students in detention listen to Frank Sinatra music. Janu said students grimaced and begged for leniency when hearing the legendary singer croon classic American songs. Teachers at Cedarbrook Middle School in Cheltenham Township, Pennsylvania, sent fighting students to a nature center to work out their differences while caring for plants and animals.

Other teachers chose punishments more traditional yet just as effective. At T.C. Williams High School in Alexandria, Virginia, students who used rainbow colors to spray paint a parking lot had to repaint it black. Joyce Perkins, a teacher in Sour Lake, Texas, forced students who cursed on the playground to call their mothers to repeat the bad language.

poral punishment too expensive and time-consuming. The Supreme Court was not willing to end corporal punishment by making it so costly.

Uncle Sam the Barbarian

Four justices dissented, which means they disagreed with the Court's decision. Justice Byron R. White wrote a dissenting opinion. He thought the Eighth Amendment prevented the government from using cruel and unusual punishment anywhere, not just in the criminal justice system. The United States adopted the amendment because "there are some punishments that are so barbaric and inhumane that we will not permit them to be imposed on anyone." White said that under the Court's decision, the Eighth Amendment protects "a prisoner who is beaten mercilessly" but not "a schoolchild who commits the same breach of discipline."

Suggestions for further reading

Ingraham v. Wright

Berry, Joy. *Every Kid's Guide to the Juvenile Justice System.* Chicago: Children's Press, 1987.

Gora, Joel M. *Due Process of Law.* National Textbook Co., 1982.

Greenberg, Keith Elliot, and Jeanne Vestal. *Adolescent Rights: Are Young People Equal under the Law?* Twenty First Century Books, 1995.

Hyde, Margaret O. *Juvenile Justice and Injustice.* New York: Franklin Watts, 1977.

Jordan, Mary. "Instead of a Hit, Sinatra." *Washington Post,* February 7, 1993.

Kowalski, Kathiann M. *Teen Rights: At Home, at School, Online.* Enslow Publishers Inc., 2000.

Landau, Elaine. *Your Legal Rights: From Custody Battles to School Searches, the Headline-Making Cases That Affect Your Life.* Walker & Co., 1995.

Marx, Trish, and Sandra Joseph Nunez. *And Justice for All: The Legal Rights of Young People.* Millbrook Press, 1997.

Olney, Ross R., and Patricia J. Olney. *Up against the Law: Your Legal Rights as a Minor.* New York: E.P. Dutton, 1985.

Riekes, Linda, Steve Jenkins, and Armentha Russell. *Juvenile Responsibility and Law.* St. Paul: West Publishing Co., 1990.

New Jersey v. T.L.O.
1985

Petitioner: State of New Jersey

Respondent: T.L.O.

Petitioner's Claim: That the assistant vice principal did not violate the Fourth Amendment when he searched T.L.O.'s purse after she had been caught smoking in the restroom.

Chief Lawyer for Petitioner: Allan J. Nodes, Deputy Attorney General of New Jersey

Chief Lawyer for Respondent: Lois De Julio

Justices for the Court: Harry A. Blackmun, Warren E. Burger, Sandra Day O'Connor, Lewis F. Powell, Jr., William H. Rehnquist, Byron R. White

Justices Dissenting: William J. Brennan, Jr., Thurgood Marshall, John Paul Stevens

Date of Decision: January 15, 1985

Decision: The Supreme Court approved the principal's search and affirmed the decision that T.L.O. was a juvenile delinquent.

Significance: With *T.L.O.,* the Supreme Court said public school officials can search students' private belongings without a warrant or probable cause. To conduct a search, public schools need only a reasonable suspicion that a student has violated the law or a school rule.

The Fourth Amendment of the U.S. Constitution protects privacy. It requires the police to get a warrant to search a person, house, or other private place for evidence of a crime. To get a warrant, police must have probable cause, which means good reason to believe the place to be searched has evidence of a crime. In *New Jersey v. T.L.O.*, the Supreme Court had to decide whether public schools needed a warrant and probable cause to search a student's purse.

Smoking in the Girl's Room

On March 7, 1980, a teacher at Piscataway High School in Middlesex County, New Jersey, found two girls smoking in a restroom. One of the girls was T.L.O. (The courts used the girl's initials to protect her privacy.) Smoking in the restroom was against school rules, so the teacher took the girls to the principal's office.

There the girls spoke to Assistant Vice Principal Theodore Choplick. T.L.O.'s friend admitted that she had been smoking in the restroom, but T.L.O. denied it. In fact, T.L.O. said she never smoked. Choplick did not believe this, so he took T.L.O. into his private office. There he demanded to see T.L.O.'s purse. When she gave it to him, Choplick opened it and found a pack a cigarettes inside. Choplick pulled the cigarettes out and accused T.L.O. of lying.

When Choplick looked back into the purse, he saw a package of cigarette rolling papers. In Choplick's experience, students with rolling papers often used marijuana, an illegal drug. Without getting permission, Choplick searched the rest of T.L.O.'s purse. Inside he found a small amount of marijuana, empty plastic bags, a lot of one dollar bills, an index card with a list of students who owed T.L.O. money, and two letters that suggested T.L.O. was selling marijuana.

Choplick notified T.L.O.'s mother of what he found and gave the evidence to the police. T.L.O.'s mother took her to the police station, where T.L.O. confessed that she had been selling marijuana. Using the confession and the evidence from T.L.O.'s purse, the state of New Jersey filed a delinquency lawsuit against T.L.O. in the Juvenile and Domestic Relations Court.

T.L.O.'s lawyer tried to get the evidence against her thrown out of court. The Fourth Amendment requires a warrant and probable cause for most searches. States, including public schools, must obey the Fourth Amendment under the Due Process Clause of the Fourteenth

Amendment. T.L.O.'s lawyer argued that Choplick violated the Fourth Amendment by searching T.L.O.'s purse without a warrant or any reason to believe she had marijuana.

The trial court ruled against T.L.O., found her delinquent, and put her on probation for one year. (Probation allows the court to supervise someone who has broken the law.) T.L.O. appealed to the Supreme Court of New Jersey. That court reversed the judgment against her because it thought Choplick violated her rights by searching her purse. As its last resort, New Jersey took the case to the U.S. Supreme Court.

Students Get Less Privacy Than Adults

With a 6–3 decision, the Supreme Court ruled in favor of New Jersey. Writing for the Court, Justice Byron R. White said the first question was whether public schools must obey the Fourth Amendment. White said they must. The United States adopted the Fourth Amendment to protect Americans from invasion of privacy by the government, not just by the police. Public schools are part of the government.

The next question was whether Choplick violated the Fourth Amendment by searching T.L.O.'s purse without a warrant. The answer depended on balancing T.L.O.'s interest in privacy against the school's interest in maintaining discipline. T.L.O. obviously had an interest in keeping her purse private. Students often carry love letters, money, diaries, and items for grooming and personal hygiene in their purses. Unlike prisoners, who cannot expect much privacy in jail, students do not shed their right to privacy at the schoolhouse gate.

Schools, however, need to maintain discipline for the sake of education. Justice White noted that schools face increasing problems with drugs, guns, and violence. School officials must react quickly to those problems to protect other students and to prevent interference with education. Forcing a school official to get a warrant with probable cause to conduct a search would frustrate quick discipline.

Balancing these interests, the Court decided schools do not need a warrant or probable cause to conduct a search. As Justice Lewis F. Powell, Jr., said in a concurring opinion, "It is simply unrealistic to think that students have the same subjective expectation of privacy as the population generally." Schools cannot, however, search anyone, anywhere, anytime for any reason. To conduct a search, schools must have a reasonable suspicion that a student has broken the law or a school rule.

HORTON V. GOOSE CREEK INDEPENDENT SCHOOL DISTRICT

In 1978, the Goose Creek Independent School District made a plan to fight drugs in school. It decided to bring drug-sniffing dogs to school to sniff students and their lockers and cars. The searches were unannounced and random. The school district used the dogs to sniff anybody, even if there was no reason to believe a student used drugs.

Heather Horton was a student in the Goose Creek school district. One day while she was in the middle of a French test, drug-sniffing dogs entered the room, went up and down the aisles, and sniffed all the students and their desks. Because Heather was afraid of big dogs, the sniff search destroyed her concentration. Although the dogs found nothing on Heather, they reacted after sniffing Robby Horton and Sandra Sanchez. School officials searched Sandra's purse and Robby's pockets, socks, and pant legs. These embarrassing searches revealed no drugs or illegal substances.

Heather, Bobby, and Sandra sued Goose Creek for violating their Fourth Amendment rights. The trial court found in favor of the school, so the students appealed to the U.S. Court of Appeals for the Fifth Circuit. That court said it was all right for the school to use drug-sniffing dogs to search lockers and cars, but not students. Sniffing people with dogs is an invasion of privacy. The court said schools cannot do that without having individual suspicion that a student is carrying drugs or alcohol.

Under this test, Choplick did not violate the Fourth Amendment when he searched T.L.O.'s purse. A teacher saw T.L.O. smoking in the restroom. When T.L.O. denied it, Choplick had good reason to suspect she was lying and that her purse would have evidence of the lie. When Choplick opened T.L.O.'s purse and found rolling papers, he had good reason to believe T.L.O. was either smoking or selling marijuana. Searching her purse to find more evidence was reasonable.

Smokescreen in the Courtroom

Three justices dissented, which means they disagreed with the Court's decision. Justice William J. Brennan, Jr., said school officials, just like the police, should need probable cause to search a student's private belongings. Brennan said, "The Fourth Amendment rests on the principle that a true balance between the individual and society depends on the recognition of 'the right to be let alone-the most comprehensive of rights and the right most valued by civilized men.'"

In his own dissenting opinion, Justice John Paul Stevens said it was wrong to give students less Fourth Amendment protection than adults. "If the Nation's students can be convicted through the use of arbitrary [random] methods destructive of personal liberty, they cannot help but feel that they have been dealt with unfairly."

Suggestions for further reading

Berry, Joy. *Every Kid's Guide to the Juvenile Justice System.* Chicago: Children's Press, 1987.

Franklin, Paula A. *The Fourth Amendment.* Englewood Cliffs: Silver Burdett Press, 1991.

Greenberg, Keith Elliot, and Jeanne Vestal. *Adolescent Rights: Are Young People Equal under the Law?* Twenty First Century Books, 1995.

Hyde, Margaret O. *Juvenile Justice and Injustice.* New York: Franklin Watts, 1977.

Kowalski, Kathiann M. *Teen Rights: At Home, at School, Online.* Enslow Publishers Inc., 2000.

Landau, Elaine. *Your Legal Rights: From Custody Battles to School Searches, the Headline-Making Cases That Affect Your Life.* Walker & Co., 1995.

Marx, Trish, and Sandra Joseph Nunez. *And Justice for All: The Legal Rights of Young People.* Millbrook Press, 1997.

Mikula, Mark, and L. Mpho Mabunda, eds. *Great American Court Cases.* Detroit: The Gale Group, 1999.

Olney, Ross R., and Patricia J. Olney. *Up against the Law: Your Legal Rights as a Minor.* New York: E.P. Dutton, 1985.

Persico, Deborah A. *Mapp v. Ohio: Evidence and Search Warrants.* Enslow Publishers, Inc., 1997.

—. *New Jersey v. T.L.O: Drug Searches in Schools.* Enslow Publishers, Inc., 1998.

Riekes, Linda, Steve Jenkins, and Armentha Russell. *Juvenile Responsibility and Law.* St. Paul: West Publishing Co., 1990.

Wetterer, Charles M. *The Fourth Amendment: Search and Seizure.* Enslow Publishers, Inc., 1998.

New Jersey
v. T.L.O.

SEARCH AND SEIZURE

Search and seizure are tools used by law enforcement officers to fight crime. When a police officer investigates a murder at the scene of the crime, she searches the place. If she finds the murder weapon, she seizes it as evidence. If the police officer finds the criminal, she arrests him. An arrest is a seizure of a person.

Before the United States was born, Great Britain conducted searches and seizures in the American colonies using general warrants and writs of assistance. These were documents that allowed British officer to enter anyone's home to look for smugglers and others who violated trade laws. British officers used these warrants to search homes and arrest people even when there was no evidence of a crime.

America's founders did not want the federal government to have such power. Privacy was something most Americans cherished. They decided to protect privacy by adopting the Fourth Amendment to the U.S. Constitution. The Fourth Amendment says law enforcement offi cials may conduct searches and seizures only when they have good reason to believe there has been a crime.

The Fourth Amendment was written to limit the power of federal law enforcement. Until the mid-1900s, state and local law enforcement did not have to obey the Fourth Amendment. The Fourteenth Amendment, however, says states may not take away liberty, or freedom, unfairly. In *Wolf v. Colorado,* the U.S. Supreme Court decided that the Fourteenth Amendment means state and local law enforcement officials must obey the Fourth Amendment.

Warrants and Probable Cause

The Fourth Amendment says, "The right of the people to be secure in their persons, houses, papers, and effects, against unreasonable searches and seizures, shall not be violated, and no Warrants shall issue, but upon probable cause, supported by Oath or affirmation, and particularly describing the place to be searched, and the persons or things to be seized." In short, the Fourth Amendment requires law enforcement to have a warrant and probable cause to conduct a search and seizure or to make an arrest.

A warrant is a document issued by a neutral person, such as a judge or magistrate. If law enforcement officials were allowed to issue their own warrants, the Fourth Amendment would not give Americans much protection. Police officers could just write a warrant anytime they wanted to enter a house or arrest a person, just like Great Britain did with general warrants. If a neutral person issues the warrant, he can make sure the police have a good reason to conduct the search or seizure.

Under the Fourth Amendment, a warrant must describe the place to be searched and the person or things to be seized. This was meant to end the British practice of using general warrants to search anywhere and arrest anyone. In the United States, for example, a warrant might specify that a police officer may search a person's business. If the officer does not find evidence of a crime, he cannot search the business owner's house and car, too.

To get a warrant, law enforcement officials must prove to the neutral judge or magistrate that they have probable cause. This is a legal term that means the officers have good reason to believe that a crime has been committed. It also means there is good reason to believe the place to be searched has either evidence of the crime or criminals to be arrested. If police officers, informants, or other citizens swear under oath to such information, a neutral magistrate can find probable cause to issue a warrant.

The warrant and probable cause requirements are the general rule under the Fourth Amendment. There are two main exceptions for arrests and automobiles.

Arrests

When a police officer sees someone commit a crime, she may arrest him without getting a warrant. For example, if an officer sees one man attacking another, she may arrest him on the spot. Making the officer get a warrant would allow the criminal to escape. The same rule applies when the police see someone who is wanted for committing a felony. (A felony is a serious crime, such as murder.) To make an arrest without a warrant, however, the officer still needs probable cause to believe the person she arrests has committed a crime.

When an officer makes an arrest, she may conduct a limited search without a warrant. The purpose of the search is to protect her safety and make sure the person she is arresting cannot destroy any evidence. This means the officer may search the person she is arresting and the area right around him. Without a search warrant, the officer cannot arrest someone and then search his entire house. That would violate the privacy the Fourth Amendment is supposed to protect.

Sometimes police officers see suspicious activity without seeing a crime. For example, an officer might see three men pacing back and forth outside a store like they are going to rob it. That is what happened in *Terry v. Ohio* (1968), in which the Supreme Court created the "stop and frisk" rule. This rule allows police officers to stop suspicious persons, frisk them to make sure they have no weapons, and ask a few questions. As long as the police have a good reason to be suspicious, they do not need a warrant or probable cause. If the stop and frisk reveals no wrongdoing, the police must quickly let the person go without making an arrest or conducting a full search of the person's clothes or surroundings.

Automobiles

The invention and widespread use of automobiles in the early 1900s presented a challenge to the Fourth Amendment. People expect to have privacy in their cars. Cars, however, are easy to move. If police officers had to get warrants to search cars, drivers could leave the state to avoid being caught.

In *Carroll v. United States* (1925), the U.S. Supreme Court created an automobile exception to the Fourth Amendment's warrant requirement. Under *Carroll,* if a police officer has probable cause to search a car, he need not get a search warrant. For example, if a police officer sees a car speeding away from a bank that was just robbed, he may stop the car and search it for stolen money without getting a search warrant. The automobile exception even allows the officer to search bags and other closed compartments in the car if he has probable cause to believe he will find evidence of a crime in them.

When police stop a car for a traffic violation, they sometimes see evidence of crimes in plain view in the car. In *Whren v. United States* (1996), police officers saw crack cocaine on the seat of a car they had stopped for making a turn without a signal. Even though the officers did not have probable cause to believe there was a drug violation when they stopped the car, they were allowed to seize the drugs that were in plain view.

There is one automobile exception that allows police to search a car without a warrant or probable cause. Police is some states use checkpoints to search for drunk drivers. At the checkpoint they stop cars and interview drivers, even if they have no reason to believe the driver is drunk. In *Michigan v. Sitz* (1990), the Supreme Court said police may use checkpoints to catch drunk drivers. The Court said checkpoint stops are a small invasion of privacy with the potential to do a lot of good by stopping drunk drivers.

Electronic Searches

The Fourth Amendment mentions people and their "houses, papers, and effects." Until 1967, the Supreme Court said the Fourth Amendment did not apply to electronic searches, such as wiretapping to hear telephone conversations. That changed in *Katz v. United States* (1967). In *Katz,* the federal government learned about illegal gambling by listening to telephone conversations in a public phone booth through a device attached outside the booth. The defendant challenged his conviction, saying the government violated the Fourth Amendment by "searching" his telephone conversations without a warrant and probable cause.

The U.S. Supreme Court agreed. It said the Fourth Amendment was not designed to protect just houses and papers. It was written to protect privacy. When a person has a telephone conversation in a closed booth, he expects it to be private. The federal government cannot invade that privacy without a warrant and probable cause.

Exclusionary Rule

The reason law enforcement officials conduct searches and seizures is to arrest criminals and find evidence to convict them in court. If an officer finds evidence by searching without a warrant, he suffers the penalty of the exclusionary rule. This rule prevents prosecutors from using evidence seized without a valid search warrant. Sometimes that means the prosecutor does not have enough evidence to convict a person who really is guilty. When that happens, the criminal is set free.

Many people have criticized the exclusionary rule. They say criminals should not be allowed to go free just because police officers make an error. The Supreme Court, however, says the exclusionary rule is necessary to make sure the government follows the law. As the Court said in **Mapp v. Ohio** (1961), "Nothing can destroy a government more quickly than its failure to observe its own laws."

Most rules, of course, have an exception, and the exclusionary rule is no different. The good faith exception applies when law enforcement uses a warrant that turns out to be invalid. A warrant is invalid, for example, if the judge issues it without probable cause. In *United States v. Leon* (1984), the Supreme Court said if law enforcement believes in good faith that a warrant is valid, prosecutors can use the evidence to convict the defendant, even if the warrant was not valid. This means criminals will not go free just because a judge or magistrate makes an error when issuing a warrant.

Suggestions for further reading

Franklin, Paula A. *The Fourth Amendment.* Englewood Cliffs: Silver Burdett Press, 1991.

Persico, Deborah A. *Mapp v. Ohio: Evidence and Search Warrants.* Enslow Publishers, Inc., 1997.

—-*New Jersey v. T.I.O: Drug Searches in Schools.* Enslow Publishers, Inc., 1998.

Shattuck, John H.F. *Rights of Privacy.* Skokie: National Textbook Co., 1977.

Wetterer, Charles M. *The Fourth Amendment: Search and Seizure.* Enslow Publishers, Inc., 1998.

Carroll v. United States
1925

Appellants: George Carroll and John Kiro

Appellee: United States

Appellants' Claim: That searching their car for illegal liquor without a search warrant violated the Fourth Amendment.

Chief Lawyer for Appellants: Thomas E. Atkinson and Clare J. Hall

Chief Lawyers for Appellee: John G. Sargent, Attorney General, and James M. Beck, Solicitor General

Justices for the Court: Louis D. Brandeis, Pierce Butler, Joseph McKenna, Edward Terry Sanford, William Howard Taft, Willis Van Devanter

Justices Dissenting: James Clark McReynolds, George Sutherland

Date of Decision: March 2, 1925

Decision: The Supreme Court affirmed appellants' convictions.

Significance: In *Carroll,* the Supreme Court decided that law enforcement officers do not need to get a warrant to search an automobile or other movable vehicle. Law enforcement only needs probable cause to believe the automobile has evidence of a crime.

The Fourth Amendment of the U.S. Constitution protects privacy. It requires law enforcement officers to get a warrant to search a house or other private place for evidence of a crime. To get a warrant, officers

must have probable cause, which means good reason to believe the place to be searched has evidence of a crime. In *Carroll v. United States,* the Supreme Court had to decide whether officers need a warrant to search an automobile.

Bootlegging

In January 1919 the United States adopted the Eighteenth Amendment to the U.S. Constitution. The Eighteenth Amendment made it illegal to manufacture, sell, and transport alcohol in the United States. Because many Americans still wanted to drink alcohol, gangs of organized criminals entered the liquor trade. They made their own alcohol for sale in the United States and smuggled alcohol in from other countries.

Chief Justice William Howard Taft.
Courtesy of the Library of Congress.

Under the Volstead Act, Congress gave federal law enforcement the power to seize vehicles and arrest persons illegally transporting alcohol. Fred Cronenwett was a federal law enforcement officer. On September 29, 1921, Cronenwett went undercover to an apartment in Grand Rapids, Michigan. There he met John Carroll, who took Cronenwett's order for three cases of whiskey. Although Carroll never delivered the whiskey, Cronenwett remembered what Carroll and his car looked like.

A few months later on December 15, Cronenwett and two other officers were driving down the highway from Grand Rapids to Detroit, Michigan, when they passed Carroll and John Kiro going the other way. Smugglers frequently used that road to bring alcohol into the country from Canada. The officers turned around, caught up to Carroll and Kiro, and told them to pull over. The officers then searched the car without a warrant and found 69 quarts of whiskey. The United States convicted Carroll and Kiro of violating the Volstead Act and the Eighteenth Amendment.

The Automobile Exception

Carroll and Kiro appealed their convictions to the U.S. Supreme Court. They said searching their car without a warrant violated the Fourth Amendment. With a 7-2 decision, the Supreme Court disagreed and affirmed their convictions.

Chief Justice William Howard Taft wrote the opinion for the Court. Taft said the Fourth Amendment protects privacy by requiring searches to be reasonable. It does not, however, require a warrant for all searches. When police believe a private home has evidence of a crime, it is reasonable to require them to get a warrant before searching the place. The house cannot go anywhere.

The case is different with automobiles and other moving vehicles. When a police officer sees an automobile that might contain evidence of a crime, there is no time to get a search warrant. The driver can hide the car or leave the state and escape the police officer's jurisdiction, or area of power. That means it is unreasonable to require the police to get a warrant to search an automobile.

Taft emphasized, however, that officers enforcing the Volstead Act could not stop and search cars at random. To conduct any search, the Fourth Amendment requires probable cause, which means good reason to believe the place to be searched has evidence of a crime. That meant officers enforcing the Volstead Act were limited to searching cars that probably contained illegal alcohol.

The Supreme Court decided that Cronenwett and his fellow officers had probable cause to search Carroll and Kiro's car. Cronenwett knew Carroll was involved in the liquor trade because Cronenwett went undercover to order illegal whiskey from Carroll. Cronenwett also knew that alcohol smugglers often used the road between Detroit and Grand Rapids. Chief Justice Taft said that when Cronenwett saw Carroll driving on that road, Cronenwett had good reason to believe the car contained illegal alcohol, which it did.

PROHIBITION

The United States adopted the Eighteenth Amendment to the U.S. Constitution in January 1919. The Eighteenth Amendment made it illegal to manufacture, sell, and transport alcohol, including liquor, beer, and wine, in the United States. This was the beginning of the period of time known as Prohibition.

Prohibition happened for many reasons. Some religious groups, especially Protestants, believed alcohol was immoral. Medical reports suggested that alcohol caused health problems and early death. Politicians in favor of prohibition said it would reduce crime. Prejudice against foreigners who used alcohol also fueled the movement for Prohibition. This was especially true of prejudice toward Germans, against whom the United States fought in World War I from 1917 to 1918.

Prohibition, however, did not work very well. Crime increased as organized criminals supplied illegal alcohol to those who wanted it. Poor people who could not afford good alcohol often were poisoned by bad alcohol. Closing saloons eliminated a popular meeting place for working class Americans. When the Great Depression hit the United States in the 1930s, Americans decided legalizing alcohol would help the economy. The United States ended prohibition with the Twenty-First Amendment to the Constitution in 1932.

Uncommon Law

Two justices dissented, meaning they disagreed with the Court's decision. Justice James Clark McReynolds wrote a dissenting opinion. McReynolds disagreed that the Fourth Amendment allows law enforcement to search a car without a warrant.

Under English common law at the time the United States adopted the Fourth Amendment, police could arrest and search a man without a warrant only if he was wanted for a felony or had committed a misdemeanor in front of the officer. (Felonies are serious crimes such as murder, while misdemeanors are less serious crimes such as reckless driving.) Because violating the Volstead Act was a misdemeanor, McReynolds thought Cronenwett needed a warrant to arrest Carroll and Kiro and search their car.

McReynolds also did not think Cronenwett had probable cause to search the car. McReynolds asked, "Has it come about that merely because a man once agreed to deliver whiskey, but did not, he may be arrested whenever thereafter he ventures to drive an automobile on the road to Detroit!"

Despite McReynolds's concerns, *Carroll* has remained good law. Federal and state law enforcement officers with probable cause to believe a car has evidence of a crime may stop and search it without a warrant.

Suggestions for further reading

Baughman, Judith S., ed. *American Decades: 1920-1929.* Detroit: Gale Research, 1996.

Franklin, Paula A. *The Fourth Amendment.* Englewood Cliffs: Silver Burdett Press, 1991.

Persico, Deborah A. *Mapp v. Ohio: Evidence and Search Warrants.* Enslow Publishers, Inc., 1997.

——. *New Jersey v. T.L.O: Drug Searches in Schools.* Enslow Publishers, Inc., 1998.

Shattuck, John H.F. *Rights of Privacy.* Skokie: National Textbook Co., 1977.

Vile, John R. *Encyclopedia of Constitutional Amendments, Proposed Amendments, and Amending Issues.* Santa Barbara: ABC-CLIO, Inc., 1996.

Wetterer, Charles M. *The Fourth Amendment: Search and Seizure.* Enslow Publishers, Inc., 1998.

Mapp v. Ohio
1961

Appellant: Dollree Mapp

Appellee: State of Ohio

Appellant's Claim: That convicting her with evidence obtained during an illegal search violated the Fourth Amendment.

Chief Lawyer for Appellant: A.L. Kearns

Chief Lawyer for Appellee: Gertrude Bauer Mahon

Justices for the Court: Hugo Lafayette Black, William J. Brennan, Jr., Tom C. Clark, William O. Douglas, Potter Stewart, Earl Warren

Justices Dissenting: Felix Frankfurter, John Marshall Harlan II, Charles Evans Whittaker

Date of Decision: June 19, 1961

Decision: The Supreme Court reversed Mapp's conviction.

Significance: Until *Mapp,* states did not have to obey the exclusionary rule, which prevents the government from using evidence its gets during an illegal search and seizure. By forcing states to obey the exclusionary rule, the Supreme Court strengthened the Fourth Amendment's protection of privacy for Americans.

A persons privacy is protected by the Fourth Amendment of the U.S. Constitution. The Fourth Amendment requires law enforcement officers to get a warrant to search a house or other private place for evidence of a

Associate Justice Tom C. Clark.
Courtesy of the Supreme Court of the United States.

crime. In *Weeks v. United States* (1914), the U.S. Supreme Court created the exclusionary rule. That rule prevents the federal government from convicting a defendant with evidence the government finds during an illegal search without a warrant.

In *Wolf v. Colorado* (1949), the Supreme Court said state and local governments must obey the Fourth Amendment by getting a warrant to conduct a search. The Court also said, however, that the exclusionary rule does not apply to the states. That allowed state prosecutors to use evidence seized during illegal searches without warrants. *Mapp v. Ohio* gave the Supreme Court the chance to overrule *Wolf* and apply the exclusionary rule to the states.

Breaking and Entering

On May 23, 1957, police officers in Cleveland, Ohio, had information that a bombing suspect was hiding in the house of Dollree Mapp. They also thought the house had illegal gambling equipment. When the police went to Mapp's house to search it, however, Mapp called her attorney and then refused to let the police in without a search warrant.

The police stationed themselves outside Mapp's home to watch the place. Three hours later they sought entrance again. When Mapp did not come to the door immediately, the police forced it open and entered the house. Mapp demanded to see a search warrant and grabbed the piece of paper the police waved at her. The police struggled with Mapp to get the paper back, hurting her in the process, and then put her in handcuffs. The paper was not really a search warrant.

The police searched Mapp's entire house, looking in rooms, leafing through photo albums and personal papers, and opening a trunk. They never found the bombing suspect or any gambling equipment. They did, however, find obscene materials that were illegal to have under Ohio's obscenity law. The police charged Mapp with violating that law and the court convicted her and put her in prison.

The police entered Dollree Mapp's house without a search warrant. Reproduced by permission of AP/Wide World Photos.

Mapp appealed her conviction. Her main argument was that Ohio's obscenity law violated her right to freedom of thought under the First Amendment. The Ohio Supreme Court rejected this argument. Mapp also argued that Ohio should not be allowed to convict her with evidence found during an illegal search without a warrant. Relying on *Wolf,* the Ohio Supreme Court also rejected this argument and affirmed Mapp's conviction. Mapp appealed her case to the U.S. Supreme Court.

EXCLUSIONARY RULE EXCEPTIONS

The exclusionary rule prevents the government from using evidence at trial that it gets during and illegal search and seizure. There are, however, two exceptions to this rule. The good faith exception applies when law enforcement uses a search warrant that turns out to be illegal. If law enforcement truly believed the warrant was valid, the government may use the illegally obtained evidence at a criminal trial.

The second exception is called the inevitable discovery rule. It applies when law enforcement conducts an illegal search and seizure to get evidence that it eventually would have found legally. Again, the government may use such evidence at trial. Under both exceptions, the Supreme Court considers the violation of the defendant's constitutional rights to be harmless compared to the cost of letting the defendant go free.

Law Over Anarchy

With a 6–3 decision, the Supreme Court reversed Mapp's conviction. Writing for the Court, Justice Tom C. Clark ignored the First Amendment issue and focused on the illegal search and seizure. Clark and the rest of the majority decided to overrule *Wolf* and apply the exclusionary rule to the states.

Clark emphasized that the Fourth Amendment was designed to protect privacy for Americans in their homes. Without the exclusionary rule, state police are encouraged to invade privacy with illegal searches and seizures. It also encourages federal law enforcement to violate the Fourth Amendment and then give the illegal evidence to the states.

Clark said the exclusionary rule not only protects privacy, but also fosters respect for the law. "Nothing can destroy a government more quickly than its failure to observe its own laws. . . . If the Government becomes a lawbreaker, it breeds contempt [disrespect] for the law; it invites every man to become a law unto himself; it invites anarchy."

**SEARCH AND
SEIZURE**

Suggestions for further reading

Franklin, Paula A. *The Fourth Amendment.* Englewood Cliffs: Silver Burdett Press, 1991.

Persico, Deborah A. *Mapp v. Ohio: Evidence and Search Warrants.* Enslow Publishers, Inc., 1997.

——. *New Jersey v. T.L.O: Drug Searches in Schools.* Enslow Publishers, Inc., 1998.

Shattuck, John H.F. *Rights of Privacy.* Skokie: National Textbook Co., 1977.

Wetterer, Charles M. *The Fourth Amendment: Search and Seizure.* Enslow Publishers, Inc., 1998.

Witt, Elder, ed. *Guide to the U.S. Supreme Court,* 2d ed. Washington, D.C.: Congressional Quarterly, 1990.

Terry v. Ohio
1968

Petitioner: John W. Terry

Respondent: State of Ohio

Petitioner's Claim: That Officer Martin McFadden violated the Fourth Amendment when he stopped and frisked petitioner on the streets of Cleveland without probable cause.

Chief Lawyer for Petitioner: Louis Stokes

Chief Lawyer for Respondent: Reuben M. Payne

Justices for the Court: Hugo Lafayette Black, William J. Brennan, Jr., Abe Fortas, John Marshall Harlan II, Thurgood Marshall, Potter Stewart, Earl Warren, Byron R. White

Justices Dissenting: William O. Douglas

Date of Decision: June 10, 1968

Decision: The Supreme Court affirmed Terry's conviction for carrying a concealed weapon.

Significance: In *Terry*, the Supreme Court said police officers do not need probable cause to stop and frisk suspicious people who might be carrying weapons.

The Fourth Amendment of the U.S. Constitution protects privacy. It requires law enforcement officers to have probable cause before they seize or arrest a person and search his belongings. Probable cause means good reason to believe that the person has committed a crime. In *Terry v.*

Ohio, the Supreme Court had to decide whether the police can stop and frisk a suspicious person in public without probable cause.

Casing the Joint

Martin McFadden, a police officer and detective for 39 years, was patrolling the streets of Cleveland, Ohio, on October 31, 1963. That afternoon, McFadden saw two men, John W. Terry and Richard D. Chilton, standing on a street corner. McFadden's experience told him the men looked suspicious, so he began to observe them from a nearby store entrance.

As McFadden watched, Terry and Chilton took turns walking past and looking inside a store window. Between them the men walked back and forth past the store twelve times. At that point a third man joined them for a brief discussion on the street corner. When the third man left, Terry and Chilton continued to take turns walking past the same store window to peer inside. Ten minutes later they headed down the street in the same direction as the third man whom they had met.

McFadden believed the three men were getting ready to rob the store they were watching. Because it was daytime, he also suspected they were armed and dangerous. McFadden followed Terry and Chilton and found them in front of Zucker's store with the third man. McFadden introduced himself as a police officer and asked for their names. When the men only mumbled in response, McFadden grabbed Terry, spun him around to face the other two men, and frisked him. McFadden felt a gun inside Terry's coat. He immediately ordered the three men to go into Zucker's store.

When everyone was inside, McFadden removed Terry's overcoat and found a .38 caliber revolver inside. McFadden ordered the three men to put their hands up on the wall. He then patted down Chilton and the third man to find a revolver in Chilton's overcoat. Ohio convicted Terry and Chilton of carrying concealed weapons.

Terry and Chilton appealed their convictions. They argued that McFadden's stop and frisk was a search and seizure under the Fourth Amendment. McFadden conducted the stop and frisk without probable cause to believe that Terry and Chilton had committed a crime. After all, there was nothing illegal about walking around the streets of Cleveland. Without probable cause, Terry and Chilton said the stop and frisk was illegal under the Fourth Amendment. If that was true, Ohio was not

ILLINOIS V. WARDLOW

In 1995, Sam Wardlow was on the streets of Chicago in an area known for drug deals. When a caravan of four police cars appeared, Wardlow fled on foot. Officers Nolan and Harvey chased and caught Wardlow on a nearby street. When Officer Nolan frisked Wardlow, he found a .38 caliber handgun. Illinois convicted Wardlow of unlawful use of a weapon by a felon.

Wardlow appealed his conviction. Wardlow argued that the police did not have any reason to be suspicious of him. That meant the stop and frisk was an illegal search and seizure under the Fourth Amendment. The Supreme Court disagreed and affirmed Wardlow's conviction. Writing for the Court, Chief Justice William H. Rehnquist said police are allowed to stop a man who flees from them in a high crime area. The circumstances of the flight give the police reason to be suspicious and to investigate.

allowed to use the evidence of the concealed weapons, meaning the cases should have been dismissed for lack of evidence.

The court of appeals rejected this argument and affirmed Terry's and Chilton's convictions. When Terry and Chilton appealed to the Ohio Supreme Court, it dismissed the appeal without considering the case. Terry and Chilton finally asked the U.S. Supreme Court to review the case. Before it did, Chilton died, so the Supreme Court was left to consider Terry's case.

Stop and Frisk Approved

With an 8–1 decision, the Supreme Court affirmed Terry's conviction. Writing for the Court, Chief Justice Earl Warren approved the stop-and-frisk tactic as a legal police procedure.

Warren said the Fourth Amendment is designed to protect privacy. A stop and frisk is a search and seizure that invades a person's privacy.

When the police stop and frisk someone who is innocent of a crime, it is especially offensive. Police, however, need to investigate suspicious activity. When they do, they need to protect themselves from people who might be armed and dangerous.

Warren rejected Terry's argument that police need probable cause to conduct a stop and frisk. He said the Fourth Amendment does not require probable cause for all searches and seizures. It only requires that a search and seizure be reasonable. When police see suspicious activity by people who might be armed and dangerous, it is reasonable to stop them for questions and frisk them for weapons. If the stop and frisk reveals no illegal activity, the police must let them go immediately. Warren said this result created the best balance between the right of privacy and needs of law enforcement.

Justice William O. Douglas wrote a dissenting opinion, meaning he disagreed with the Court's decision. Douglas said the Fourth Amendment requires probable cause for every search and seizure. When the Court creates an exception, Americans lose protection for privacy. Despite Douglas's concern, *Terry* remains the law of the land. Police are allowed to stop suspicious people and frisk them for weapons without reason to believe they have committed a crime.

Suggestions for further reading

Franklin, Paula A. *The Fourth Amendment.* Englewood Cliffs: Silver Burdett Press, 1991.

Greenhouse, Linda. "Supreme Court Roundup; Flight Can Justify Search By Police, High Court Rules." *New York Times,* January 13, 2000.

Persico, Deborah A. *Mapp v. Ohio: Evidence and Search Warrants.* Enslow Publishers, Inc., 1997.

——. *New Jersey v. T.L.O: Drug Searches in Schools.* Enslow Publishers, Inc., 1998.

Shattuck, John H.F. *Rights of Privacy.* Skokie: National Textbook Co., 1977.

Wetterer, Charles M. *The Fourth Amendment: Search and Seizure.* Enslow Publishers, Inc., 1998.

United States v. Santana
1976

Petitioner: United States

Respondents: Mom Santana, et al.

Petitioner's Claim: That the police did not violate the
Fourth Amendment when they arrested Mom Santana in
her home and searched her for drug money.

Chief Lawyer for Petitioner: Frank H. Easterbrook

Chief Lawyer for Respondent: Dennis H. Eisman

Justices for the Court: Harry A. Blackmun, Warren E. Burger,
Lewis F. Powell, Jr., William H. Rehnquist, John Paul Stevens,
Potter Stewart, Byron R. White

Justices Dissenting: William J. Brennan, Jr., Thurgood Marshall

Date of Decision: June 24, 1976

Decision: The Supreme Court said the police did not
violate the Fourth Amendment.

Significance: With *Santana,* the Supreme Court said police officers in hot pursuit of a criminal suspect do not need a warrant to
chase her into her home and arrest her.

The Fourth Amendment of the U.S. Constitution protects privacy. It
requires police officers to have a warrant and probable cause before they
arrest a person and search her in her home. A warrant is a document that
a neutral magistrate issues when there is probable cause to arrest some-

one. Probable cause means good reason to believe the person has committed a crime. In *United States v. Santana* (1976), the Supreme Court had to decide whether the police need a warrant to arrest a person who retreats into her home after the police begin to chase her.

Drug Bust

Michael Gilletti was an undercover officer with the Philadelphia Narcotics Squad. On August 16, 1974, Gilletti arranged to buy heroin, a narcotic drug, from Patricia McCafferty. McCafferty told Gilletti the heroin would cost $115 and that they would get it from Mom Santana.

Gilletti told his supervisors about the plan and the Narcotics Squad planned a drug bust. Gilletti recorded the serial numbers for $110 in marked bills and went to meet McCafferty, who got into Gilletti's car and directed him to Mom Santana's house. There McCafferty took the money from Gilletti and went inside. When she returned a short time later, McCafferty got into Gilletti's car and they drove away together. When McCafferty pulled envelopes with heroin out of her bra, Gilletti stopped the car, showed McCafferty his badge, and arrested her.

McCafferty told Gilletti that Mom Santana had the marked money. Gilletti told this to Sergeant Pruitt, who went with his officers back to Mom Santana's house while Gilletti took McCafferty to the police station. At the house, Pruitt and his officers saw Mom Santana standing in the doorway holding a brown paper bag. The police stopped their car fifteen feet from Santana and got out of the car shouting "police" and showing their badges. As the officers approached Santana, she retreated into her home.

The police followed Mom Santana inside and caught her in the foyer. During a brief struggle, two bundles of packets with powder fell out of the brown paper bag. The powder turned out to be heroin. When the police ordered Santana to empty her pockets, she produced $70 of Gilletti's marked money.

The United States filed criminal charges against Mom Santana for possessing heroin with the intention of selling it. At her trial, Santana made a motion to exclude the evidence of the heroin and the marked money. Santana said the police violated her Fourth Amendment rights by arresting and searching her in her home without a warrant. The government is not allowed to use evidence it finds when it violates the Fourth Amendment. Without the heroin and the marked money, the government would not have a case against Santana.

MINNESOTA V. OLSON

On July 18, 1987, Joseph Ecker robbed an Amoco gasoline station in Minneapolis, Minnesota, killed the station manager, and escaped in a car driven by Rob Olson. Police found and arrested Ecker that same day. The next day, police received a call from a woman who said Olson was hiding in a house where he was staying with two women.

Police surrounded the house and then telephoned to ask Olson to come out. The woman who answered the phone said Olson was not there, but police heard Olson tell her to say that. Without a warrant, the police entered the home, found Olson hiding in a closet, and arrested him. Olson soon confessed to the crime and was convicted of murder, robbery, and assault.

On appeal, the Minnesota Supreme Court reversed Olson's conviction and the U.S. Supreme Court agreed. The Supreme Court said Olson expected privacy in the house where he was staying. The Fourth Amendment protects that privacy by requiring police officers to get a warrant before entering a home. Unlike in *Santana,* the police were not in hot pursuit of Olson. Instead, they surrounded the home to prevent Olson from escaping. There was plenty of time to get a warrant before entering the home to arrest Olson. Because the police failed to get a warrant, Olson's arrest and confession were illegal under the Fourth Amendment.

The trial court granted Santana's motion. It said the government cannot enter a person's house to arrest her without a warrant. The court of appeals affirmed this decision, so the United States took the case to the U.S. Supreme Court.

Mom Busted

With a 7–2 decision, the Supreme Court ruled in favor of the United States. Writing for the Court, Justice William H. Rehnquist said the Fourth Amendment protects privacy by requiring probable cause before an arrest. From what McCafferty told Gilletti, the police had probable cause to believe Mom Santana was selling drugs.

Justice Rehnquist said the Fourth Amendment does not require police to have a warrant for every arrest. Police only need a warrant to enter a private place, such as a home. Mom Santana was not in her home when Sergeant Pruitt and his team tried to arrest her. She was standing in the doorway in full view of the public. Anything people choose to expose to the public is not private.

Rehnquist said Santana could not frustrate a legal arrest by retreating into her home. Rehnquist called this the "hot pursuit" doctrine. When police are in hot pursuit of a criminal suspect, they may follow her into her home if stopping to get a warrant would frustrate the arrest. In this case, Santana could have gotten rid of the marked money while police went to get a warrant. Under those circumstances, the police were allowed to follow Santana into her house. They did not violate the Fourth Amendment.

Suggestions for further reading

Franklin, Paula A. *The Fourth Amendment.* Englewood Cliffs: Silver Burdett Press, 1991.

Persico, Deborah A. *Mapp v. Ohio: Evidence and Search Warrants.* Enslow Publishers, Inc., 1997.

—. *New Jersey v. T.L.O: Drug Searches in Schools.* Enslow Publishers, Inc., 1998.

Shattuck, John H.F. *Rights of Privacy.* Skokie: National Textbook Co., 1977.

Wetterer, Charles M. *The Fourth Amendment: Search and Seizure.* Enslow Publishers, Inc., 1998.

Arkansas v. Sanders
1979

Petitioner: State of Arkansas

Respondent: Lonnie James Sanders

Petitioner's Claim: That the police did not violate the
Fourth Amendment by searching Sanders's suitcase
without a search warrant.

Chief Lawyer for Petitioner: Joseph H. Purvis, Deputy
Attorney General of Arkansas

Chief Lawyer for Respondent: Jack T. Lassiter

Justices for the Court: Warren E. Burger,
Thurgood Marshall, Lewis F. Powell, Jr., John Paul Stevens,
Potter Stewart, Byron R. White

Justices Dissenting: Harry A. Blackmun, William H. Rehnquist

Date of Decision: June 20, 1979

Decision: The Supreme Court said the search
violated the Fourth Amendment.

Significance: With *Sanders,* the Supreme Court said police may
not search luggage without a warrant unless there are exigent, or
urgent, circumstances.

A person's privacy is protected by the Fourth Amendment of the U.S.
Constitution. The Fourth Amendment requires searches and seizures by
the government to be reasonable. In most cases, law enforcement officers
must get a warrant to search a house or other private place for evidence of

a crime. To get a warrant, officers must have probable cause, which means good reason to believe the place to be searched has evidence of a crime.

There are exceptions to the warrant requirement. The automobile exception allows police to stop and search a car without a warrant when they have probable cause to believe the car is holding evidence of a crime. There are two reasons for the automobile exception. First, because a car can be moved, police might lose the evidence if they were forced to get a warrant. Second, Americans have less privacy in their cars than in their homes. In *Arkansas v. Sanders,* the U.S. Supreme Court had to decide whether police could search a suitcase in the trunk of a car without a warrant.

The Man With the Green Suitcase

David Isom was an officer with the police department in Little Rock, Arkansas. On April 23, 1976, an informant told Isom that at 4:35 in the afternoon, Lonnie James Sanders would arrive at the Little Rock airport carrying a green suitcase with marijuana inside. Isom believed the informant because just three months earlier, the informant gave the police information that led to Sanders's arrest and conviction for possessing marijuana.

Acting on the informant's tip, Isom and two other police officers placed the airport under surveillance. As the informant predicted, Sanders appeared at gate No. 1, deposited some luggage in a taxicab, and then went to the baggage claim area. There Sanders met a man named David Rambo. Rambo waited while Sanders retrieved a green suitcase from the airport baggage service. Sanders gave the suitcase to Rambo and then went to his taxicab, where Rambo joined him a short while later. Rambo put the suitcase into the trunk and rode off in the taxicab with Sanders.

Isom and one of his fellow officers pursued the taxicab. With help from a patrol car, they stopped the taxicab several blocks from the airport. At the request of the police, the taxi driver opened the trunk of the car, where the officers found the green suitcase. Without asking for permission, the police opened the suitcase and found 9.3 pounds of marijuana in ten plastic bags.

On October 14, 1976, Arkansas charged Sanders and Rambo with possession of marijuana with intent to deliver. Before trial, Sanders made a motion to suppress, or get rid of, the marijuana evidence. When the government violates the Fourth Amendment, it is not allowed to use the evidence it finds to convict the defendant. Sanders said the police violated his Fourth Amendment rights by opening the suitcase without a search warrant. Arkansas argued that the search was legal under the automobile exception to the warrant requirement.

The trial court denied Sanders's motion, the jury convicted him, and the court sentenced him to ten years in prison and fined him $15,000. Sanders appealed to the Supreme Court of Arkansas. That court ruled in his favor, saying the trial court should have suppressed the marijuana evidence because the police violated the Fourth Amendment. Faced with having to dismiss the case against Sanders, Arkansas took the case to the U.S. Supreme Court.

Privacy Prevails

With a 7–2 decision, the Supreme Court ruled in favor of Sanders. Writing for the Court, Justice Lewis F. Powell, Jr., said the automobile exception did not apply to the search of Sanders's suitcase. Once the police had the suitcase, there was no danger that it would be taken away like an automobile.

Powell said people usually keep personal belongings in their luggage. That means they expect the luggage to be private. The Fourth Amendment protects privacy by requiring the police to get a warrant by proving they have probable cause to search a private item. After seizing Sanders's suitcase, Isom and his fellow officer should have asked a judge or magistrate for a warrant before searching it. Because they did not, Arkansas could not use the marijuana evidence to convict Sanders of a crime.

Criminal Justice Fails?

Two justices dissented, which means they disagreed with the Court's opinion. Justice Harry A. Blackmun wrote a dissenting opinion. Blackmun thought Isom was allowed to search the suitcase under the automobile exception to the warrant requirement. Why should Isom have stopped the search when he found a piece of luggage that was supposed to contain criminal evidence? Blackmun thought the Court's decision created an unrealistic difference between searching cars and searching things found in cars. He feared this would allow many guilty people to go free.

THE WAR ON DRUGS

The South American country of Colombia is a major battleground in the war on drugs. According to estimates by the U.S. Drug Enforcement Administration, 80 percent of the cocaine and heroin in the United States comes from Colombia.

In January 2000, President William J. Clinton announced a plan to make the Colombian government a partner in the war on drugs. Clinton asked Congress to approve a $1.3 billion aid package to Colombia. Most of the aid would equip and fund the Colombian military. Clinton's request included thirty Black Hawk helicopters and fifteen UH-1N Huey helicopters.

Clinton's plan received criticism from members of Congress. Many Republicans think the United States should fund American drug-fighting police instead of the Colombian military. They say the Colombian military uses aid packages to fight guerrillas (independent bands of soldiers) who are trying to overthrow the Colombian government. Amnesty International and many Democrats added concerns that the Colombian military is responsible for many human rights violations, including restricting military service to uneducated people. The Clinton administration, however, believes fighting Colombian guerrillas is a necessary part of winning the war on drugs.

Suggestions for further reading

Deyoung, Karen. "Clinton Plans to Seek $1.3 Billion to Stem Colombian Drug Flow." *Washington Post,* January 12, 2000.

Deyoung, Karen. "Colombia Anti-Drug Plan Draws Hill Fire." *Washington Post,* February 16, 2000.

Franklin, Paula A. *The Fourth Amendment.* Englewood Cliffs: Silver Burdett Press, 1991.

Persico, Deborah A. *Mapp v. Ohio: Evidence and Search Warrants.* Enslow Publishers, Inc., 1997.

Peters, Ralph. "The U.S. Is Setting a Trap for Itself in Colombia." *Washington Post,* March 5, 2000.

Shattuck, John H.F. *Rights of Privacy.* Skokie: National Textbook Co., 1977.

Wetterer, Charles M. *The Fourth Amendment: Search and Seizure.* Enslow Publishers, Inc., 1998.

Arkansas v. Sanders

New York v. Belton
1981

Petitioner: State of New York

Respondent: Roger Belton

Petitioner's Claim: That a police officer did not violate the Fourth Amendment by searching Belton's jacket in a car without a search warrant.

Chief Lawyer for Petitioner: James R. Harvey

Chief Lawyer for Respondent: Paul J. Cambria, Jr.

Justices for the Court: Harry A. Blackmun, Warren E. Burger, Lewis F. Powell, Jr., William H. Rehnquist, John Paul Stevens, Potter Stewart

Justices Dissenting: William J. Brennan, Jr., Thurgood Marshall, Byron R. White

Date of Decision: July 1, 1981

Decision: The Supreme Court approved the police officer's search.

Significance: With *Belton,* the Supreme Court said whenever the police arrest people in a car, they may search the passenger compartment without a warrant.

The Fourth Amendment of the U.S. Constitution protects privacy. Any searches and seizures undertaken by the government are required to be reasonable. In most cases, law enforcement officers must get a warrant to search a house or other private place for evidence of a crime. To get a warrant, officers must have probable cause, which means good reason to believe the place to be searched has evidence of a crime.

There are exceptions to the warrant requirement. When police officers see a person commit a felony or misdemeanor, they may arrest the person without a warrant. During the arrest, the police need to protect themselves from any weapons the criminal might have. Police also need to make sure the criminal does not destroy any evidence during the arrest. Because of these needs, police are allowed to search a person and his surroundings without a warrant when they arrest him. In *New York v. Belton,* the Supreme Court had to decide whether police could search inside a car after arresting the car's occupants.

Smoking

On April 9, 1978, New York State Trooper Douglas Nicot was driving an unmarked police car on the New York Thruway. An automobile passed Nicot going well over the speed limit. Nicot chased the car and ordered it's driver to pull off the road. There were four men in the car, including Roger Belton.

Nicot asked to see the driver's license and automobile registration. He learned that none of the four men owned the car or was related to its owner. During the stop, Nicot smelled burnt marijuana and saw an envelope marked "Supergold" on the floor of the car. In Nicot's experience, Supergold meant marijuana. Because possessing marijuana was illegal, Nicot ordered the four men to get out of the car and arrested them.

After separating the men outside the car and patting them down, Nicot returned to the car to search it. Inside the envelope he found marijuana, just as he suspected he would. Nicot then searched the entire passenger compartment. On the back seat he found a black leather jacket. Nicot unzipped the pockets and found cocaine and Belton's identification card inside. Nicot finally took everyone to a nearby police station.

New York charged Belton with criminal possession of cocaine, a controlled substance. At Belton's trial, he made a motion to get rid of the cocaine evidence. Belton argued that Nicot violated the Fourth Amendment by searching his jacket without a search warrant. Belton said Nicot did not need to search the jacket to protect himself or the evidence because the four men already were out of the car.

The trial court denied Belton's motion. Belton pleaded guilty to a lesser offense and reserved his right to appeal the issue of whether Nicot

POTTER STEWART

Potter Stewart, who wrote the Supreme Court's opinion in *New York v. Belton,* was born on January 23, 1915, in Jackson, Michigan. After graduating from Yale Law School in 1941, Stewart worked in law firms in New York City and Cincinnati before entering Cincinnati politics in 1949. After Stewart supported Dwight D. Eisenhower's presidential campaign in 1952, Eisenhower appointed Stewart to the Sixth Circuit Court of Appeals in 1954. At thirty-nine, Stewart was the youngest federal judge in the country.

Eisenhower appointed Stewart to the Supreme Court in 1958. Stewart was a moderate justice, often casting the deciding vote in close cases. In 1962, he was the only dissenter in a case banning prayer in public schools. In an obscenity case in 1964, Stewart said that while he could not define obscenity, "I know it when I see it." In 1969, press reports suggested that Stewart was being considered to succeed Earl Warren as chief justice of the Supreme Court. Privately, Stewart asked President Richard M. Nixon not to name him to that post. In 1981 at age sixty-six, Stewart became the youngest justice to resign from the Supreme Court. He died on December 7, 1985, after suffering a stroke.

violated the Fourth Amendment. On appeal, the Appellate Division said Nicot's search was lawful. The New York Court of Appeals, however, reversed. It said Nicot did not need to search Belton's jacket to protect himself or the evidence. Belton, then, should have gotten a warrant before searching the jacket. Faced with having to dismiss Belton's case, New York took the case to the U.S. Supreme Court.

Bright-Line Rules

With a 6–3 decision, the Supreme Court reversed again and ruled in favor of New York. Writing for the Court, Justice Potter Stewart said confusing cases were making it hard for police officers to know what they could search without a warrant. The Supreme Court decided to change that with a clear, bright-line rule. It held that when police officers lawfully arrest the occupants of an automobile, they may search the entire passenger compartment and anything in it without a search warrant. With a clear rule, police would have no doubt what their powers are under the Fourth Amendment.

This new rule made Nicot's search lawful under the Fourth Amendment. Nicot was allowed to arrest Belton and his companions without a warrant because he saw them with marijuana. That arrest allowed Nicot to search the passenger compartment of the car, including Belton's jacket in the back seat. Because Nicot found the cocaine without violating the Fourth Amendment, New York was allowed to use the cocaine to charge Belton with criminal possession of a controlled substance.

Fourth Amendment Falls

Three justices dissented, which means they disagreed with the Court's decision. Justice William J. Brennan wrote a dissenting opinion. Brennan said the Fourth Amendment is an important tool for protecting privacy in the United States. Exceptions to the warrant requirement must be narrow if privacy is to survive. The Court's decision hurt privacy by allowing police officers to search cars without a warrant, probable cause, or any danger to police officers and evidence. Brennan did not think helping police officers with a bright-line rule was a good reason for disregarding the Fourth Amendment.

Suggestions for further reading

Franklin, Paula A. *The Fourth Amendment.* Englewood Cliffs: Silver Burdett Press, 1991.

Gareffa, Peter M., ed. *Contemporary Newsmakers.* Detroit: Gale Research Company, 1986.

Persico, Deborah A. *Mapp v. Ohio: Evidence and Search Warrants.* Enslow Publishers, Inc., 1997.

Shattuck, John H.F. *Rights of Privacy.* Skokie: National Textbook Co., 1977.

Wetterer, Charles M. *The Fourth Amendment: Search and Seizure.* Enslow Publishers, Inc., 1998.

Washington v. Chrisman
1982

Petitioner: State of Washington

Respondent: Neil Martin Chrisman

Petitioner's Claim: That a police officer did not violate the Fourth Amendment by searching Chrisman's dormitory room for illegal drugs without a warrant.

Chief Lawyer for Petitioner: Ronald R. Carpenter

Chief Lawyer for Respondent: Robert F. Patrick

Justices for the Court: Harry A. Blackmun, Warren E. Burger, Sandra Day O'Connor, Lewis F. Powell, Jr., William H. Rehnquist, John Paul Stevens

Justices Dissenting: William J. Brennan, Jr., Thurgood Marshall, Byron R. White

Date of Decision: January 13, 1982

Decision: The Supreme Court approved the police officer's search and seizure.

Significance: With *Chrisman,* the Supreme Court said if police are lawfully in a person's private home, they may seize any criminal evidence they see in plain view.

$\mathbf{A}$ person's privacy is protected under the Fourth Amendment of the U.S. Constitution. The Fourth Amendment requires searches and seizures by the government to be reasonable. In most cases, law enforcement officers must get a warrant to search a house or other private place for evidence of a crime. To get a warrant, officers must have probable cause, which means good reason to believe the place to be searched has evidence of a crime. The warrant must specifically describe the evidence the police may look for.

There are exceptions to the warrant requirement. One of the exceptions is called the "plain view" doctrine. Under this doctrine, police who have a warrant to look for specific evidence may seize any other evidence that is in plain view in the place they are searching. In *Washington v. Chrisman,* the U.S. Supreme Court had to decide whether a policeman in a dormitory room without a search warrant could seize evidence in plain view.

Party Time

Officer Daugherty worked for the Washington State University police department. On the evening of January 21, 1978, Daugherty saw Carl Overdahl, a student, leave a dormitory carrying a half-gallon bottle of gin. University regulations outlawed alcoholic beverages on university property. State law also made it illegal for anyone under twenty-one to possess alcoholic beverages.

Because Overdahl appeared to be under twenty-one, Daugherty stopped him and asked for identification. Overdahl said he would have to go back to his room to get it. Daugherty arrested Overdahl and said he would have to accompany Overdahl back to the room. Overdahl's roommate, Neil Martin Chrisman, was in the room when Overdahl and Daugherty arrived. Chrisman, who was putting a small box into a medicine cabinet, became nervous.

Daugherty stood in the doorway while Overdahl went to get his identification. While in the doorway, Daugherty noticed seeds and a seashell pipe sitting on a desk. Without asking for permission or getting a search warrant, Daugherty entered the room to examine the seeds, which were marijuana seeds. Daugherty arrested Chrisman and read both gentlemen their rights, including the right to remain silent. He then asked whether they had any other drugs in the room. Chrisman handed Daugherty the small box he had been putting away. The box had three small plastic bags with marijuana and $112 in cash.

Daugherty radioed for a second officer to help him. Both officers said they would have to search the whole room, but that Chrisman and

Overdahl could force them to get a search warrant first. After discussing the matter in whispers, Chrisman and Overdahl allowed the officers to search the whole room without a warrant. Daugherty and his fellow officer found more marijuana and some LSD, another illegal drug.

Time to Pay the Piper

The State of Washington charged Chrisman with one count of possessing more than 40 grams of marijuana and one count of possessing LSD, both felonies. Before his trial, Chrisman made a motion to exclude the drug evidence that Daugherty had seized. Chrisman said the entire search was illegal under the Fourth Amendment because Daugherty entered the room to look at the seeds without a search warrant. The trial court denied Chrisman's motion and the jury convicted him on both counts.

The Washington Court of Appeals affirmed the convictions, but the Supreme Court of Washington reversed. It said although Overdahl was under arrest, Daugherty had no reason to enter the dormitory room. There was no indication that Overdahl was getting a weapon, destroying evidence, or trying to escape. Absent such problems, Daugherty was

Illegal drugs can come in many shapes and forms, but the police are trained to recognize them all.
AP/Wide World Photos.

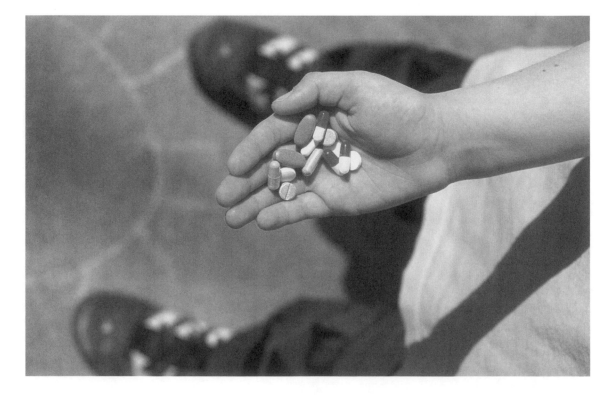

DRUG SNIFFING DOGS

The U.S. Customs Service guards the United States's borders to prevent illegal drugs from getting into the country. In 1970, Customs faced increasing drug traffic with a shrinking staff. That year, a manager suggested that dogs could sniff for illegal drugs. Working with dog experts from the U.S. Air Force, Customs developed a program to train dogs for drug detection.

Customs selects dogs that are natural-born retrievers for drug detection programs. The dogs it uses most often are golden retrievers, Labrador retrievers, and German short-hair retrievers. Customs trains the dogs to detect a drug by linking drug detection with positive feedback. In effect, the dog learns that it will get praise if it finds a certain drug. Trainers must make sure that all items used during training smell like the drug to be found. Otherwise the dog might look for odors that are not associated with an illegal drug.

obliged to remain outside the room. Without a warrant, he was not allowed to enter to search for illegal drugs. Faced with having to dismiss the charges against Chrisman, Washington took the case to the U.S. Supreme Court.

The Plain View Rule

With a 6–3 decision, the Supreme Court reversed again and ruled in favor of Washington. Writing for the Court, Chief Justice Warren E. Burger applied the plain view doctrine to decide the case. He said Officer Daugherty legally arrested Overdahl for having alcohol. After arresting Overdahl, Daugherty was allowed to stay with him wherever Overdahl went. Police need to stay with arrested people to protect themselves, to protect evidence, and to prevent escape.

Because Daugherty was allowed to stay with Overdahl, he was allowed to go into Overdahl's room when Overdahl went to get his identification. Once in the room, the plain view doctrine allowed Daugherty

to seize any evidence of a crime that he saw in plain view. After he seized the marijuana seeds, Chrisman voluntarily handed over three bags of marijuana and then gave Daugherty permission to search the entire room. The whole search was lawful under the Fourth Amendment.

Invasion of Privacy

Three justices dissented, which means they disagreed with the Court's decision. Justice Byron R. White wrote a dissenting opinion. Justice White disagreed that Daugherty was allowed to go into Overdahl's private home just because Daugherty had arrested him. White said Daugherty could go in only if necessary to protect himself or prevent escape. There was no indication that Overdahl was getting a weapon, and Daugherty was preventing escape by standing in the doorway.

White said that without a valid reason to enter the room, Daugherty was not allowed to enter just because he saw seeds that looked like marijuana seeds. Otherwise, police officers can snoop around people's homes looking inside for evidence of a crime. That would destroy the privacy the Fourth Amendment is supposed to protect.

Suggestions for further reading

Franklin, Paula A. *The Fourth Amendment.* Englewood Cliffs: Silver Burdett Press, 1991.

Jaffe, Jerome H., ed. *Encyclopedia of Drugs and Alcohol.* New York: Macmillan Library Reference USA, 1995.

Persico, Deborah A. *Mapp v. Ohio: Evidence and Search Warrants.* Enslow Publishers, Inc., 1997.

Shattuck, John H.F. *Rights of Privacy.* Skokie: National Textbook Co., 1977.

Wetterer, Charles M. *The Fourth Amendment: Search and Seizure.* Enslow Publishers, Inc., 1998.

Hudson v. Palmer
1984

Petitioner: Ted S. Hudson

Respondent: Russel Thomas Palmer. Jr.

Petitioner's Claim: That the Fourth Amendment does not apply to prison inmates.

Chief Lawyer for Petitioner: William G. Broaddus, Deputy Attorney General of Virginia

Chief Lawyer for Respondent: Deborah C. Wyatt

Justices for the Court: Warren E. Burger, Sandra Day O'Connor, Lewis F. Powell, Jr., William H. Rehnquist, Byron R. White

Justices Dissenting: Harry A. Blackmun, William J. Brennan, Jr., Thurgood Marshall, John Paul Stevens

Date of Decision: July 3, 1984

Decision: The Supreme Court said the Fourth Amendment does not apply to prison inmates.

Significance: After *Hudson,* prisoners who are treated unfairly during cell searches must sue under state law to recover their damages.

The Fourth Amendment of the U.S. Constitution protects privacy. It requires searches and seizures by the government to be reasonable. In most cases, law enforcement officers must get a warrant to search a house or other private place for evidence of a crime. To get a warrant, officers must have probable cause, which means good reason to believe the place to be searched has evidence of a crime. Requiring law enforcement officers to get a warrant prevents them from harassing people for no good reason. In *Hudson v. Palmer,* the U.S. Supreme Court had to decide whether the Fourth Amendment protects prisoners in their jail cells.

Shakedown

Russel Thomas Palmer, Jr,. was an inmate at the Bland Correctional Center in Bland, Virginia. Palmer was serving sentences for forgery, grand larceny (theft), and bank robbery convictions. Ted S. Hudson was an officer at the correctional center.

On September 16, 1981, Hudson and a fellow officer searched Palmer's prison locker and cell. They were looking for contraband, which means illegal items such as weapons. During the search they found a ripped prison pillow case in a trash can near Palmer's bed. The prison filed a disciplinary charge against Palmer for destroying state property. Palmer was found guilty. The prison forced him to pay for the pillow case and entered a reprimand on his prison record.

Afterwards, Palmer filed a lawsuit against Hudson. He said Hudson searched his cell just to harass him. Palmer accused Hudson of destroying some of Palmer's personal property during the search. Palmer said the harassing and destructive search violated his constitutional rights. He sought to recover his damages under a federal statute for people whose constitutional rights are violated.

Without holding a trial, the federal court entered judgment in Hudson's favor. The court said Hudson did not violate any of Palmer's constitutional rights. It said if Hudson destroyed personal property, Palmer could file a property damage lawsuit under state law.

The federal court of appeals, however, reversed. It said Palmer had a constitutional right of privacy in his jail cell under the Fourth Amendment. If Hudson violated that privacy with a harassing and destructive search, Palmer could recover damages for violation of his constitutional rights. The trial court would have to hold a trial to determine if that is what happened. Wishing to avoid the trial, Hudson took the case to the U.S. Supreme Court.

ATTICA TORTURE CASE

On September 9, 1971, prison inmates at the Attica Correctional
Facility near Buffalo, New York, rioted. They took control of an
exercise yard and held forty-nine prison guards hostage. The
prisoners rioted because of inhumane conditions at the facility.
Prisoners had to work in a metal shop where the temperature was
over 100 degrees Fahrenheit. They got only one shower and one
roll of toilet tissue each month. Spanish-speaking prisoners could
not get their mail, and Muslim prisoners demanded meat other
than pork.

After four days of unsuccessful negotiations to end the crisis,
New York governor Nelson Rockefeller ordered state troopers to
take control of the situation. After bombing the yard with tear
gas, troopers stormed in, shooting blindly through the gas. In the
end, thirty-two inmates and eleven prison officers were dead.

After regaining control of the facility, prison guards punished
and tortured the inmates. They forced inmates to strip and crawl
over broken glass. They shoved a screwdriver up one man's rec-
tum. They forced another man to lie naked for hours with a football under his chin. Guards told the inmate he would be killed or
castrated if he dropped the ball.

In 1974, lawyers for the inmates filed a lawsuit seeking $100
million for injuries suffered during the torture. On February 16,
2000, a judge finally approved a settlement to end the case.
Under the settlement, New York State will pay $8 million, to be
divided among the inmates who were injured.

Struck Down

With a 5–4 decision, the Supreme Court ruled in favor of Hudson.
Writing for the Court, Chief Justice Warren E. Burger began by saying
prisoners do not give up all of their constitutional rights. For example,
prisoners have First Amendment rights to freedom of speech and religion. The Eighth Amendment says prisoners cannot receive cruel and

unusual punishments. In short, there is no "iron curtain" separating prisoners from all constitutional rights.

Prisoners, however, do give up some constitutional rights. Prisoners are confined because they have broken the law. Prisons need to maintain order and discipline among these criminals. Prison officials especially need to protect themselves, visitors, and other inmates from violence by the prisoners.

The ultimate question, then, was whether the Fourth Amendment protects prisoners from unreasonable searches and seizures. The Supreme Court said it does not. Because prison officials need to search jail cells for weapons, drugs, and other dangers, prisoners have no right of privacy in their cells. That means Hudson did not violate Palmer's Fourth Amendment rights by conducting a harassing and destructive search. As a prisoner, Palmer had no Fourth Amendment rights in his jail cell.

Chief Justice Warren emphasized that Palmer had other remedies available. If Hudson destroyed his property, Palmer could file a property damage suit under state law. He just could not recover for violation of constitutional rights.

Imprisoning Property Rights

Four justices dissented, which means they disagreed with the Court's decision. Justice John Paul Stevens wrote a dissenting opinion. He did not think the Fourth Amendment protects only privacy. He said it also protects property from unreasonable seizures. Surely it is unreasonable for a prison official to seize and destroy personal property such as personal letters, photographs of family members, a hobby kit, a diary, or a Bible. Justice Stevens said that for prisoners, holding onto such personal items marks "the difference between slavery and humanity."

Suggestions for further reading

Boyd, Herb. "Long Time Coming, but Welcome." *New York Amsterdam News,* January 6, 2000.

Chen, David W. "Judge Approves $8 Million Deal for Victims of Attica Torture." *Washington Post,* February 16, 2000.

Franklin, Paula A. *The Fourth Amendment.* Englewood Cliffs: Silver Burdett Press, 1991.

Haberman, Clyde. "Attica: Exorcising Demons, Redeeming the Deaths." *Washington Post,* January 9, 2000.

Persico, Deborah A. *Mapp v. Ohio: Evidence and Search Warrants.* Enslow Publishers, Inc., 1997.

Shattuck, John H.F. *Rights of Privacy.* Skokie: National Textbook Co., 1977.

Wetterer, Charles M. *The Fourth Amendment: Search and Seizure.* Enslow Publishers, Inc., 1998.

Hudson v. Palmer

California v. Ciraolo
1986

Petitioner: State of California

Respondent: Dante Carlo Ciraolo

Petitioner's Claim: That the police did not violate the Fourth Amendment by searching Ciraolo's backyard from an airplane without a warrant.

Chief Lawyer for Petitioner: Laurence K. Sullivan, Deputy Attorney General of California

Chief Lawyer for Respondent: Marshall Warren Krause

Justices for the Court: Warren E. Burger, Sandra Day O'Connor, William H. Rehnquist, John Paul Stevens, Byron R. White

Justices Dissenting: Harry A. Blackmun, William J. Brennan, Jr., Thurgood Marshall, Lewis F. Powell, Jr.

Date of Decision: May 19, 1986

Decision: The Supreme Court said the search did not violate the Fourth Amendment.

Significance: With *Ciraolo,* the Supreme Court said people in enclosed yards cannot expect privacy from air traffic above.

A person's right to privacy is guaranteed under the Fourth Amendment of the U.S. Constitution. The Fourth Amendment requires any searches and seizures by the government to be reasonable. In most cases, law enforcement officers must get a warrant to search a house or other private place for evidence of a crime. To get a warrant, officers must have probable cause, or believe the place to be searched has evidence of a crime.

In *Oliver v. United States* (1984), the Supreme Court said people can expect privacy not just inside their houses, but in the curtilage too. The curtilage is the yard that a person encloses or considers to be private. Because the curtilage is private, law enforcement officers usually must have a warrant and probable cause to search it. In *California v. Ciraolo,* the U.S. Supreme Court had to decide whether the police violated the Fourth Amendment by searching a backyard from an airplane without a warrant.

Flying Low

Dante Carlo Ciraolo lived in Santa Clara, California. On September 2, 1982, Santa Clara police received an anonymous tip that Ciraolo was growing marijuana in his backyard. The police could not see the backyard from the ground because Ciraolo enclosed it with a six-foot outer fence and a ten-foot inner fence. Later that day, Officer Shutz hired a private plane to fly him and Officer Rodriguez over Ciraolo's backyard at an altitude of 1,000 feet.

Shutz and Rodriguez both were trained in marijuana identification. From the airplane they saw marijuana plants growing eight- to ten-feet high in a fifteen-by-twenty-five-foot plot. The officers photographed Ciraolo's backyard and those of surrounding neighbors. Six days later they used the photographs and their observations to get a warrant to search Ciraolo's entire house and yard. During the search they seized seventy-three marijuana plants.

Florida charged Ciraolo with cultivating, or growing, marijuana. At his trial, Ciraolo asked the court to suppress, or get rid of, the marijuana evidence against him. When the government violates the Fourth Amendment, it may not use the evidence it finds to convict the defendant. Ciraolo said Officers Shutz and Rodriguez violated the Fourth Amendment by searching his backyard from an airplane without a warrant.

The trial court denied Ciraolo's motion, so he pleaded guilty to the charge against him and appealed to the California Court of Appeals. That court reversed his conviction, saying the police violated the Fourth Amendment. Faced with having to dismiss its case against Ciraolo, California took the case to the U.S. Supreme Court.

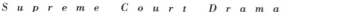

FLORIDA V. RILEY

Three years after deciding *Ciraolo,* the Supreme Court decided another case involving aerial surveillance. In *Florida v. Riley,* police used a helicopter to hover 400 feet over a greenhouse that had two panels missing from its roof. From the helicopter they were able to see and photograph marijuana plants through the open panels. At his trial for possession of marijuana, Michael A. Riley asked the court to suppress the marijuana evidence because the police violated the Fourth Amendment.

The trial court ruled in Riley's favor, but the Supreme Court reversed. Relying on its decision in *Ciraolo,* the Court said Riley could not expect privacy from helicopters hovering above his greenhouse. In a dissenting opinion, Justice William J. Brennan, Jr., warned that the Court was creating a dictatorial society such as George Orwell described in his novel *1984:*

> The black-mustachio'd face gazed down from every commanding corner. There was one on the house front immediately opposite. BIG BROTHER IS WATCHING YOU, the caption said. . . . In the far distance a helicopter skimmed down between the roofs, hovered for an instant like a bluebottle, and darted away again with a curving flight. It was the Police Patrol, swooping into people's windows.

High Court Rules

With a 5–4 decision, the Supreme Court reversed and ruled in favor of California. Writing for the Court, Chief Justice Warren E. Burger said the Fourth Amendment only protects reasonable expectations of privacy. By putting a fence around his yard, Ciraolo had a reasonable expectation that nobody would invade his privacy from the ground.

Ciraolo did not, however, cover his yard from the airspace above. It was unreasonable for Ciraolo to think that nobody would see his yard from airplanes and other flying machines. After all, public airplanes were allowed to fly over Ciraolo's yard at the same height flown by Officers Shutz and Rodriguez. Quoting from a prior Supreme Court case, Burger said, "What a person knowingly exposes to the public, even in his own home or office, is not a subject of Fourth Amendment protection."

Because Ciraolo could not expect privacy from above his backyard, the police did not need a warrant to search from the airplane. "The Fourth Amendment simply does not require the police traveling in the public airways at this altitude to obtain a warrant to observe what is visible to the naked eye."

Low Down Dirty Shame

Four justices dissented, which means they disagreed with the Court's decision. Justice Lewis F. Powell, Jr., wrote a dissenting opinion. He said Ciraolo did all he needed to do to protect privacy in his backyard by erecting fences. The Court's decision called Ciraolo's privacy expectation reasonable on the ground but unreasonable from the air. That meant police could not use a ladder to see into Ciraolo's yard, but they could use an airplane.

Powell said that in reality, public and commercial airplane passengers cannot see backyards very well from the air. That means people do not expect invasions of privacy from airplanes. The police were able to see Ciraolo's backyard only because they hired a plane that positioned them to see the marijuana plot. Letting them do that without a search warrant was unfaithful to privacy, which is what the Fourth Amendment is supposed to protect.

Suggestions for further reading

Franklin, Paula A. *The Fourth Amendment.* Englewood Cliffs: Silver Burdett Press, 1991.

Mikula, Mark, and L. Mpho Mabunda, eds. *Great American Court Cases.* Detroit: The Gale Group, 1999.

Persico, Deborah A. *Mapp v. Ohio: Evidence and Search Warrants.* Enslow Publishers, Inc., 1997.

Shattuck, John H.F. *Rights of Privacy.* Skokie: National Textbook Co., 1977.

Wetterer, Charles M. *The Fourth Amendment: Search and Seizure.* Enslow Publishers, Inc., 1998.

General Bibliography

Aaseng, Nathan. *Great Justices of the Supreme Court*. Minneapolis: Oliver Press, 1992.

Arthur, Joe. *Justice for All: The Story of Thurgood Marshall*. New York: Yearling Books, 1995.

Bains, Rae. *Thurgood Marshall: Fight for Justice*. Mahwah, NJ: Troll Assoc., 1993.

Bernstein, Richard, and Jerome Agel. *Into the Third Century: The Supreme Court*. New York: Walker & Co., 1989.

Cornelius, Kay. *The Supreme Court*. New York: Chelsea House Publishers, 2000.

Coy, Harold. *The Supreme Court*. New York: Franklin Watts, 1981.

Deegan, Paul J. *Anthony Kennedy*. Edina, MN: Abdo & Daughters, 1992.

——. *Antonin Scalia*. Edina, MN: Abdo & Daughters, 1992.

——. *Chief Justice William Rehnquist*. Edina, MN: Abdo & Daughters, 1992.

——. *David Souter*. Edina, MN: Abdo & Daughters, 1992.

——. *Supreme Court Book*. Edina, MN: Abdo & Daughters, 1992.

Deegan, Paul J., and Bob Italia. *John Paul Stevens*. Edina, MN: Abdo & Daughters, 1992.

——. *Sandra Day O'Connor*. Edina, MN: Abdo & Daughters, 1992.

Feinburg, Barbara Silberdick. *Constitutional Amendments*. Twenty First Century Books, 1996.

General Bibliography

Friedman, Leon. *The Supreme Court.* New York: Chelsea House, 1987.

Friedman, Leon, and Fred L. Israel. *The Justices of the United States Supreme Court: Their Lives and Major Opinions.* New York: Chelsea House Publishers, 1995.

Goldish, Meish. *Our Supreme Court.* Brookfield: Millbrook Press, 1994.

Harrison, Michael. *Landmark Decisions of the United States Supreme Court.* San Diego: Excellent Books, 1991.

Health, David. *The Supreme Court of the United States.* New York: Capstone, 1998.

Holland, Gini. *Sandra Day O'Connor.* Austin: Raintree/Steck Vaughn, 1997.

Irons, Peter H. *The Courage of Their Convictions: Sixteen Americans Who Fought Their Way to the Supreme Court.* New York: Penguin, 1990.

Italia, Bob, and Paul Deegan. *Ruth Bader Ginsburg.* Edina, MN: Abdo & Daughters, 1994.

Kallen, Stuart A. *Thurgood Marshall.* Edina, MN: Abdo & Daughters, 1993.

Kent, Deborah. *Thurgood Marshall and the Supreme Court.* Chicago: Children's Press, 1997.

Krull, Kathleen. *A Kids' Guide to America's Bill of Rights: Curfews, Censorship, and the 100-Pound Giant.* New York: Avon Books, 1999.

Macht, Norman L., Christopher E. Henry, and Nathan I. Huggins. *Clarence Thomas: Supreme Court Justice.* New York: Chelsea House Publishers, 1995.

Peterson, Helen Stone. *The Supreme Court in America's Story.* Scarsdale: Garrard Pub. Co., 1976.

Prentzas, G.S. *Thurgood Marshall.* New York: Chelsea House Publishers, 1994.

Prolman, Marilyn. *The Constitution.* Chicago: Children's Press, Inc., 1995.

Reef, Catherine. *The Supreme Court.* New York: Dillon Press, 1994.

Rierden, Anne B. *Reshaping the Supreme Court: New Justices, New Directions.* New York: Franklin Watts, 1988.

Sagarin, Mary. *Equal Justice under Law: Our Court System and How It Works.* New York: Lothrop, Lee & Shephard Co., Inc., 1966.

Stein, R. Conrad. *The Powers of the Supreme Court.* Chicago: Children's Press, Inc., 1995.

——. *The Bill of Rights.* Chicago: Children's Press, Inc., 1992.

White, G. Edward. *Oliver Wendell Holmes: Sage of the Supreme Court.* New York: Oxford University Press Children's Books, 2000.

Justices of the Supreme Court

The Justices are listed by year of appointment and in what way they served the court—as an Associate Justice or Chief Justice.

John Jay (Chief: 1789 - 1795)

John Rutledge (Associate: 1790 - 1791, Chief: 1795 - 1795)

William Cushing (Associate: 1790 - 1810)

James Wilson (Associate: 1789 - 1798)

John Blair (Associate: 1790 - 1795)

James Iredell (Associate: 1790 - 1799)

Thomas Johnson (Associate: 1792 - 1793)

William Paterson (Associate: 1793 - 1806)

Samuel Chase (Associate: 1796 - 1811)

Oliver Ellsworth (Chief: 1796 - 1800)

Bushrod Washington (Associate: 1799 - 1829)

Alfred Moore (Associate: 1800 - 1804)

John Marshall (Chief: 1801 - 1835)

William Johnson (Associate: 1804 - 1834)

Brockholst Livingston (Associate: 1807 - 1823)

Thomas Todd (Associate: 1807 - 1826)

Justices of the Supreme Court

Gabriel Duvall (Associate: 1811 - 1835)

Joseph Story (Associate: 1812 - 1845)

Smith Thompson (Associate: 1823 - 1843)

Robert Trimble (Associate: 1826 - 1828)

John McLean (Associate: 1830 - 1861)

Henry Baldwin (Associate: 1830 - 1844)

James M. Wayne (Associate: 1835 - 1867)

Roger B. Taney (Chief: 1836 - 1864)

Philip P. Barbour (Associate: 1836 - 1841)

John Catron (Associate: 1837 - 1865)

John McKinley (Associate: 1838 - 1852)

Peter V. Daniel (Associate: 1842 - 1860)

Samuel Nelson (Associate: 1845 - 1872)

Levi Woodbury (Associate: 1845 - 1851)

Robert C. Grier (Associate: 1846 - 1870)

Benjamin R. Curtis (Associate: 1851 - 1857)

John A. Campbell (Associate: 1853 - 1861)

Nathan Clifford (Associate: 1858 - 1881)

Noah Swayne (Associate: 1862 - 1881)

Samuel F. Miller (Associate: 1862 - 1890)

David Davis (Associate: 1862 - 1877)

Stephen J. Field (Associate: 1863 - 1897)

Salmon P. Chase (Chief: 1864 - 1873)

William Strong (Associate: 1870 - 1880)

Joseph P. Bradley (Associate: 1870 - 1892)

Ward Hunt (Associate: 1873 - 1882)

Morrison R. Waite (Chief: 1874 - 1888)

John M. Harlan (Associate: 1877 - 1911)

William B. Woods (Associate: 1881 - 1887)

Stanley Matthews (Associate: 1881 - 1889)

Horace Gray (Associate: 1882 - 1902)

Samuel Blatchford (Associate: 1882 - 1893)

Lucius Q.C. Lamar (Associate: 1888 - 1893)

Melville W. Fuller (Chief: 1888 - 1910)

David J. Brewer (Associate: 1890 - 1910)

Henry B. Brown (Associate: 1891 - 1906)

George Shiras, Jr. (Associate: 1892 - 1903)

Howell E. Jackson (Associate: 1893 - 1895)

Edward D. White (Associate: 1894 - 1910, Chief: 1910 - 1921)

Rufus Peckham (Associate: 1896 - 1909)

Joseph McKenna (Associate: 1898 - 1925)

Oliver W. Holmes, Jr. (Associate: 1902 - 1932)

William R. Day (Associate: 1903 - 1922)

William H. Moody (Associate: 1906 - 1910)

Horace H. Lurton (Associate: 1910 - 1914)

Charles E. Hughes (Associate: 1910 - 1916, Chief: 1930 - 1941)

Willis Van Devanter (Associate: 1911 - 1937)

Joseph R. Lamar (Associate: 1911 - 1916)

Mahlon Pitney (Associate: 1912 - 1922)

James C. McReynolds (Associate: 1914 - 1941)

Louis D. Brandeis (Associate: 1916 - 1939)

John H. Clarke (Associate: 1916 - 1922)

William Howard Taft (Chief: 1921 - 1930)

George Sutherland (Associate: 1922 - 1938)

Pierce Butler (Associate: 1923 - 1939)

Edward T. Sanford (Associate: 1923 - 1930)

Harlan Fiske Stone (Associate: 1925 - 1941, Chief: 1941 - 1946)

Owen J. Roberts (Associate: 1930 - 1945)

Benjamin N. Cardozo (Associate: 1932 - 1938)

Hugo L. Black (Associate: 1937 - 1971)

Stanley Reed (Associate: 1938 - 1957)

Felix Frankfurter (Associate: 1939 - 1962)

Justices of the Supreme Court

Justices of the Supreme Court

William O. Douglas (Associate: 1939 - 1975)

Frank Murphy (Associate: 1940 - 1949)

James F. Byrnes (Associate: 1941 - 1942)

Robert H. Jackson (Associate: 1941 - 1954)

Wiley B. Rutledge (Associate: 1943 - 1949)

Harold Burton (Associate: 1945 - 1958)

Fred M. Vinson (Chief: 1946 - 1953)

Tom C. Clark (Associate: 1949 - 1967)

Sherman Minton (Associate: 1949 - 1956)

Earl Warren (Chief: 1953 - 1969)

John M. Harlan (Associate: 1955 - 1971)

William J. Brennan (Associate: 1956 - 1990)

Charles E. Whittaker (Associate: 1957 - 1962)

Potter Stewart (Associate: 1959 - 1981)

Byron R. White (Associate: 1962 - 1993)

Arthur J. Goldberg (Associate: 1962 - 1965)

Abe Fortas (Associate: 1965 - 1969)

Thurgood Marshall (Associate: 1967 - 1991)

Warren E. Burger (Chief: 1969 - 1986)

Harry A. Blackmun (Associate: 1970 - 1994)

Lewis F. Powell, Jr. (Associate: 1972 - 1987)

William H. Rehnquist (Associate: 1972 - 1986, Chief: 1986 -)

John Paul Stevens (Associate: 1975 -)

Sandra Day O'Connor (Associate: 1981 -)

Antonin Scalia (Associate: 1986 -)

Anthony Kennedy (Associate: 1988 -)

David H. Souter (Associate: 1990 -)

Clarence Thomas (Associate: 1991 -)

Ruth Bader Ginsburg (Associate: 1993 -)

Stephen Gerald Breyer (Associate: 1994 -)

The Constitution
of the United States

On February 21, 1787, Congress adopted the resolution that a convention of delegates should meet to revise the Articles of Confederation. The Constitution was signed and submitted to Congress on September 17 of that year. Congress then sent it to the states for ratification; the last state to sign, Rhode Island, did so May 29, 1790.

We The People of the United States, in Order to form a more perfect Union, establish Justice, insure domestic Tranquility, provide for the common defence, promote the general Welfare, and secure the Blessings of Liberty to ourselves and our Posterity, do ordain and establish this Constitution for the United States of America.

Art. I

Sec. 1. All legislative Powers herein granted shall be vested in a Congress of the United States, which shall consist of a Senate and House of Representatives.

Sec. 2. The House of Representatives shall be composed of Members chosen every second Year by the People of the several States, and the Electors in each State shall have the Qualifications requisite for Electors of the most numerous Branch of the State Legislature.

No Person shall be a Representative who shall not have attained to the Age of twenty five Years, and been seven Years a Citizen of the

United States, and who shall not, when elected, be an Inhabitant of that State in which he shall be chosen.

Representatives and direct Taxes shall be apportioned among the several States which may be included within this Union, according to their respective Numbers, which shall be determined by adding to the whole Number of free Persons, including those bound to Service for a Term of Years, and excluding Indians not taxed, three fifths of all other Persons. The actual Enumeration shall be made within three Years after the first Meeting of the Congress of the United States, and within every subsequent Term of ten Years, in such Manner as they shall by Law direct. The Number of Representatives shall not exceed one for every thirty Thousand, but each State shall have at Least one Representative; and until such enumeration shall be made, the State of New Hampshire shall be entitled to chuse three, Massachusetts eight, Rhode-Island and Providence Plantations one, Connecticut five, New-York six, New Jersey four, Pennsylvania eight, Delaware one, Maryland six, Virginia ten, North Carolina five, South Carolina five, and Georgia three.

When vacancies happen in the Representation from any State, the Executive Authority thereof shall issue Writs of Election to fill such Vacancies.

The House of Representatives shall chuse their Speaker and other Officers; and shall have the sole Power of Impeachment.

Sec. 3. The Senate of the United States shall be composed of two Senators from each State, chosen by the Legislature thereof, for six Years; and each Senator shall have one Vote.

Immediately after they shall be assembled in Consequence of the first Election, they shall be divided as equally as may be into three Classes. The Seats of the Senators of the first Class shall be vacated at the Expiration of the second Year, of the second Class at the Expiration of the fourth Year, and of the third Class at the Expiration of the sixth Year, so that one third may be chosen every second Year; and if Vacancies happen by Resignation, or otherwise, during the Recess of the Legislature of any State, the Executive thereof may make temporary Appointments until the next Meeting of the Legislature, which shall then fill such Vacancies.

No Person shall be a Senator who shall not have attained to the Age of thirty Years, and been nine Years a Citizens of the United States, and who shall not, when elected, be an Inhabitant of that State for which he shall be chosen.

The Vice President of the United States shall be President of the Senate, but shall have no Vote, unless they be equally divided.

The Senate shall chuse their other Officers, and also a President protempore, in the Absence of the Vice President, or when he shall exercise the Office of President of the United States.

The Senate shall have the sole Power to try all Impeachments. When sitting for that Purpose, they shall be on Oath or Affirmation. When the President of the United States is tried, the Chief Justice shall preside: And no Person shall be convicted without the Concurrence of two thirds of the Members present.

Judgment in Cases of Impeachment shall not extend further than to removal from Office, and disqualification to hold and enjoy any Office of honor, Trustor Profit under the United States: but the Party convicted shall nevertheless be liable and subject to Indictment, Trial, Judgment and Punishment, according to Law.

Sec. 4. The Times, Places and Manner of holding Elections for Senators and Representatives, shall be prescribed in each State by the Legislature thereof; but the Congress may at any time by Law make or alter such Regulations, except as to the Places of chusing Senators.

The Congress shall assemble at least once in every Year, and such Meeting shall be on the first Monday in December, unless they shall by Law appoint a different Day.

Sec. 5. Each House shall be the Judge of the Elections, Returns and Qualifications of its own Members, and a Majority of each shall constitute a Quorum to do Business; but a smaller Number may adjourn from day to day, and may be authorized to compel the Attendance of absent Members, in such Manner, and under such Penalties as each House may provide.

Each House may determine the Rules of its Proceedings, punish its Members for disorderly Behaviour, and, with the Concurrence of two thirds, expel a Member.

Each House shall keep a Journal of its Proceedings, and from time to time publish the same, excepting such Parts as may in their Judgment require Secrecy; and the Yeas and Nays of the Members of either House on any question shall, at the Desire of one fifth of those Present, be entered on the Journal.

Neither House, during the Session of Congress, shall, without the Consent of the other, adjourn for more than three days, nor to any other Place than that in which the two Houses shall be sitting.

Sec. 6. The Senators and Representatives shall receive a Compensation for their Services, to be ascertained by Law, and paid out of the Treasury of the United States. They shall in all Cases, except Treason, Felony and Breach of the Peace, be privileged from Arrest during their Attendance at the Session of their respective Houses, and in going to and returning from the same; and for any Speech or Debate in either House, they shall not be questioned in any other Place.

No Senator or Representative shall, during the Time for which he was elected, be appointed to any civil Office under the Authority of the United States which shall have been created, or the Emoluments whereof shall have been encreased during such time; and no Person holding any Office under the United States, shall be a Member of either House during his Continuance in Office.

Sec. 7. All Bills for raising Revenue shall originate in the House of Representatives; but the Senate may propose or concur with Amendments as another Bills.

Every Bill which shall have passed the House of Representatives and the Senate, shall, before it become a Law, be presented to the President of the United States; If he approve he shall sign it, but if not he shall return it, with his Objections to that House in which it shall have originated, who shall enter the Objections at large on their Journal, and proceed to reconsider it. If after such Reconsideration two thirds of that House shall agree tapes the Bill, it shall be sent, together with the Objections, to the other House, by which it shall likewise be reconsidered, and if approved by two-thirds of that House, it shall become a Law. But in all such Cases the Votes of both Houses shall be determined by yeas and Nays, and the Names of the Persons voting for and against the Bill shall be entered on the Journal of each House respectively. If any Bill shall not be returned by the President within ten Days (Sundays excepted) after it shall have been presented to him, the Same shall be a Law, in like Manner as if he had signed it, unless the Congress by their Adjournment prevent its Return, in which Case it shall note a Law.

Every Order, Resolution, or Vote to which the Concurrence of the Senate and House of Representatives may be necessary (except on a question of Adjournment) shall be presented to the President of the United States; and before the Same shall take Effect, shall be approved by him, or being disapproved by him, shall be repassed by two thirds of the Senate and House of Representatives, according to the Rules and Limitations prescribed in the Case of a Bill.

Sec. 8. The Congress shall have Power To lay and collect Taxes, Duties, Imposts and Excises, to pay the Debts and provide for the common Defence and general Welfare of the United States; but all Duties, Imposts and Excises shall be uniform throughout the United States;

To borrow Money on the credit of the United States;

To regulate Commerce with foreign Nations, and among the several States, and with the Indian Tribes;

To establish an uniform Rule of Naturalization, and uniform Laws on the subject of Bankruptcies throughout the United States;

To coin Money, regulate the Value thereof, and of foreign Coin, and fix the Standard of Weights and Measures;

To provide for the Punishment of counterfeiting the Securities and current Coin of the United States;

To establish Post Offices and post Roads;

To promote the Progress of Science and useful Arts, by securing for limited Times to Authors and Inventors the exclusive Right to their respective Writings and Discoveries;

To constitute Tribunals inferior to the supreme Court;

To define and punish Piracies and Felonies committed on the high Seas, and Offences against the Law of Nations;

To declare War, grant Letters of Marque and Reprisal, and make Rules concerning Captures on Land and Water;

To raise and support Armies, but no Appropriation of Money to that Use shall be for a longer Term than two Years;

To provide and maintain a Navy;

To make Rules for the Government and Regulation of the land and naval forces;

To provide for calling forth the Militia to execute the Laws of the Union, suppress Insurrections and repel Invasions;

To provide for organizing, arming, and disciplining, the Militia, and for governing such Part of them as may be employed in the Service of the United States, reserving to the States respectively, the Appointment of the Officers, and the Authority of training the Militia according to the discipline prescribed by Congress;

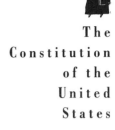

The
Constitution
of the
United
States

To exercise exclusive Legislation in all Cases whatsoever, over such District (not exceeding ten Miles square) as may, by Cession of particular States, and the Acceptance of Congress, become the Seat of the Government of the United States, and to exercise like Authority over all Places purchased by the Consent of the Legislature of the State in which the Same shall be, for the Erection of Forts, Magazines, Arsenals, dock-Yards, and other needful Buildings;—And

To make all Laws which shall be necessary and proper for carrying into Execution the foregoing Powers, and all other Powers vested by this Constitution in the Government of the United States, or in any Department or Officer thereof.

Sec. 9. The Migration or Importation of such Persons as any of the States now existing shall think proper to admit, shall not be prohibited by the Congress prior to the Year one thousand eight hundred and eight, but a Tax or daytime be imposed on such Importation, not exceeding ten dollars for each Person.

The Privilege of the Writ of Habeas Corpus shall not be suspended, unless when in Cases of Rebellion or Invasion the public Safety may require it.

No Bill of Attainder or ex post facto Law shall be passed.

No Capitation, or other direct, Tax shall be laid, unless in Proportionate the Census or Enumeration herein before directed to be taken.

No Tax or Duty shall be laid on Articles exported from any State.

No Preference shall be given by any Regulation of Commerce or Revenue to the Ports of one State over those of another: nor shall Vessels bound to, or from, one State, be obliged to enter, clear, or pay Duties in another.

No Money shall be drawn from the Treasury, but in Consequence of Appropriations made by Law; and a regular Statement and Account of the Receipts and Expenditures of all public Money shall be published from time to time.

No Title of Nobility shall be granted by the United States: And no Person holding any Office of Profit or Trust under them, shall, without the Consent of the Congress, accept of any present, Emolument, Office, or Title, of any kind whatever, from any King, Prince or foreign State.

Sec. 10. No State shall enter into any Treaty, Alliance, or Confederation; grant Letters of Marque and Reprisal; coin Money; emit

Bills of Credit; make any Thing but gold and silver Coin a Tender in Payment of Debts; pass any Bill of Attainder, ex post facto Law, or Law impairing the Obligation of Contracts, or grant any Title of Nobility.

No State shall, without the Consent of the Congress, lay any Impostor Duties on Imports or Exports, except what may be absolutely necessary for executing it's inspection Laws: and the net Produce of all Duties and Imposts, laid by any State on Imports or Exports, shall be for the Use of the Treasury of the United States; and all such Laws shall be subject to the Revision and Controul of the Congress.

No State shall, without the Consent of Congress, lay any Duty of Tonnage, keep Troops, or Ships of War in time of Peace, enter into any Agreement or Compact with another State, or with a foreign Power, or engage in War, unless actually invaded, or in such imminent Danger as will not admit of delay.

Art. II

Sec. 1. The executive Power shall be vested in a President of the United States of America. He shall hold his Office during the Term of four Years, and, together with the Vice President, chosen for the same Term, be elected, as follows.

Each State shall appoint, in such Manner as the Legislature thereof may direct, a Number of Electors, equal to the whole Number of Senators and Representatives to which the State may be entitled in the Congress: but no Senator or Representative, or Person holding an Office of Trust or Profit under the United States, shall be appointed an Elector.

The Electors shall meet in their respective States, and vote by Ballot for two Persons, of whom one at least shall not be an Inhabitant of the same State with themselves. And they shall make a List of all the Persons voted for, and of the Number of Votes for each; which List they shall sign and certify, and transmit sealed to the Seat of the Government of the United States, directed to the President of the Senate. The President of the Senate shall, in the Presence of the Senate and House of Representatives, open all the Certificates, and the Votes shall then be counted. The Person having the greatest Number of Votes shall be the President, if such Number be a Majority of the whole Number of Electors appointed; and if there be more than one who have such Majority, and have an equal Number of Votes, then the House of Representatives shall immediately chuse by Ballot one of them for

President; and if no personae a Majority, then from the five highest on the List the said House shallon like Manner chuse the President. But in chusing the President, the Votes shall be taken by States, the Representation from each State having one Vote; A quorum for this Purpose shall consist of a Member or Members from two thirds of the States, and a Majority of all the States shall be necessary to a Choice. In every Case, after the Choice of the President, the Person having the greatest Number of Votes of the Electors shall be the Vice President. But if there should remain two or more who have equal Votes, the Senate shall chuse frothed by Ballot the Vice President.

The Congress may determine the Time of chusing the Electors, and the day on which they shall give their Votes; which Day shall be the same throughout the United States.

No Person except a natural born Citizen, or a Citizen of the United States, at the time of the Adoption of this Constitution, shall be eligible the Office of President; neither shall any Person be eligible to that Office who shall not have attained to the Age of thirty five Years, and been fourteen Years a Resident within the United States.

In Case of the Removal of the President from Office, or of his Death, Resignation, or Inability to discharge the Powers and Duties of the said Office, the Same shall devolve on the Vice President, and the Congress may by Law provide for the Case of Removal, Death, Resignation or Inability, both of the President and Vice President, declaring what Officer shall then act as President, and such Officer shall act accordingly, until the Disability be removed, or a President shall be elected.

The President shall, at stated Times, receive for his Services, a Compensation, which shall neither be encreased nor diminished during the Period for which he shall have been elected, and he shall not receive within that Period another Emolument from the United States, or any of them.

Before he enter on the Execution of his Office, he shall take the following Oath or Affirmation:—"I do solemnly swear (or affirm) that I will faithfully execute the Office of President of the United States, and will to the bestow my Ability, preserve, protect and defend the Constitution of the United States."

Sec. 2. The President shall be Commander in Chief of the Army and Navy of the United States, and of the Militia of the several States, when called into the actual Service of the United States; he may require the Opinion, in writing, of the principal Officer in each of the executive

Departments, upon any Subject relating to the Duties of their respective Offices, and he shall have Power to grant Reprieves and Pardons for Offences against the United States, except in Cases of Impeachment.

He shall have Power, by and with the Advice and Consent of the Senate, to make Treaties, provided two thirds of the Senators present concur; Andie shall nominate, and by and with the Advice and Consent of the Senate, shall appoint Ambassadors, other public Ministers and Consuls, Judges of the supreme Court, and all other Officers of the United States, whose Appointments are not herein otherwise provided for, and which shall be established by Law: but the Congress may by Law vest the Appointment of such inferior Officers, as they think proper, in the President alone, in the Courts of Law, or in the Heads of Departments.

The President shall have Power to fill up all Vacancies that may happen during the Recess of the Senate, by granting Commissions which shall expire at the End of their next Session.

Sec. 3. He shall from time to time give to the Congress Information of the State of the Union, and recommend to their Consideration such Measures as he shall judge necessary and expedient; he may, on extraordinary Occasions, convene both Houses, or either of them, and in Case of Disagreement between them, with Respect to the Time of Adjournment, he may adjourn them to such Time as he shall think proper; he shall receive Ambassadors and other public Ministers; he shall take Care that the Laws be faithfully executed, and shall Commission all the Officers of the United States.

Sec. 4. The President, Vice President and all civil Officers of the United States, shall be removed from Office on Impeachment for, and Conviction of, Treason, Bribery, or other high Crimes and Misdemeanors.

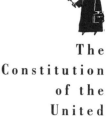
Art. III

Sec. 1. The judicial Power of the United States, shall be vested none supreme Court, and in such inferior Courts as the Congress may from time to time ordain and establish. The Judges, both of the supreme and inferior Courts, shall hold their Offices during good Behaviour, and shall, at stated Times, receive for their Services, a Compensation, which shall not be diminished during their Continuance in Office.

Sec. 2. The judicial Power shall extend to all Cases, in Law and Equity, arising under this Constitution, the Laws of the United States, and Treaties made, or which shall be made, under their Authority;—to all Cases affecting Ambassadors, other public Ministers and Consuls;—to all Cases of admiralty and maritime Jurisdiction;—to Controversies to which the United States shall be a Party;—to Controversies between two or more States;—between a State and Citizens of another State;—between Citizens of different States,—between Citizens of the same State claiming Lands under Grandson different States, and between a State, or the Citizens thereof, and foreign States, Citizens or Subjects.

In all Cases affecting Ambassadors, other public Ministers and Consuls, and those in which a State shall be Party, the supreme Court shall have original Jurisdiction. In all the other Cases before mentioned, the supreme Court shall have appellate Jurisdiction, both as to Law and Fact, with such Exceptions, and under such Regulations as the Congress shall make.

The Trial of all Crimes, except in Cases of Impeachment, shall be by Jury; and such Trial shall be held in the State where the said Crimes shall have been committed; but when not committed within any State, the Trial shall be at such Place or Places as the Congress may by Law have directed.

Sec. 3. Treason against the United States, shall consist only in levying War against them, or in adhering to their Enemies, giving them Aid and Comfort. No Person shall be convicted of Treason unless on the Testimony of two Witnesses to the same overt Act, or on Confession in open Court.

The Congress shall have Power to declare the Punishment of Treason, but no Attainder of Treason shall work Corruption of Blood, or Forfeiture except during the Life of the Person attainted.

Art. IV

Sec. 1. Full Faith and Credit shall be given in each State to the Public Acts, Records, and judicial Proceedings of every other State. And the Congressman by general Laws prescribe the Manner in which such Acts, Records and Proceedings shall be proved, and the Effect thereof.

Sec. 2. The Citizens of each State shall be entitled to all Privileges and Immunities of Citizens in the several States.

A Person charged in any State with Treason, Felony, or other Crime, who shall flee from Justice, and be found in another State, shall on

Demand of the executive Authority of the State from which he fled, be delivered up, to be removed to the State having Jurisdiction of the Crime.

No Person held to Service or Labour in one State, under the Laws thereof, escaping into another, shall, in Consequence of any Law or Regulation therein, be discharged from such Service or Labour, but shall be delivered up on Claim of the Party to whom such Service or Labour may be due.

Sec. 3. New States may be admitted by the Congress into this Union; but no new States shall be formed or erected within the Jurisdiction of another State; nor any State be formed by the Junction of two or more States, or Parts of States, without the Consent of the Legislatures of the States concerned as well as of the Congress.

The Congress shall have Power to dispose of and make all needful Rules and Regulations respecting the Territory or other Property belonging to the United States; and nothing in this Constitution shall be so construed as to Prejudice any Claims of the United States, or of any particular State.

Sec. 4. The United States shall guarantee to every State in this Union a Republican Form of Government, and shall protect each of them against Invasion; and on Application of the Legislature, or of the Executive (when the Legislature cannot be convened) against domestic Violence.

Art. V

The Congress, whenever two thirds of both Houses shall deem it necessary, shall propose Amendments to this Constitution, or, on the Application of the Legislatures of two thirds of the several States, shall call a Convention for proposing Amendments, which, in either Case, shall be valid to all Intents and Purposes, as Part of this Constitution, when ratified by the Legislatures of three fourths of the several States, or by Conventions in three fourths thereof, as the one or the other Mode of Ratification may be proposed by the Congress; Provided that no Amendment which may be made prior to the Year One thousand eight hundred and eight shall in any Manner affect the first and fourth Clauses in the Ninth Section of the first Article; and that no State, without its Consent, shall be deprived of it's equal Suffrage in the Senate.

Art. VI

All Debts contracted and Engagements entered into, before the Adoption of this Constitution, shall be as valid against the United States under this Constitution, as under the Confederation.

This Constitution, and the Laws of the United States which shall be made in Pursuance thereof; and all Treaties made, or which shall be made, under the Authority of the United States, shall be the supreme Law of the Land; and the Judges in every State shall be bound thereby, any Thing in the Constitution or Laws of any State to the Contrary notwithstanding.

The Senators and Representatives before mentioned, and the Members of the several State Legislatures, and all executive and judicial Officers, both of the United States and of the several States, shall be bound by Oath or Affirmation, to support this Constitution; but no religious Test shall ever be required as a Qualification to any Office or public Trust under the United States.

Art. VII

The Ratification of the Conventions of nine States, shall be sufficient for the Establishment of this Constitution between the States so ratifying the Same.

The Bill of Rights

Articles in addition to, and Amendment of the Constitution of the United States of America, proposed by Congress, and ratified by the Legislatures of the several States, pursuant to the fifth Article of the original Constitution.

[The first ten amendments went into effect November 3, 1791.]

Art. I

Congress shall make no law respecting an establishment of religion, or prohibiting the free exercise thereof; or abridging the freedom of speech, or of the press; or the right of the people peaceably to assemble, and to petition the government for a redress of grievances.

Art. II

A well regulated Militia, being necessary to the security of a free State, the right of the people to keep and bear Arms, shall not be infringed.

Art. III

No Soldier shall, in time of peace be quartered in any house, without the consent of the Owner, nor in time of war, but in a manner to be prescribed by law.

Art. IV

The right of the people to be secure in their persons, houses, papers, and effects, against unreasonable searches and seizures, shall not be violated, and no Warrants shall issue, but upon probable cause, supported by Oath or affirmation, and particularly describing the place to be searched, and the persons or things to be seized.

Art. V

No person shall be held to answer for a capital, or otherwise infamous crime, unless on a presentment or indictment of a Grand Jury, except in cases arising in the land or naval forces, or in the Militia, when in actual service in time of War or public danger; nor shall any person be subject for the same offence to be twice put in jeopardy of life or limb; nor shall be compelled in any criminal case to be a witness against himself, nor be deprived of life, liberty, or property, without due process of law; nor shall private property be taken for public use, without just compensation.

Art. VI

In all criminal prosecutions, the accused shall enjoy the right to a speedy and public trial, by an impartial jury of the State and district wherein the crime shall have been committed, which district shall have been previously ascertained by law, and to be informed of the nature and cause of the accusation; to be confronted with the witnesses against him; to have compulsory process for obtaining witnesses in his favor, and to have the Assistance of Counsel for his defence.

Art. VII

In Suits at common law, where the value in controversy shall exceed twenty dollars, the right of trial by jury shall be preserved, and no fact tried by a jury, shall be otherwise re-examined in any Court of the United States, than according to the rules of the common law.

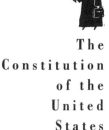

Art. VIII

Excessive bail shall not be required, nor excessive fines imposed, nor cruel and unusual punishments inflicted.

Art. IX

The enumeration in the Constitution, of certain rights, shall not be construed to deny or disparage others retained by the people.

Art. X

The powers not delegated to the United States by the Constitution, nor prohibited by it to the States, are reserved to the States respectively, or to the people.

Further Amendments to the Constitution

Art. XI
Jan. 8, 1798

The Judicial power of the United States shall not be construed to extend to any suit in law or equity, commenced or prosecuted against one of the United States by Citizens of another State, or by Citizens or Subjects of any Foreign State.

Art. XII
Sept. 25, 1804

The Electors shall meet in their respective states, and vote by ballot for President and Vice-President, one of whom, at least, shall not be an inhabitant of the same state with themselves; they shall name in their ballots the person voted for as President, and in distinct ballots the person voted for as Vice-President, and they shall make distinct lists of all persons voted for as President, and of all persons voted for as Vice-

President, and of the number of votes for each, which lists they shall sign and certify, and transmit sealed to the seat of the government of the United States, directed to the President of the Senate;—The President of the Senate shall, in the presence of the Senate and House of Representatives, open all the certificates and the votes shall then be counted;—The person having the greatest number of votes for President, shall be the President, if such number be a majority of the whole number of Electors appointed; and if no person have such majority, then from the persons having the highest numbers not exceeding three on the list of those voted for as President, the House of Representatives shall choose immediately, by ballot, the President. But in choosing the President, the votes shall be taken by states, the representation from each state having one vote; a quorum for this purpose shall consist of a member or members from two-thirds of the states, and a majority of all the states shall be necessary to a choice. And if the House of Representatives shall not choose a President whenever the right of choice shall devolve upon them, before the fourth day of March next following, then the Vice-President shall act as President, as in the case of the death or other constitutional disability of the President.—The person having the greatest number of votes as Vice-President, shall be the Vice-President, if such number be a majority of the whole number of Electors appointed, and if no person have a majority, then from the two highest numbers on the list, the Senate shall choose the Vice-President; a quorum for the purpose shall consist of two-thirds of the whole number of Senators, and a majority of the whole number shall be necessary to a choice. But no person constitutionally ineligible to the office of President shall be eligible to that of Vice-President of the United States.

Art. XIII
Dec. 18, 1865

Sec. 1. Neither slavery nor involuntary servitude, except as a punishment for crime whereof the party shall have been duly convicted, shall exist within the United States, or any place subject to their jurisdiction.

Sec. 2. Congress shall have power to enforce this article by appropriate legislation.

Art. XIV
July 28, 1868

Sec. 1. All persons born or naturalized in the United States, and subject to the jurisdiction thereof, are citizens of the United States and of the State wherein they reside. No State shall make or enforce any law which shall abridge the privileges or immunities of citizens of the United States; nor shall any State deprive any person of life, liberty, or property, without due process of law; nor deny to any person within its jurisdiction the equal protection of the laws.

Sec. 2. Representatives shall be apportioned among the several States according to their respective numbers, counting the whole number of persons in each State, excluding Indians not taxed. But when the right to vote at any election for the choice of electors for President and Vice President of the United States, Representatives in Congress, the Executive and Judicial officers of a State, or the members of the Legislature thereof, is denied to any of the male inhabitants of such State, being twenty-one years of age, and citizens of the United States, or in any way abridged, except for participation in rebellion, or other crime, the basis of representation therein shall be reduced in the proportion which the number of such male citizens shall bear to the whole number of male citizens twenty-one years of age in such State.

Sec. 3. No person shall be a Senator or Representative in Congress, or elector of President and Vice President, or hold any office, civil or military, under the United States, or under any State, who, having previously taken an oath, as a member of Congress, or as an officer of the United States, or as a member of any State legislature, or as an executive or judicial officer of any State, to support the Constitution of the United States, shall have engaged in insurrection or rebellion against the same, or given aid or comfort to the enemies thereof. But Congress may by a vote of two-thirds of each House, remove such disability.

Sec. 4. The validity of the public debt of the United States, authorized by law, including debts incurred for payment of pensions and bounties for services in suppressing insurrection or rebellion, shall not be questioned. But neither the United States nor any State shall assume or pay any debt or obligation incurred in aid of insurrection or rebellion against the United States, or any claim for the loss or emancipation of any slave; but all such debts, obligations and claims shall be held illegal and void.

Sec. 5. The Congress shall have power to enforce, by appropriate legislation, the provisions of this article.

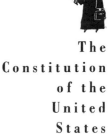
Art. XV
March 30, 1870

Sec. 1. The right of citizens of the United States to vote shall not be denied or abridged by the United States or by any State on account of race, color, or previous condition of servitude.

Sec. 2. The Congress shall have power to enforce this article by appropriate legislation.

Art. XVI
February 25, 1913

The Congress shall have power to lay and collect taxes on incomes, from whatever source derived, without apportionment among the several States and without regard to any census or enumeration.

Art. XVII
May 31, 1913

The Senate of the United States shall be composed of two senators from each State, elected by the people thereof, for six years; and each Senator shall have one vote. The electors in each State shall have the qualifications requisite for electors of the most numerous branch of the State legislature.

When vacancies happen in the representation of any State in the Senate, the executive authority of such State shall issue writs of election to fill such vacancies: *Provided*, That the legislature of any State may empower the executive thereof to make temporary appointments until the people fill the vacancies by election as the legislature may direct.

This amendment shall not be so construed as to affect the election or term of any senator chosen before it becomes valid as part of the Constitution.

Art. XVIII
January 29, 1919

After one year from the ratification of this article, the manufacture, sale, or transportation of intoxicating liquors within, the importation thereof into, or the exportation thereof from the United States and all territory subject to the jurisdiction thereof for beverage purposes is hereby prohibited.

The Congress and the several States shall have concurrent power to enforce this article by appropriate legislation.

This article shall be inoperative unless it shall have been ratified as an amendment to the Constitution by the legislatures of the several States, as provided in the Constitution, within seven years from the date of the submission thereof to the States by Congress.

Art. XIX
August 26, 1920

The right of citizens of the United States to vote shall not be denied or abridged by the United States or by any States on account of sex.

The Congress shall have power by appropriate legislation to enforce the provisions of this article.

Art. XX
February 6, 1933

Sec. 1. The terms of the President and Vice-President shall end at noon on the twentieth day of January, and the terms of Senators and Representatives at noon on the third day of January, of the years in which such terms would have ended if this article had not been ratified; and the terms of their successors shall then begin.

Sec. 2. The Congress shall assemble at least once in every year, and such meeting shall begin at noon on the third day of January, unless they shall by law appoint a different day.

Sec. 3. If, at the time fixed for the beginning of the term of the President, the President-elect shall have died, the Vice-President-elect shall become President. If a President shall not have been chosen before the time fixed for the beginning of his term, or if the President-elect shall have failed to qualify, then the Vice-President-elect shall act as President until a President shall have qualified; and the Congress may by law provide for the case wherein neither a President-elect nor a Vice-President-elect shall have qualified, declaring who shall then act as President, or the manner in which one who is to act shall be selected, and such person shall act accordingly until a President or Vice-President shall have qualified.

Sec. 4. The Congress may by law provide for the case of the death of any of the persons from whom the House of Representatives may choose a President whenever the right of choice shall have devolved upon them, and for the case of the death of any of the persons from whom the Senate may choose a Vice-President whenever the right of choice shall have devolved upon them.

Sec. 5. Sections 1 and 2 shall take effect on the 15th day of October following the ratification of this article.

Sec. 6. This article shall be inoperative unless it shall have been ratified as an amendment to the Constitution by the legislatures of three-fourths of the several States within seven years from the date of its submission.

Art. XXI
December 5, 1933

Sec. 1. The eighteenth article of amendment to the Constitution of the United States is hereby repealed . . .

Art. XXII
February 26, 1951

Sec. 1. No person shall be elected to the office of the President more than twice, and no person who has held the office of President, or acted as President for more than two years of a term to which some other person was elected President shall be elected to the office of the President more than once. But this Article shall not apply to any person holding the office of President when this Article was proposed by the Congress, and shall not prevent any person who may be holding the office of President, or acting as President, during the term within which this Article becomes operative from holding the office of President or acting as President during the remainder of such term.

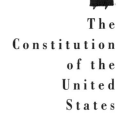

The
Constitution
of the
United
States

Article XXIII
March 29, 1961

SEC. 1. The District constituting the seat of Government of the United States shall appoint in such manner as the Congress may direct:

A number of electors of President and Vice-President equal to the whole number of Senators and Representatives in Congress to which the District would be entitled if it were a State, but in no event more than the least populous state; they shall be in addition to those appointed by the states, but they shall be considered, for the purposes of the election of President and Vice-President, to be electors appointed by a state; and they shall meet in the District and perform such duties as provided by the twelfth article of amendment.

SEC. 2. The Congress shall have power to enforce this article by appropriate legislation.

Article XXIV
January 24, 1964

SEC. 1. The right of citizens of the United States to vote in any primary or other election for President or Vice-President, for electors for President or Vice-President, or for Senator or Representative in Congress, shall not be denied or abridged by the United States or any stateby reason of failure to pay any poll tax or other tax.

SEC. 2. The Congress shall have power to enforce this article by appropriate legislation.

Article XXV
February 23, 1967

SEC. 1. In case of the removal of the President from office or his death or resignation, the Vice-President shall become President.

SEC. 2. Whenever there is a vacancy in the office of the Vice-President, the President shall nominate a Vice-President who shall take the office upon confirmation by a majority vote of both houses of Congress.

SEC. 3. Whenever the President transmits to the President pro tempore of the Senate and the Speaker of the House of Representatives his written declaration that he is unable to discharge the powers and duties of his office, and until he transmits to them a written declaration to the contrary, such powers and duties shall be discharged by the Vice-President as Acting President.

SEC. 4. Whenever the Vice-President and a majority of either the principal officers of the executive departments, or of such other body as Congress may by law provide, transmit to the President pro tempore of the Senate and the Speaker of the House of Representatives their written declaration that the President is unable to discharge the powers and duties of his office, the Vice-President shall immediately assume the powers and duties of the office as Acting President.

Thereafter, when the President transmits to the President pro tempore of the Senate and the Speaker of the House of Representatives his written declaration that no inability exists, he shall resume the powers and duties of his office unless the Vice-President and a majority of either the principal officers of the executive department, or of such other body as Congress may by law provide, transmit within four days to the President pro tempore of the Senate and the Speaker of the House of Representatives their written declaration that the President is unable to discharge the powers and duties of his office. Thereupon Congress shall decide the issue, assembling within 48 hours for that purpose if not in session. If the Congress, within 21 days after receipt of the latter written declaration, or, if Congress is not in session, within 21 days after Congress is required to assemble, determines by two-thirds vote of both houses that the President is unable to discharge the powers and duties of his office, the Vice-President shall continue to discharge the same as Acting President; otherwise, the President shall resume the powers and duties of his office.

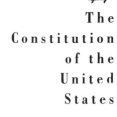

Article XXVI
July 7, 1971

Sec. 1. The right of citizens of the United States, who are eighteen years of age or older, to vote shall not be denied or abridged by the United States or by any State on account of age.

Sec. 2. The Congress shall have power to enforce this article by appropriate legislation.

Index

Page numbers in bold text indicate the primary article on a topic or court case. Page numbers in italics indicate illustrations.

Index

Index

Index

D

Index

Index

Index

Index

Index

Index

Index

Index

Korematsu v. United States
(1944), 3:580–581
Murray v. Maryland (1936), 3:764

N

NAACP, 1:3, 1:11–15, 1:192,
3:763–764, 3:790
Marshall, Thurgood, 3:780–781
Powell v. Alabama (1932),
2:305–306
NAACP v. Alabama ex rel. Patterson
(1958), 1:3–4, **1:11–15**
National Association for the
Advancement of Colored People
(NAACP). *See* NAACP
National bank, 4:874–879
National Labor Relations Act, 4:999
National Labor Relations Board
(NLRB), 4:999
National security and publication of
sensitive material, 1:31, 1:42–43
Native Americans, **4:1063–1092**
assimilation, 4:1067–1068
Cherokee Nation v. Georgia
(1831), 4:1079–1086
Johnson v. McIntosh (1823),
4:1072–1078
land transfers, 4:1072–1078,
4:1089
religious practices, 1:93, 1:110
vs. state power, 4:955,
4:1079–1086
Trail of Tears, 4:1085–1086
tribal organization, 4:1068,
4:1069
Worcester v. Georgia (1832),
4:1079–1086
Nazis. *See* American Nazi party
Near, J. M., 1:35–37
Near v. Minnesota (1931), 1:31,
1:35–39
Nebbia, Leo, 4:974–975
Nebbia v. New York (1934), **4:972–977**
Nebraska, Meyer v., (1923), 3:739
Nebraska Press Association v. Stuart
(1976), 1:33, **1:55–59**

Nebraska state law
on teaching evolution, 1:127
Nelson, Baker v., (1971), 2:348
New Deal, 4:1032
New Hampshire, Chaplinsky v.,
(1942), 1:160, **1:170–173**
New Hampshire, Cox v., (1941),
1:3, 1:163
New Hampshire state law
offensive speech, 1:171
New Jersey state law transporting
children to school, 1:112, 1:114–116
New Jersey v. T.L.O. (1985),
2:426–431
New Mexico state law on teaching
evolution, 1:127
New York, Feiner v., (1951),
1:179–183
New York, Gitlow v., (1925), 1:158
New York, Lochner v., (1905),
4:826, 4:839, 4:956, 4:997,
4:1003–1009, 4:1011
New York, Mayor of, v. Miln
(1837), 4:973
New York City, Train v., (1975), 4:929
New York (colony)
seditious libel law, 1:64
*New York State Crime Victims Board,
Simon & Schuster v.,* (1991),
1:242–247
New York state law
assisted suicide ban, 3:525–530
Bakeshop Act, 4:1004–1006
disorderly conduct law, 1:180
drug control law, 1:85–89
Milk Control Act of 1934,
4:974–975
Son of Sam law, 1:242–247
steamship rights, 4:969
New York Times, Pentagon Papers,
1:42–43
New York Times Co. v. United States
(1971), 1:31, **1:40–46**
New York Times Company v. Sullivan
(1964), 1:32, 1:62, 1:63, **1:189–193**
New York v. Belton (1981), **2:462–465**
New York, Near v., (1934), **4:972–977**
News reporters. *See* Journalists

Index

Index

emotional distress, 1:63–64
gag order, 1:33
Hazelwood School District v. Kuhlmeier (1988), 1:56–60
Hustler Magazine v. Falwell (1988), 1:61–65
invasion of privacy, 1:63–64
libel, 1:63–64
Near v. Minnesota (1931), 1:35–39
Nebraska Press Association v. Stuart (1976), 1:51–55
New York Times Co. v. United States (1971), 1:40–45
responsibility, 1:48
revealing sources, 1:32–33, 1:46–49
students, 1:56–60
Price, Victoria, 2:304–306
Priddy, Albert, 3:673, 3:675
Prigg, Edward, 3:552–556
Prigg v. Pennsylvania (1842), 3:552–556
Prior restraint, 1:30–31, 1:35–39, 1:40. *See also* Censorship; Press
gag order, 1:33, 1:36–37, 1:53
Prisons and freedom of speech, 1:162
Privacy, 1:64, 1:82, 2:299, 2:329, 2:447
vs. Congressional inquiries, 1:76–79
death, 1:71–72
family life, 1:70–71
freedom of association and, 1:13–14
freedom of speech and, 1:239–240
Griswold v. Connecticut (1964), 1:80–84
marriage, 1:68–69, 1:83, 1:219
personal information, 1:72–73, 1:85–89
refuse medical treatment, 3:515–516
sexual relations, 1:68–70, 3:691, 3:747–752
Watkins v. United States (1957), 1:74–79
Whalen v. Roe (1977), 1:85–89
Privacy, invasion of, 1:63–64

Privacy, right to, **1:67–89**
Privacy Protection Act of 1974, 1:71
Private schools. *See* Schools, private
Pro-choice movement, 3:696, *3:699, 3:706,* 3:710. *See also* Abortion; Reproductive rights
Pro-Choice of Western New York, Schenck v., (1997), 3:669
Pro-life movement, *3:690,* 3:695–696, *3:699, 3:700, 3:708,* 3:710. *See also under* Abortion; Reproductive rights
Probable cause, 2:299, 2:329, 2:433–434, 2:434–435
Probation, 2:301
Profanity and freedom of speech, 1:172, 1:186, 1:216–220. *See also* Blasphemy and freedom of speech; Obscene material
Prohibition, 2:442
Property, 2:344–345
Proposition 21, 2:417
Protests
abortion, 1:237–241, 3:669, *3:690, 3:699, 3:700, 3:706, 3:708*
affirmative action, *3:490*
picketing, 1:237–241
police brutality, 1:2, 1:8
racism, 1:161–162
segregation, 1:16–22
Vietnam War, 1:159
Public accomodations and *Civil Rights Cases* (1883), 3:563–568
Public health, conflict with First Amendment rights, 1:88, 1:93
Public schools. *See* Schools, Public
Public trial, right to, 4:1043
Public Utilities Commission v. Pollak (1952), 1:68
Public Works Employment Act of 1977
Fullilove v. Klutznick (1980), 3:501–506
Puerto Rico v. Branstad (1987), **4:990–994**
Pynchon, William, *The Meritorious Price of Our Redemption,* 1:229

Index

Index

Index

Index

V

Index

Index

Index